Mac OS® X Lion™
PORTABLE GENIUS

Mac OS® X Lion™

PORTABLE GENIUS

by Dwight Spivey

WILEY

John Wiley & Sons, Inc.

Mac OS® X Lion™ Portable Genius

Published by
John Wiley & Sons, Inc.
10475 Crosspoint Blvd.
Indianapolis, IN 46256
www.wiley.com

Copyright © 2011 by John Wiley & Sons, Inc., Indianapolis, Indiana

Published simultaneously in Canada

ISBN: 978-1-118-02239-9

Manufactured in the United States of America

10   9   8   7   6   5   4   3   2   1

For general information on our other products and services or to obtain technical support, please contact our Customer Care Department within the U.S. at (877) 762-2974, outside the U.S. at (317) 572-3993 or fax (317) 572-4002.

John Wiley & Sons, Inc. also publishes its books in a variety of electronic formats and by print-on-demand. Some content that appears in standard print versions of this book may not be available in other formats. For more information about Wiley products, visit us at www.wiley.com.

Library of Congress Control Number: 2011936811

WILEY

About the Author

Dwight Spivey is the author of several Mac books, including *Mac OS X Leopard Portable Genius* and *Mac OS X Snow Leopard Portable Genius*. He is also a software and support engineer for Konica Minolta, where he specializes in working with Mac operating systems, applications, and hardware, as well as color and monochrome laser printers. He teaches classes on Mac usage, writes training and support materials for Konica Minolta, and is a member of the Apple Developer Program. Dwight lives on the Gulf Coast of Alabama with his beautiful wife Cindy and their four amazing children, Victoria, Devyn, Emi, and Reid. He studies theology, draws comic strips, and roots for the Auburn Tigers ("War Eagle!") in his ever-decreasing spare time.

Credits

Executive Editor
Jody Lefevere

Project Editor
Amanda Gambill

Technical Editor
Guy Hart-Davis

Senior Copy Editor
Kim Heusel

Editorial Director
Robyn Siesky

Business Manager
Amy Knies

Senior Marketing Manager
Sandy Smith

Vice President and Executive Group Publisher
Richard Swadley

Vice President and Executive Publisher
Barry Pruett

Project Coordinator
Patrick Redmond

Graphics and Production Specialists
Jennifer Henry
Julie Trippetti

Quality Control Technicians
Rebecca Denoncour
Lauren Mandelbaum
Susan Moritz

Proofreading and Indexing
Debbye Butler
Potomac Indexing, LLC

For Carrie Leigh Spivey and Jerad Lee Spivey.

I miss you both so much.

I love you, my dear cousins, and thank God that I'll see you again.

Acknowledgments

 I must thank my family and friends for putting up with my many absences during the writing of this book. I love you all!

Many thanks to my agent, Carole Jelen, for keeping me rolling!

Sincere appreciation goes to Jody Lefevere and Amanda Gambill. Thank you both for being so good to me from start to finish of this book. Jody and Amanda, you have both been a joy to work with, and my work benefits mightily because of you.

Very special thanks to my favorite technical editor, Guy Hart-Davis, for always having my back.

To everyone else who has had a hand in getting this book from raw manuscript to the beautiful publication that it is, I cannot thank you enough. You make my work so much better than I deserve. I sincerely thank you for all of your hard work and dedication to this book.

Contents
at a Glance

Contents

How Can I Customize Lion?   32

chapter 3

How Do I Change the Lion
System Preferences?   56

chapter 4

How Do I Manage User Accounts?   80

chapter 5

What Can I Do with Applications? 100

Mac OS X Lion — Chat

mosxlionpg@gmail.com (Jabber)
Away – Idle (27 min)

I am Lionn! Heaare me rooaar!@

Excuse me?

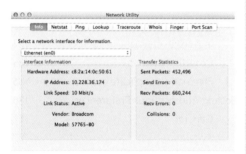

chapter 8

How Do I Organize My Life with
iCal and Address Book?   168

Publish calendar

Publish calendar as: Home

Publish on: MobileMe

☐ Publish changes automatically   ☐ Publish alerts
☑ Publish titles and notes   ☐ Publish attachments
☐ Publish to do items

Cancel   Publish

chapter 9

How Do I Master the Web
with Safari?   192

chapter 10

How Do I Stay Connected with Mail? 216

How Can I Use iTunes with Multimedia? 244

How Do I Work with Images and Video? 274

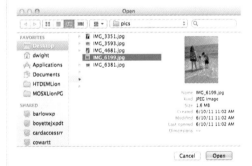

chapter 13

How Do I Print and Share?   306

chapter 14

How Can I Automate My Mac? 334

Apple Inc.

main   1-800-MY-APPLE
homepage   http://www.apple.com
work   1 Infinite Loop
Cupertino CA 95014
United States

Dictionary (3 found)

Q genius

All **Dictionary** Thesaurus Apple Wikipedia

genius
genius loci
geniuses

gen·ius | jēnyəs |
noun (pl. **geniuses**)
1 exceptional intellectual or creative power or other natural ability: *she was a teacher of genius* | *Gardner had a real **genius for** tapping wealth.*
2 a person who is exceptionally intelligent or creative, either generally or in some particular respect: *one of the great musical geniuses of the 20th century.*
3 (pl. **genii** | jēnē,ī |) (in some mythologies) a guardian spirit associated with a person, place, or institution.
• a person regarded as exerting a powerful influence over another for good or evil: *he sees Adams as the man's evil genius.*
4 (pl. **genii**) the prevalent character or spirit of something such as a nation or age: *Boucher's paintings did not suit the austere genius of neoclassicism.*

ORIGIN late Middle English: from Latin, *'attendant spirit present from one's birth, innate ability or inclination,'*

Introduction

Thank you, Apple! Once again you've raised the bar for your competitors and knocked the socks off the rest of us. Lion isn't only the best-looking operating system around, it's also the most functional and easy to use.

Some of you may be rolling your eyes right now; all computers use the file and folder concept and some sort of colorful user interface, so there couldn't be that much difference between Mac OS X and its competitors, right? Wrong! I don't just say this because of some blind devotion to all things Apple. I've actually used different flavors of Windows and Linux for more than 16 years, right alongside my trusty Mac, so experience has been my teacher. If I have any devotion to Apple, there are plenty of good reasons why, the subject of this book being the first.

Readers of this book who are already Mac users understand exactly what I'm talking about. For those of you moving from other computing platforms, it's my desire that by the end of this book you have a new perspective on computing and see what it means to have fun while working with your computer.

With *Mac OS X Lion Portable Genius,* you learn much more than the basics. You learn the subtle nuances, and little tips and tricks that make using your Mac that much easier. I cover the gamut, from printing files, surfing the Internet, and using e-mail, to partitioning your hard drive, automating repetitive tasks, and troubleshooting pesky problems (with a little bit of geeky humor thrown in for good measure).

I hope this book does Mac OS X Lion justice, because it isn't just a computer operating system — it's an art form.

How Do I Get Started with Lion?

You are about to embark on the world's most advanced operating system experience, courtesy of Apple. In this chapter, I show you how to get Mac OS X Lion up and running, as well as how to navigate Lion using the Finder application, which helps you find just about anything on your Mac. I also cover how to view a file without opening its parent application, how to find items on your Mac, easy ways to manipulate numerous open windows, and the latest and greatest method for launching your applications.

System Requirements for Installing Lion

As eager as you probably are to get started, make sure that your Mac meets all the necessary hardware requirements for properly installing and running Lion. Table 1.1 lists the requirements.

Table 1.1 Requirements for Installing Lion

Requirement	Minimum Specifications
Processor	Intel Core 2 Duo processor or better.
Memory	2GB is needed to run all the bells and whistles at a decent speed.
Media	Internet access is required to upgrade your Mac to Lion. You will also need to be running Mac OS X Snow Leopard 10.6.7 or higher to install Lion from the Mac App Store.
Hard drive space	At least 8GB of free space.

What's New in Lion?

Apple has been busy: Lion adds more than 250 new features to Mac OS X! But it's not the quantity of features that impresses — it's the quality. Let's check out some of the more prominent Lion goodies:

- **Accessibility.** Features in Lion are unmatched. VoiceOver (a utility that allows your Mac to speak to you) now supports 23 languages. There is also built-in support for 80 braille tables.

- **FaceTime video calling.** You can now talk to your favorite pals with a true video phone using your Mac and FaceTime.

- **AutoSave.** Applications developed with AutoSave automatically save any changes you make to your documents. There's no longer any need to constantly press ⌘+S to save your files after each change.

- **Lion is now distributed online.** You can download the entire Mac OS through the Mac App Store and install with just a few clicks.

- **Full-screen applications.** You can run many of your applications in full-screen mode, which cuts down on external distractions and keeps you focused.

- **Recovery mode.** You no longer need discs to reinstall or restore Mac OS X because Lion includes a built-in restore partition on your hard drive. Just press ⌘+R during a restart to boot into Recovery mode.

- **Launchpad.** This literally launches all of the apps on your Mac. You can see most (if not all) of them with a click of your mouse or a swipe of your trackpad. You can also organize your applications into folders, a process with which iPhone and iPad users are already familiar.

- **Mission Control.** Mission Control allows you to see everything that's happening on your Mac in one window.

- **Multi-Touch gestures.** Multi-Touch gestures make your Magic Mouse, Magic Trackpad, or your laptop trackpad absolutely rock! Properly orchestrated finger swipes instantly scroll through web pages, open Launchpad, zoom in, and much more.

- **Versions.** Lion saves versions of all of your documents once an hour while you work. You can browse between versions of your documents if you mistakenly remove an item and need to restore it. You can restore parts of older versions or you can restore the entire document. Lion saves only the information that has changed from version to version so your hard drive space won't be eaten up with duplicate information.

- **Resume.** Resume allows you to open an application in the exact same state you left it when you last closed it. Any windows that were open, any palettes that were on-screen, and even the position of the cursor, remain exactly as they were when you last used the application. You can also restart your Mac, and any applications or windows that were open before you restarted are restored upon reboot.

Upgrading to Lion

Let's get started with your upgrade to the latest feline from Apple. Follow these steps:

1. **Make sure you are connected to the Internet.**

Caution

Back up your files before performing the upgrade to Lion! Years of experience have taught me not to make a major leap (such as an operating system upgrade) without backing up first. If you don't, Murphy's Law dictates that something will erase Grandma's recipes which have been passed down for generations.

2. **Check the version of Mac OS X you currently have installed by choosing Apple menu ⇨ About This Mac in the upper-left corner of your screen.** You must have at least Mac OS X 10.6.7 to install Lion (10.7).

3. **Open the App Store and type Lion into the search field in the upper-right corner.**

4. **Select and buy Lion from the App Store.** You must have an Apple ID to do so. If you don't have one, click Create an Apple ID when prompted.

5. **After Lion downloads, it begins the installation process**. Follow the on-screen instructions to complete your upgrade. You are now fully Lionized!

Working with the Finder

After your Mac boots or when you first log in, take a look at that smiley-face guy grinning at you near the bottom-left corner of your screen. That's the Finder (see Figure 1.1), and it's one of the most important items in all of Mac OS X Lion.

The Finder is an application that always runs in Lion and it has been a part of Mac OS since its inception. The Finder is what Mac fans have used for decades to browse their computer drives and discs.

It has evolved into a great tool that I can't imagine not having (especially as you can't view the contents of your hard drive without it). For Windows converts, think of the Finder as the Mac OS X equivalent to Windows Explorer. In this section, I show you how to use the basic features in Finder, and also give you tips that I've learned to make it even easier and more productive to use.

1.1 The Finder icon.

The Lion desktop at a glance

The desktop is what you see when you first start up or log in to your Mac. This is where all the action in your applications takes place. The desktop is a major part (and actually, the starting point) of the Finder.

Figure 1.2 should mirror your own Mac screen very closely after you log in. It shows the major parts that you see when the Finder first comes up.

Apple menu   Menu bar   Volume   Clock   Spotlight

Finder File Edit View Go Window Help

Paul's iPod

Dock   Documents stack | Trash
Downloads stack

image courtesy of Paul McFedries

1.2 The Finder desktop in all its default glory.

Now that you know the names of the items you see in the Finder, you can use Table 1.2 to decipher what functionality they provide.

Table 1.2 Finder Items

Item	Function
Apple menu	Provides quick access to functions such as Sleep, Restart, Shut Down, Recent Items, and System Preferences. Windows users find that it functions similarly to the Start menu.
Menu bar	Use the menu bar in the Finder and in other applications to print, copy and paste, and change application preferences.

continued

Table 1.2 continued

Item	Function
Desktop	Functions like the desktop on your desk. It's where everything else (such as documents and applications) sits while you are working. You can easily change the desktop picture (see Chapter 2 for more details).
Volume	Adjusts the Mac volume.
Clock	Displays the current date and time.
Spotlight	Searches your Mac for files and folders. More on this later in the chapter.
Dock	Houses icons that link to applications and other items that you use most frequently. You can modify the Dock, as you see later in this chapter.
Trash	Contains files and folders that you want to remove from your Mac. Former Windows users will find it similar to the Recycle Bin.
Downloads stack	Provides fast access to items in your home folder's Downloads folder.
Documents stack	Provides fast access to items in your home folder's Documents folder.

Now that you are more familiar with the features of the desktop, let's examine a Finder window, which is the mechanism you need to view files and folders on your drives. Figure 1.3 shows a default Finder window.

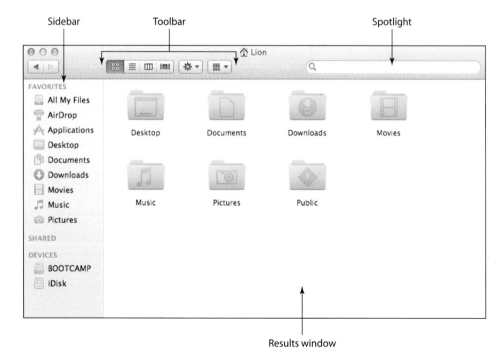

1.3 Finder windows are used for browsing your drives, files, and folders.

Table 1.3 gives a brief breakdown of each noteworthy item in the Finder window.

Table 1.3 Finder Window Components

Component	Description
Folders	Used to store files and other subfolders.
Toolbar	Contains tools for accessing files and folders.
Sidebar	Provides quick links to drives, favorite folders, shared folders, and preconfigured searches.
Spotlight	Type a search term to look for it in the current folder.
Results window	Shows the files and subfolders that reside in a folder and also displays search results.

Setting the Finder preferences

You'll notice throughout this book that you can modify most things in Lion to match your personal preferences and tastes (to one degree or another), and that's the way I like it. The Finder is no exception (see Chapter 2 for a lot of Finder customization tips). To access its preferences, choose Finder⇨ Preferences or press ⌘+,. Let's take a look at the preferences that the Finder allows you to control.

General

The options listed in the General tab of the Finder Preferences window, as shown in Figure 1.4, are fairly self-explanatory (with the exception of spring-loaded folders and windows, which are so cool that they get their own sidebar).

1.4 Options available in the General tab.

The available options allow you to do the following:

- **Show certain items (such as hard or external drives, CDs, DVDs, iPods, or servers) on the desktop.**

- **Choose which folder automatically opens when you open a new Finder window.**

- **Decide whether to always open folders in new (separate) windows.** I do not recommend that you use this feature unless you regularly use or compare multiple windows.

Spring-Loaded Folders and Windows

Spring-loaded folders and windows are a neat feature of the Finder but are foreign to many Mac users, especially the new recruits. Enabling spring-loaded folders and windows lets you move items between folders and drives with minimal effort.

With this feature enabled, you can drag an item over any folder, hold it there for just a split second, and the folder automatically opens. Continue to hold the mouse button down while you position the item over each subfolder and they all behave accordingly — automatically opening and allowing you to drill down into the subfolders as far as you need to. Finally, drop the item into the folder you want to move it to by releasing the mouse button. Reading a description of this feature can be pretty boring, so give it a try on your own to master this nifty little trick.

Labels and Sidebar

The Labels tab of the Finder Preferences window allows you to assign color labels to categories that you determine. You can then assign these labels to files and folders by right-clicking them (or Control+clicking if you don't have a two-button mouse), and then selecting a label from the list, as shown in Figure 1.5.

The Sidebar tab of the Finder Preferences window simply lets you choose which types of items to display in the sidebar of every Finder window.

Advanced

Table 1.4 explains the options that are available in the Advanced tab of the Finder Preferences window.

Open

Move to Trash

Get Info
Compress "Important!"
Burn "Important!" to Disc...
Duplicate
Make Alias
Quick Look "Important!"

Copy "Important!"

Clean Up Selection
Show View Options

Label:

"BigTime Important"

New Email With Attachment
Folder Actions Setup...

1.5 Assigning a label color to a folder.

Table 1.4 Advanced Tab Options

Option	Function
Show all filename extensions	Each file has an extension at the end of its name that is hidden by default. This extension helps Lion know what type of document it is, and with which application it is associated. Unless you understand these extensions, it is best to leave this option deselected.
Show warning before changing an extension	Lion warns you that you are about to change the extension of a file. This warning is beneficial so that you don't accidentally change an extension, which could cause your document to open in a different application than intended, or not open at all.
Show warning before emptying the Trash	Lion prompts you to confirm that you mean to empty the Trash before allowing you to do so. This option is designed to help prevent accidental deletions of important info.
Empty Trash securely	Select this option to make certain that all traces of a file are removed from the hard drive when you empty the Trash. This is a feature security nuts love, but it prevents you from ever recovering any files you may have accidentally deleted. Use this option with caution.
When performing a search	Determine the default location for searches by selecting an option from this pop-up menu.

Genius You can securely empty the Trash on a case-by-case basis instead of enabling it all the time. To do so, place the item you want to permanently delete in the Trash, and then choose Finder ⇨ Secure Empty Trash.

Moving around in the Finder

Mac OS X employs the same basic navigation techniques as any other graphical operating system. Double-clicking opens files and folders, while right-clicking (or Control+clicking) items opens contextual menus with which you can alter or perform an action on an item (like the Labels example earlier in this chapter). You can also click and drag items to move them to and fro. As I'm sure you're all experienced at the basics of mouse operations, I'll move on to more Finder-centric tasks and options.

Finder viewing options

You can change the way files and folders are displayed in Finder windows by choosing one of the four View options in the toolbar: Icon, list, columns, or Cover Flow. Let's look at how each option displays the contents of the same folder so that you can clearly see the differences between each view.

Icon view

Icon view shows each file and folder as large icons in the window, as shown in Figure 1.6.

1.6 A folder in icon view.

List view

List view does just what it says: it displays the files and folders in a list. You can arrange the list by filenames, the date the files were modified, the size of the file or folder, and the kind of item it is.

Columns view

My personal favorite is columns view. This view arranges the contents of a folder into columns, with each column displaying the contents of the subsequent folder.

Quickly Open Commonly Used Folders

I can't speak for other Mac users, but the Finder menu that I most wish I had discovered years ago is the Go menu, which you see in the menu bar when the Finder is active. The Go menu gives you instant access to the most commonly used folders in Lion, but for some reason I overlooked it for a good portion of the years I've used Mac OS X. Click the Go menu to quickly go to the Applications or Utilities folders, your Network, and more.

Better yet, familiarize yourself with the keyboard shortcuts (listed to the right of each command in the Go menu) used to access those items. If an item you want to jump to isn't in the Go menu, press ⌘+Shift+G to open the Go to Folder window, type the path of the folder you want, and then click Go to jump over to it.

Cover Flow view

Cover Flow is hands down the coolest viewing option at your disposal. As shown in Figure 1.7, files and folders are displayed as they really appear when opened in an application, which can be a great help when searching for a particular document or picture.

1.7 In Cover Flow view, you can zoom through all of the files in a folder.

13

Getting Information on Files and Folders

You can never have too much information, and Mac OS X is more than happy to provide you with what you need to know about the files and folders on your computer. To find out what there is to know about an item, click (just once) the file or folder you want information about, and then press ⌘+I, or choose File➪Get Info. Figure 1.8 shows a typical Info window.

To quickly get information on multiple items without having to open separate Info windows for each one, you can use the Inspector, which is a floating version of the Get Info window. To do this, follow these steps:

1. **Open the folder that contains the items about which you want to see information.**

2. **Press ⌘+Option+I to open the Inspector window (it looks just like a standard Info window).**

3. **Click each file in the folder to see its information in the Inspector window.** The Inspector changes information for each file you select. You can move between files by using the arrow keys on the keyboard.

1.8 A file Info window with most of the categories expanded.

Table 1.5 explains the categories that are available in the Info window.

Table 1.5 Information Categories

Category	Information Displayed
Spotlight Comments	Type information about the file that helps you find it using a Spotlight search. More on this later in the chapter.
General	Tells you information such as what kind of item you're viewing, its size, where it's located, and when it was created and/or modified.
More Info	The information shown here varies depending on the type of item this is. If the file is an image, you might see its dimensions and color space.
Name & Extension	Allows you to change the name and extension of the file, and to hide the extension.
Open with	Select the default application that you want to use to open this type of file. This option only displays when getting info about a file.
Preview	Shows a small thumbnail version of the file.
Sharing & Permissions	Allows you to change access permissions for the item. Click the lock icon in the bottom-right corner to change the permissions. Click the plus (+) or minus (–) signs to add or remove users from the permissions list.

Using Quick Look

Quick Look is one of the best features in Lion. It allows you to see the contents of a file without actually opening it in its native application. For example, you can see every page of a Word document without having to open Word itself. This makes it really easy to find a document if you've forgotten its name but know the content that you're looking for, or when you're looking for just the right image but don't want to wait for Photoshop to load. To use Quick Look, follow these steps:

1. **Find the file you want to view and click it once to highlight it.**

2. **Press the spacebar to open the file in Quick Look view, an example of which is shown in Figure 1.9.**

3. **To see the item in Full Screen mode, click the diagonal arrows at the top right of the window.** To exit Full Screen mode, click the arrows again.

4. **To open the item in its default application, click Open with in the upper-right corner of the window.** In Figure 1.9, it says Open with Preview.

5. **If the file contains multiple pages you can scroll through them using the sidebar on the right side of the window.**

6. **Close the Quick Look window by clicking the X in the upper-left corner or by pressing the spacebar again.**

1.9 A file being viewed in Quick Look.

Working with Removable Media

When you insert or connect removable media, such as CDs, DVDs, external hard drives, and USB flash drives, Lion automatically mounts and makes them immediately available for use. The media icon appears on your desktop, in a Finder window, or both, depending on how you configure your Finder preferences. Figure 1.10 shows a flash drive (BACKUP) and a CD (Audio CD) in the sidebar of the Finder window under Devices. You can also double-click the icon on the desktop to see the media contents, just as you would any other hard drive or folder.

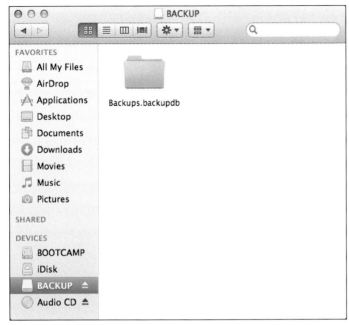

1.10 A flash drive and audio CD as they appear in the sidebar of the Finder.

Perform one of the following actions to disconnect or eject removable media:

- Click the Eject icon to the right of the media in the sidebar of the Finder window.

- Click and drag the media icon from the desktop, and drop it on the Trash icon in the Dock.

- Right-click (or Control+click) the media icon on the desktop or in the sidebar, and then select Eject from the contextual menu.

- Click the icon for the media once to highlight it and press ⌘+E.

Searching for Items

Apple introduced Spotlight in Mac OS X Tiger and instantly changed the way Mac users look for items on their computers. Spotlight finds things on your Mac much faster than you could if you were poking around every file and folder. In fact, it's the quickest way I've ever seen to find things on a computer.

When you first log in to your Mac, OS X creates an index of every file and folder it contains. Lion knows everything there is to know about every single thing that occupies your Mac, whether the item is visible or not. Lion stores this information, or metadata, and Spotlight uses the information,

17

along with filenames and content, to find what you are looking for. Every time you add or remove an item, or add or remove something within that item (like text within a document), Lion updates its index files, thereby keeping all your searches up-to-the-minute accurate.

You might think that with all this information to look through a search could take forever, but that's not the case at all. Spotlight can find items containing your search words almost as quickly as you can type them.

Searching with Spotlight

Chances are good that no matter how long it's been since you've seen the file you're looking for, Spotlight can dig it up for you. Let's see how to use this amazing feature:

1. **Click the Spotlight icon (the magnifying glass) in the upper-right corner of the Mac window to reveal the Search text field, as shown in Figure 1.11.**

1.11 Type your search words into Spotlight.

2. **Type your search criteria in the text field.** Some applications have Spotlight Search fields in their toolbars, which you can use to type search words when specifically searching for items within that application (for example, when searching for an e-mail within Mail).

3. **Spotlight immediately begins searching your Mac and displays the information it finds that matches the criteria you typed in Step 2.**

4. **Scan the list for the item you want and then click to open it in its default application.** Spotlight only shows the top matches in each category. To see all of the matches, click Show All at the top of the list.

You can easily modify Spotlight to search where and how you want it to, using its preferences. Choose Apple menu ➪ System Preferences, and then click the Spotlight icon in the Personal section to access the Spotlight preferences pane, as shown in Figure 1.12.

Genius Did you notice that Spotlight doesn't only show you items such as documents and folders that contain your search words? Spotlight literally searches every file on your Mac for your search criteria, including e-mails, web pages you've visited, contacts, music, movies, images, and PDF files. Spotlight can even search other Macs on your network if they have file sharing enabled.

1.12 The Spotlight preferences let you search the way you want.

Figure 1.12 shows the Search Results section of the preferences pane. This section lists the categories of files that appear in the search results window. Select the check box next to those categories you want Spotlight to search and deselect those you want it to leave alone.

For example, if you don't want Spotlight to check your e-mail when performing a search, simply deselect the Messages & Chats check box. You can also click and drag the categories into the order in which you prefer the results to be displayed.

Click the Privacy tab at the top of the preferences pane to reveal the Privacy list. This section allows you to specify directories (folders) on your Mac that you want to exclude from any searches.

To modify the Privacy list, follow these steps:

1. **Click the plus sign (+) under the bottom-left corner of the list.**

2. **Browse your Mac for the folder you want to exclude from searches, highlight it, and then click Choose.** The folder is now shown in the Privacy list.

3. **You can remove a folder from the list by highlighting it and then clicking the minus sign (–) under the bottom-left corner of the list.**

The two check boxes at the bottom of the preferences pane allow you to enable Spotlight keyboard shortcuts for opening a Spotlight menu or window with the stroke of a couple of keys, as shown in Table 1.6. You can also select which keys perform these functions by choosing a key combination from the pop-up menus next to each option.

Table 1.6 Spotlight Keyboard Shortcuts

Function	Keys
Open the Spotlight menu	⌘+spacebar
Open the Spotlight (Finder) window	⌘+Option+spacebar
Jump to the first item in the next heading	⌘+Down arrow
Jump to the first item in the prior heading	⌘ +Up arrow
Show an item in the Finder	Click the item while holding down ⌘

Searching with the Spotlight menu is certainly fast and easy, but it doesn't always yield the best results. In fact, it may give you so many results that you could never realistically review them all in a reasonable amount of time. To remedy this situation, Spotlight brings in your trusty friend, the Finder.

Searching within a Finder window

The Finder gives you much more leverage to enhance your search beyond the Spotlight menu's capabilities.

To perform a basic Spotlight search within a Finder window, follow these steps:

1. **Open a Finder window by pressing ⌘+N while the Finder is activated**. If the Finder isn't the activated (or foremost) application, click the Finder icon on the left side of the Dock.

2. **Browse your Mac for the folder that includes the files you're looking for (or through) and click it to highlight it.**

3. **Type the search criteria into the Search text field in the upper-right corner of the Finder window.** Your results are displayed in the Finder.

Any search utility worth using allows a lot of flexibility to narrow searches and Spotlight is as flexible as they come.

Figure 1.13 shows a Finder search window that has been assigned several search attributes to act as filters for your search results. These attributes allow you to specify the type of file you want, including its name, when it was last opened, and many other specifications.

1.13 Customize your searches in Spotlight.

To add attributes to a search, follow these steps:

1. **Click the plus sign (+) next to Save in the upper-right area of the Finder window to add the first attribute.**

2. **Choose the type of attribute to use by clicking the pop-up menu, as shown in Figure 1.13.** There are many more attributes preconfigured by Apple that you can access by choosing Other from the attribute list. You can also add other conditions (specifically, the All, Any, or None of the following are true criteria) to the search by holding down the Option key while clicking the plus sign (+). Also, some attributes have several pop-up menus that you can change to customize them.

3. **Make any setting changes to the attribute to narrow your search.**

4. **Your new filtered search results are displayed almost instantly after you add an attribute.**

5. **Continue to add or remove (by clicking the minus sign) as many attributes as necessary.**

21

Genius

Use Boolean operators such as AND, OR, and NOT to logically narrow your search. You may also use quotes around text to specify that the words in the quotes must be found in exactly the order you typed them.

Managing Windows with Mission Control

Mission Control is a feature that is new to Lion. It allows you to see every open window, Dashboard, and all of your Spaces (more on those later in this chapter). Individual windows are grouped according to the application to which they belong. Figure 1.14 shows Mission Control in action.

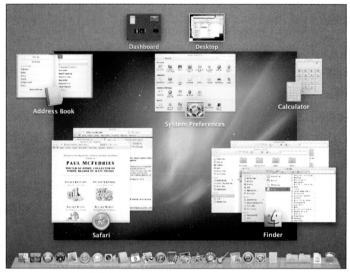

Image courtesy of Paul McFedries.

1.14 Mission Control shows every open window and other items, such as Dashboard, all in one location.

Manipulating open windows

You can launch Mission Control in a few ways:

- **Click the Mission Control icon in the Dock.**

- **Swipe up on your trackpad or Magic Mouse using three fingers.**

- **Press the Mission Control key on your keyboard, or press F9 (or fn+F9 for laptops) if you don't have a Mission Control key.** Consult the documentation for your Mac to find out if you have a Mission Control key.

Now that Mission Control is running, you can use it to move or copy files from location to location.

Moving a file from a folder to the desktop

You can easily move files from a folder to the desktop using Mission Control. Follow these steps:

1. **Find the file you want to move to your desktop and click to select it.**

2. **Start dragging the file while simultaneously pressing ⌘+Mission Control (use F11 if you don't have a Mission Control key or fn+F11 on a laptop) to hide all windows.**

3. **To move the file, just drop it onto the desktop.**

    - **To copy the file to the desktop, press Option before dropping it.**

    - **To create an alias for the file, press ⌘+Option before dropping it onto the desktop.**

Copying text and graphics to the desktop

You can use Mission Control to quickly copy text or graphics from another item (such as a document or website). To do so:

1. **In the window that you want to copy from, select the text or graphics you want to copy to the desktop.**

2. **Start dragging the text or graphics, and then press ⌘+Mission Control at the same time.** If you don't have a Mission Control key, use F11 (or fn+F11 on a laptop).

3. **Drop the text or graphics onto the desktop by releasing the mouse or trackpad button.**

Copying text and graphics from one window to another

Mission Control affords the flexibility to copy text and graphics from one open window to another. The window could be a folder, a website, or a document. To copy from one window to another, follow these steps:

1. **Open the window containing the text or graphics you want to copy, and then select them.**

2. **Start dragging the text or graphics by performing one of these options:**

    - **If copying the text or graphic into another window in the same application, press Control+Mission Control (F10 if you don't have a Mission Control key, or fn+F10 for laptops).**

- **If copying the text or graphics into a window from another application, press Mission Control (F9 if you don't have a Mission Control key, or fn+F9 on a laptop).**

3. **Hold the text or graphics over the window to which you want to copy them, and then press the same keys that you used in Step 2.**

4. **Copy the text or graphics to the other window by releasing the mouse or trackpad button.**

Setting Mission Control preferences

You can control several behaviors of Mission Control through the use of preferences. I'm very big on preferences, as they let you control more of the action.

Open the Mission Control preferences, shown in Figure 1.15, by choosing Apple menu ⇨ System Preferences, and then selecting the Mission Control icon in the Personal section.

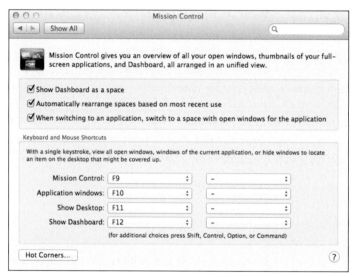

1.15 Configure the Mission Control preferences to suit your needs and work habits.

The preferences allow you to do the following:

- **Determine whether to show the Dashboard as a space.**

- **Arrange spaces automatically according to those you use the most.**

- Switch to a space automatically when choosing an application that has a window open within it.
- Configure keyboard and mouse shortcuts for launching Mission Control, switching to application windows, showing the desktop, or showing Dashboard.

Managing Windows with Exposé

Exposé is a great feature for helping clear up the jumbled mess of windows that can grind your productivity to a halt. Exposé arranges your windows in one of three ways, using three of the function keys at the top of your keyboard: F9, F10, and F11. You've actually already used Exposé in conjunction with Mission Control if you performed any of the Mission Control tasks earlier in this chapter.

Note As with Mission Control, if you have a laptop you have to hold down the fn key in conjunction with the F3, Control+F3, and ⌘+F3 keys for them to function correctly with Exposé.

Press F3 to arrange the open windows so that they can all be seen. Move the mouse pointer over the windows to see which applications they belong to. Click the window you want to bring to the forefront, or press F9 to return the Finder to its previous state.

Press Control+F3 to bring all of the open windows for the current application to the forefront. Press ⌘+F3 to cause all of the open windows to scram out of the way so that you can see the desktop. To return the windows to their previous position, press either Control+F3 or ⌘+F3, depending on which one you used to move the windows.

Using Multiple Desktops with Spaces

Spaces is an organizational tool that lets you create multiple spaces for certain tasks. Spaces are essentially additional desktops. You could have a space for surfing the web and checking e-mail, another space to watch your stocks, a third space to work on a spreadsheet, and so on.

Adding and removing spaces

You can have as many as 16 spaces at one time. There's nothing magical about adding or removing spaces:

1. **Launch Mission Control.**

2. **Move your mouse pointer to the
   upper-right corner of the screen and
   a plus sign (+) appears, as shown in
   Figure 1.16.**

3. **Click the plus sign (+) to add a new
   space to the top of the Mission
   Control window.**

You can remove spaces just as easily as you
add them:

1. **Launch Mission Control.**

2. **Move your mouse pointer to the
   upper-left corner of the space you
   want to remove and a small circle
   containing an X appears, as shown in
   Figure 1.17.**

3. **Click the X to remove the space.**

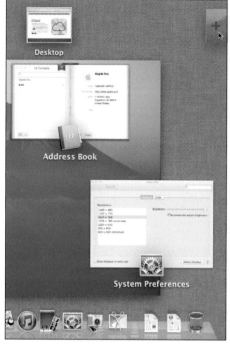

1.16 Click the plus sign (+) to add new spaces.

Moving between spaces

There are a few ways to jump from space to space:

- Launch Mission Control and click the space to which you want to move.

- Press Control and the corresponding number key of the space to which you want to
  jump. For example, if you want to move to the fourth space, press Control+4.

- Press Control and the right- or left-arrow key to scroll from space to space.

- The coolest way is to swipe three fingers to the left or the right to scroll through
  your spaces.

26

Image courtesy of Guy Hart-Davis.

1.17 To remove a space, click the X.

Moving windows between spaces

You can easily move a window from one space to another:

- **Launch Mission Control from within the space that contains the window to which you want to move.** Drag and drop the window into the space you want it.

- **Place the mouse pointer over the window you want to move.** Press Control and the corresponding number key of the space to which you want to move the window, or press the right- or left-arrow key to find the desired space. Release the keys to drop the window into its new space.

- **Drag the window you want to move all the way to the edge of the screen and hold it there for a moment.** Lion detects that you want to move the window to another space and automatically switches to the next space. When you get to the space to which you want the window moved, release the mouse or trackpad button.

Assigning applications to spaces

One feature I love in Spaces is the ability to assign applications to always open in a specific space. To assign applications to spaces, click and hold the application icon in the Dock to open the shortcut menu. If you don't see the application icon, open it so the icon appears in the Dock.

Select one of the following options to assign an application to a space (or all spaces):

- **Assign the application to open in one assigned space.** Choose Options ⇨ This Desktop, as shown in Figure 1.18. The application now opens only in the assigned space.

- **Assign the application to open in all spaces.** Choose Options ⇨ All Desktops. When you open the application, it is available across all the spaces you have in Mission Control.

- **Assign the application to only open in the space in which you are currently working.** Choose Options ⇨ None.

1.18 Choose the space in which your applications are assigned to open.

Managing Applications with Launchpad

Launchpad is an application launcher instantly familiar to folks who've used an iPhone, iPad, or iPod touch because of its obvious tie to iOS (the operating system used by those devices).

Launchpad displays all the apps installed on your Mac in full-screen mode, as shown in Figure 1.19.

Launching installed applications

Launching an application in Launchpad doesn't get much easier than this: simply click the icon of the application you want to open. That's it!

If you don't see the application you want to open in the initial Launchpad window, it may be because you have so many applications installed that they cannot all fit into one window. If that's the case, notice the dots at the bottom of the Launchpad window (see Figure 1.19); these indicate that there is more than one Launchpad window. Swipe the trackpad or Magic Mouse with two fingers to see the contents of the other Launchpad windows.

1.19 Launchpad affords a quick, easy solution to finding and launching applications.

Grouping applications with folders

You can group applications according to their type to help you organize them in the Launchpad window. For example, Launchpad automatically groups your utilities in a Utilities folder, as shown in Figure 1.20.

To group apps into folders, follow these steps:

1. **Click and drag the application you want to add to a folder on top of another application that you want to add to the same folder.**

2. **Drop the first application onto the icon of the second to create a new folder.**

3. **Click the name of the folder once to highlight it and then type a descriptive name for it.**

To access the applications in a folder, click the folder and then click the app icon to launch it. To remove applications from a folder, click the folder and drag the app icon from the folder to the Launchpad window.

1.20 In Launchpad, you can group similar applications into folders.

How Can I Customize Lion?

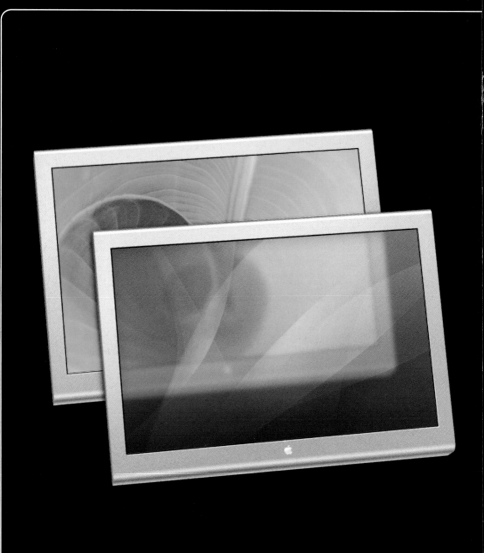

As attractive as Lion already is, it's always fun to customize your Mac to match your personality and preferences. Customizing creates a more enjoyable work and play environment. One of the slickest ways to customize Lion is with Dashboard and its widgets. These miniature applications can help you do a multitude of things, such as keep up with the weather or flight information. This chapter explores the numerous ways you can tweak Lion so that you feel as comfortable in front of your computer as you do in your living room.

The General Preferences Pane

The General preferences pane, shown in Figure 2.1, is your first stop on the Mac customization tour. Here, you can modify the basic color and textual elements of your Finder windows. To open this pane, click the System Preferences icon in the Dock, or choose Apple menu⇨System Preferences. Next, click the General icon in the Personal category of the System Preferences window.

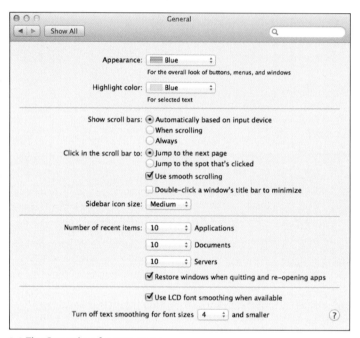

2.1 The General preferences pane.

Color modifications

The Appearance menu lets you choose the color you prefer for your system-wide menus and buttons. I hope either blue or graphite suits your taste because those are your only options.

You can change the default color used to highlight text with the Highlight color menu. Thankfully, there's a lengthy list of color choices available to you here.

Scrolling options

There are several different options for viewing information that doesn't fit your screen. For example, scroll bars usually appear, as shown in Figure 2.2.

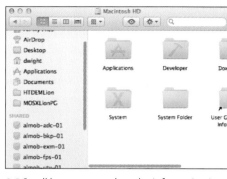

2.2 Scroll bars appear when the information in the window is too large to fit.

The options shown in Table 2.1 allow you to control how your Mac scrolls through documents or web pages that are too large for the screen.

Table 2.1 Scrolling Options

Option	Description
Show scroll bars	Scroll bars typically only appear in a window when the items within it don't quite fit, and you are using a mouse or trackpad to maneuver within the window. This behavior is the Automatically based on input device option and it's also the default. You can choose the When scrolling option to have the scroll bars appear only when scrolling, or Always to always display the scroll bars in windows.
Click in the scroll bar to	Select the Jump to the next page option for each click in the scroll bar to advance you one page in the document. The Jump to the spot that's clicked option moves you to the spot in the document that you are clicking. If you click the top of the scroll bar, then you jump to the first page of the document.
Use smooth scrolling	Scroll through your documents or web pages smoothly instead of jumping from page to page.
Double-click a window's title bar to minimize	Causes a window to minimize to the Dock when you double-click its title bar.
Sidebar icon size	Change the size of the icons in the sidebar to small, medium, or large.

Genius

You can switch between the Jump to the next page and Jump to the spot that's clicked options by holding down the Option key while clicking in the scroll bar.

Accessing recently used items

There's a very handy way to see and quickly access applications, documents, and servers that you've used recently. Simply click the Apple menu and hold your mouse over Recent Items, as shown in Figure 2.3. The Number of Recent Items pop-up menus in the General preferences pane let you choose how many of each item type you want to list.

Viewing fonts

Mac OS X uses a technique called anti-aliasing (or font smoothing) to help fonts appear without jagged edges. To enable or disable font smoothing in Lion, toggle the check box for Use LCD font smoothing when available (see Figure 2.1).

2.3 Looking at items that you've recently used.

The only possible downside to font smoothing is that it may cause some fonts to appear fuzzy Smaller font sizes can be almost impossible to read, so the General pane offers the option to turr off font smoothing for fonts smaller than the point size you choose at the bottom of the pane (see Figure 2.1).

Changing the Desktop

No two things personalize your Mac quite as much as great desktop pictures and really cool screer savers. From photos of the kids to fantastic paintings of faraway space battles, desktop picture: and screen savers can be very personal displays of individual taste and style.

Choosing a desktop picture

Open System Preferences by clicking its icon in the Dock or by choosing Apple menu ⇨ System Preferences. Click the Desktop & Screen Saver icon in the Personal category, and then click the Desktop tab at the top of the pane.

The left side of the Desktop tab, shown in Figure 2.4, lists the desktop pictures available on your system. Apple has taken the liberty of supplying you with a lot of different pictures and has even arranged them into subject folders.

2.4 The Desktop tab of the Desktop & Screen Saver preferences pane.

You can also add your personal collection of desktop pictures to this list by following these steps:

1. **Click the plus sign (+) below the list.**

2. **Browse the hard drive for the folder that contains the pictures you want to use.**

3. **Click Choose.**

To remove folders from the list, simply highlight the folder to be removed and then click the minus sign (–) below the list. To set an image as your default desktop picture, browse the list for the picture you want to use and click it once.

Should you quickly get bored with your choice of desktop picture, or if it's just too hard to decide which one you like best, select the Change picture check box at the bottom of the pane. Use the pop-up menu next to this check box to determine how often you want your Mac to change its desktop background. To add even more spice, select the Random order check box. This allows your Mac to use its own discretion when choosing a desktop picture.

Toggle the Translucent menu bar option to enable or disable translucency in the menu bar at the top of your screen. Some people love the translucent bar, others not so much, so it's nice of Apple to let you decide how you want it displayed.

Selecting a screen saver

Screen savers look really great on a Mac screen and they're somewhat useful for security purposes, but if not for these factors, screen savers would be obsolete in today's computing world. At one time, screen savers were a necessary tool to prevent *burn-in* from occurring on CRT-based monitors. Burn-in is when a latent image appears on a monitor after it is turned off. New monitors are typically LCD or plasma, and burn-in is no longer a concern.

To choose a screen saver that meets your personal standards of coolness, do the following:

1. **Open the Desktop & Screen Saver pane in System Preferences (Apple menu ⇨ System Preferences ⇨ Desktop & Screen Saver), and click the Screen Saver tab.**

2. **Browse the list of screen savers on the left side of the pane and find the one that grabs your attention.**

3. **Click Test to see the screen saver as it will look when engaged during normal use.** Move the mouse or press any key on your keyboard to exit the test.

4. **Select the Use random screen saver check box to allow Mac OS X to choose the screen saver it uses.**

5. **Select the Show with clock check box if you want a digital clock displayed on-screen with the screen saver.**

6. **Click and drag the Start screen saver slider to set the amount of time that your Mac is idle before the screen saver starts.**

7. **Finalize your selection and close System Preferences.**

Setting the screen saver options

Some screen savers allow you to change the way they behave by supplying an Options button underneath the Preview window, as shown in Figure 2.5. Click Options to make adjustments to the look of the chosen screen saver. For example, select the Flurry screen saver from the Screen Savers list on the left of the pane. Click Options and you see the options that are specific to that screen saver.

Finding Desktop Pictures on the Web

The Internet is chock-full of great websites for downloading desktop pictures. You can find a desktop picture to suit just about any mood or taste by performing a search on Google for the terms "desktop picture" or "wallpaper." If you want to find Mac-specific desktop pictures, simply add Mac OS X or Mac to your search criteria.

Here are a few sites you may want to check out:

- **www.macdesktops.com**
- **www.theapplecollection.com/desktop/**
- **http://interfacelift.com/wallpaper/downloads/date/any/**
- **www.pixelgirlpresents.com/desktops.php**
- **http://browse.deviantart.com/customization/wallpaper/**

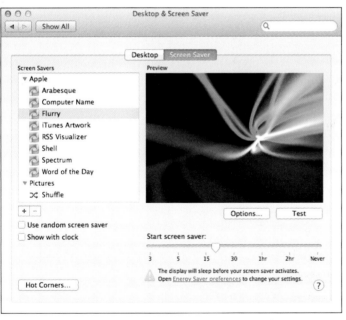

2.5 The Screen Saver tab of the Desktop & Screen Saver preferences pane.

Usually, options for screen savers are very straightforward. Choose an option from the Color pop-up menu to change the color of the streams. Move the sliders to change the number of streams, their thickness, or the speed at which they move.

Note   Mac OS X comes loaded with several really neat screen savers, but there are plenty that can be downloaded from the web, so you can personalize to your heart's content. Open Safari and search Mac OS X screen savers on Google to find more than you can shake a stick at.

Using hot corners

Have you noticed the Hot Corners button in the bottom-left corner of the pane? Click it to see the Hot Corners preferences sheet, similar to the one shown in Figure 2.6. Here, you can set actions for your Mac to take when you move the mouse pointer to one of the four corners of your screen.

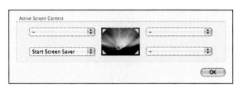

2.6 The Hot Corners preferences sheet, also known as Active Screen Corners.

Click one of the four pop-up menus to select an action for the corresponding screen corner. Table 2.2 lists actions that you can select for hot corners.

Table 2.2 Hot Corner Actions

Action	Result
Start Screen Saver and Disable Screen Saver	These two options speak, quite clearly, for themselves.
All Windows	All open windows are arranged in the screen so that they can be seen. This is the same function that Mission Control performs with the F9 key, as described in Chapter 1.
Application Windows	All open windows for the currently active application are neatly arranged so that each of their contents can be displayed at once. This is also achieved with the F10 key and Mission Control, as discussed in Chapter 1.
Desktop	This is yet another feature of Mission Control (using the F11 key), which causes all open windows to zoom off the screen so the desktop can clearly be seen. On current keyboards, this feature is mapped to ⌘+F3; on laptops, it's fn+F11.
Dashboard	Opens when the mouse is moved to the hot corner. See sections later in this chapter for more information on Dashboard.
Put Display to Sleep	Causes the monitor to go into sleep mode.
- (Minus sign)	Disables the hot corner.

Customizing the Finder

The Finder is the application you use most often on your Mac, so you may as well customize it to suit your needs and preferences. Mac OS X gives you a lot of latitude when it comes to customizing the Finder, and I'll show you a few of my favorite tweaks to this quintessential Mac OS standby in this section. While Chapter 1 covers the ins and outs of using the Finder, in this chapter you can discover how to give it that personal touch.

Finder windows

The Finder is a great tool for navigating your Mac, and I like to take full advantage of the available customization to make the Finder work for me.

Figure 2.7 is an example of the Finder modified to my specs. One of the differences between my customized Finder window and the default configuration is that the toolbar and sidebar have been changed significantly. This gives me quick access to the tools and folders that I use the most. I've also changed my view from Icons to Columns and there are two new additions to the bottom of the window: the path and status bars.

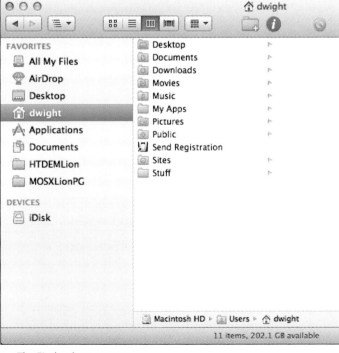

2.7 The Finder done my way.

Note The path bar is an easy way to see where you've been and to quickly get back there. To enable it, open a new Finder window and choose View⇨ Show Path Bar. It then appears in the bottom of the Finder window. The folders in the path bar change as you browse your hard drive. Double-click one of the folders in the path bar to zoom back to it. It's sort of like taking a tiny step back in time!

In the rest of this section, I show you how I customized Finder. Of course, you don't have to make the same changes to yours. In fact, I encourage you to experiment with all of the options the Finder affords, including those I don't touch on, so that you can find the combination that works best for you.

Modifying the toolbar

The toolbar gives you fast access to common tasks and actions, and helps you navigate your Mac more efficiently. You can change the default set of tools in the toolbar by adding items that you use more than others or removing those that you don't need. All of this is done in the Customize Toolbar sheet, shown in Figure 2.8.

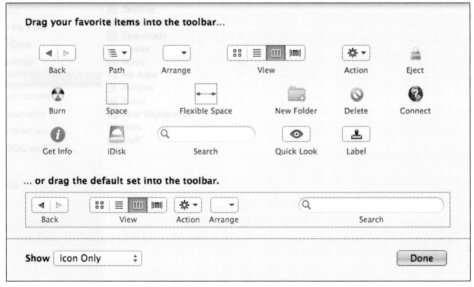

2.8 The Customize Toolbar sheet allows you to edit the tools available in the toolbar.

Follow these steps to customize the Finder toolbar:

1. **Activate the Finder by clicking its icon on the left side of the Dock.**

2. **Open a new Finder window by pressing ⌘+N.**

3. **Choose View ⇨ Customize Toolbar to open the Customize Toolbar sheet.**

4. **To add an item to the toolbar, drag and drop it from the sheet to the position in the toolbar that you desire.**

5. **To remove an item from the toolbar, simply drag and drop its icon anywhere outside of the Finder window, and it disappears in a puff of smoke!**

6. **If the arrangement of the icons in the toolbar doesn't suit you, just click and drag them to the spot where they work best.** As you drag an icon, the other icons move automatically to make room for it.

7. **Once you have everything just right, click Done to close the sheet.**

Table 2.3 gives an overview of the function of each item in the Customize Toolbar Sheet to help you make informed decisions about those you want to include.

Table 2.3 Customize Toolbar Sheet Items

Item	Description/Action
Back	Navigate forward or backward in the folder path.
Path	Click to see the current folder path.
Arrange	Select a method for organizing items in the Finder window. Select from Name, Kind, Application, Date Last Opened, Date Added, Date Last Modified, Date Created, Size, Label, or None to return to the default arrangement.
View	Quickly change the view for the current Finder window.
Action	Choose from a list of common actions, such as creating a new folder or getting information on an item.
Eject	Eject a disc or other removable media.
Burn	Burn a CD or DVD.
Space and Flexible Space	Use to separate items and groups of items.
New Folder	Creates a new folder within the current one.
Delete	Moves the selected file or folder to the Trash.
Connect	Opens the Connect to Server window, allowing you to quickly connect to other computers.
Get Info	Shows all information relative to the selected file or folder.
iDisk	Connects to your iDisk (a subscription to Apple's MobileMe service is required).
Search	Type the name of the item(s) you need to find on your hard drive.
Quick Look	Provides a glance at the contents of a file without having to open the application that created it.
Label	Add a color-coded label to a file or folder by selecting the item in the Finder window. Next, click and hold the Label button to select a color.

Genius

The fastest way to alter items already on the toolbar (or even the toolbar itself) is by using the trusty ⌘ key. To quickly rearrange items on the toolbar, hold down the ⌘ key, and then click and drag the item to its new location. To remove an item, simply press ⌘+click and drag it out of the toolbar, and then drop it.

Changing the sidebar

The sidebar contains links (or shortcuts) to folders, discs, and servers to which you often need access. You can modify the contents of the sidebar in a number of ways:

- **To remove an item you don't use, right-click (or Control+click) it and select Remove from Sidebar.**

- **Add your favorite folders by dragging their icons into the sidebar under the Favorites section, as shown in Figure 2.9.** The other items in the sidebar shift as necessary to make room for their new neighbor.

- **Adjust the size of the sidebar by clicking and dragging the divider bar.**

- **Hide the sidebar from view altogether by choosing View ⇨ Hide Sidebar from the menu, or by pressing ⌘+Option+S.**

- **Rearrange items in the sidebar by clicking and dragging them to their new location.**

2.9 Make the sidebar conform to your needs.

Note

See Chapter 1 to discover how to choose which Devices, Shared, Places, and Search For items are displayed by default in your sidebar.

Adding a background image or color

One trick that adds a touch of class and functionality to your Finder windows is to add a background picture or color to them. These can be used for simple decoration or to differentiate the contents of each folder. For example, if you keep records of your children's homework on your Mac, you could assign a picture of each child to the folder containing her homework. When you then open one of these folders in a Finder window, a light background picture of your little darling instantly identifies whose homework you're checking. This option is especially helpful if you have multiple windows open at once. To add a background image or color to your Finder windows, do the following:

1. **Open the folder to which you want to add the image or color.**

2. **Choose View ⇨ Show View Options or press ⌘+J.**

3. **Select the Color option in the Background section to add a color to the window or select the Picture option to place an image in the background, as shown in Figure 2.10.**

   - **If you choose to use a color, click inside the white square to the right of the option button to open the Colors palette.** Select the color that you want to use for the background and close the Colors palette.

   - **If you select Picture, drag an image into the Drag image here box next to the Picture option button.**

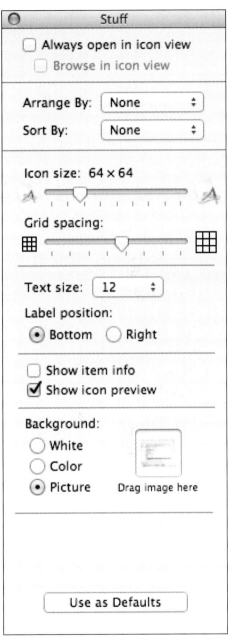

2.10 You can make changes to the background of a folder window in the Background section of the View Options window.

Note You must be in Icon view in order to use a background or color image in the Finder window. To do so, simply click the Icon view icon in the toolbar of the Finder window.

Caution A potential oops when using an image is that if it is too large to fit in the window you only see part of it. The Preview application that comes loaded with Mac OS X Lion is a great tool for easily resizing images. See Chapter 12 for step-by-step instructions.

Changing icons

A very popular method for redecorating your Mac is using custom icons for applications, folders, and files. You can change a plain folder icon into something more suitable for its contents. For example, you might use a football icon for the folder in which you keep your child's practice and game schedules. I've seen many a Mac on which icons were changed system-wide, from top to bottom!

Here's how to change any icon in Mac OS X Lion:

1. **Highlight the icon you want to use and press ⌘+I (Get Info) to open the Info window.**

2. **Click the icon picture in the upper-left corner of the Info window, as shown in Figure 2.11, and then copy the icon by pressing ⌘+C or choosing Edit ⇨ Copy.**

3. **Close the Info window.**

4. **Highlight the item with the icon you want to change and open its Info window by pressing ⌘+I.**

5. **Click the icon in the upper-left corner of the Info window and paste the new one there by pressing ⌘+V or choosing Edit ⇨ Paste.**

6. **Close the Info window of the changed item.**

2.11 Change an icon from within its Info window.

Genius There are utilities that you can purchase on the Internet to greatly ease your icon revamping. One such tool is CandyBar (www.panic.com/candybar), which makes icon customization and organization a breeze.

Adding and removing items in the Dock

You can add and remove items to and from the Dock as you please, and it's really easy to do:

- **To add an item to the Dock, simply drag its icon to the Dock and drop it where you want it.** You can also reposition an item in the Dock by simply dragging and dropping it in its new location.

- **If you have an application open that you want to keep in the Dock, click and hold the icon, hold your pointer over Options, and then select Keep in Dock from the contextual menu that appears, as shown in Figure 2.12.**

- **To remove an item, drag its icon from the Dock and let go of the mouse button.** The icon disappears in a puff of smoke! Don't worry — the original item is still in its location, you've just removed its alias.

2.12 Keep an icon in the Dock if you use it often.

Changing the appearance or placement of the Dock

You can tame the Dock by setting its preferences to meet your needs. Open the Dock preferences by right-clicking (or Control+clicking) the divider line and selecting Dock Preferences.

The Dock preferences window lets you make several changes:

- **Increase or decrease the size of the Dock by moving the Size slider.**

- **If your icons are too small to see clearly, select the Magnification check box and adjust the slider to increase or decrease the amount of magnification.** To magnify the icons, hold the mouse pointer over the Dock.

- **The Dock can be positioned on the left, right, or bottom of the window, which is the default setting.**

- **The Minimize windows using option lets you choose the special effect that occurs when you minimize a window into the Dock.** To minimize a window, click the yellow button in its upper-left corner.

- **To save tons of space in the Dock, check the box called Minimize windows into application icon.** To access minimized windows using this method, click and hold the icon for the application that owns the window. You then see the window in the contextual menu; click to maximize it.

- **Select the Animate opening applications check box to cause the icon of an item you are opening to bounce up and down in the Dock.**

- **If you don't like the Dock cramping your style — or your desktop space — you can hide it by selecting the Automatically hide and show the Dock check box.** When you inevitably have to use the Dock again, hold your mouse pointer at the bottom of the window for a second. The Dock temporarily pops back into view and goes back into hiding when you finish.

- **Select the Show indicator lights for open applications check box if you want bright white dots to appear beneath the icons of applications that are open.**

Working with Widgets

Lion includes an application called Dashboard that affords you another fun way to customize your Mac. With Dashboard, you can access and manage a multitude of widgets to track packages, get driving directions, browse the Yellow Pages, check stocks, see the latest weather forecasts, find out what movies are playing at your local multiplex, play Sudoku, and the list goes on. Widgets are one of those rare things that make your life easier and are cool to use at the same time. In the next few sections, I show you how to access, use, customize, and even create your own widgets.

Genius

If you have a Mac laptop with a multitouch trackpad, or if you have the Magic Trackpad for your desktop Mac, simply swipe three fingers from left to right to flick over to the Dashboard screen.

To open Dashboard and see the default set of running widgets, do one of the following:

- **Click the Dashboard icon in your Dock.**

- **Press F4 if you have a newer keyboard (F12 if it's a bit older).**

In the main body of the screen, you see the four widgets that Lion runs out of the gate: Calculator, iCal, Weather, and World Clock. These are very basic widgets that you can use to get your feet wet in the world of widgetry. To get a quick feel for using a widget, click the Calculator to bring it to the forefront and use your mouse to perform calculations on the virtual keypad, or use your keyboard to type information.

Notice the plus sign (+) in the small circle that appears in the lower-left corner of the screen when you activate Dashboard (see Figure 2.13). Click it to open the widget bar. This grants access to all the widgets that Lion so graciously includes. It also allows you to change those you have running.

Peruse the Widget bar until you see a widget that strikes your fancy, and then click to open it. When you click the widget you want to open, Dashboard drops it on your screen.

To close any widget, click the X in the upper-left corner. Dashboard even has a neat effect for this action — the widget is sucked into the X until it disappears. If that's not cool enough for you, hold down the Shift key while clicking the X to watch it disappear in slow motion.

The Lion preinstalled widgets

Because there are quite a few widgets that come preinstalled on Lion, I want to give you a quick synopsis of what's available and what each one can do. Table 2.4 spells out the details.

Table 2.4 Lion Widgets

Widget	Function
Widgets	Opens the Widget manager.
Address Book	Lets you quickly search your Address Book and displays information for the contact.
Calculator	Performs basic mathematical computations.

continued

Table 2.4 continued

Dictionary	A fast way to look up definitions. Also doubles as a thesaurus.
ESPN	Finds all the latest scores and sports news.
Flight Tracker	When you type a flight number, Flight Tracker details its status.
iCal	Displays your schedule for the day selected.
Movies	Gives you the movie showtimes for local theaters. You can also view trailers or buy tickets online.
People	Finds people by their name and city.
Ski Report	You can type the name of your favorite ski resort to get the latest information on skiing conditions.
Stickies	You can use them just like you would the real thing: to keep little notes all over your Mac!
Stocks	Keeps up with all the latest Wall Street comings and goings for stocks that you specify.
Tile Game	Keeps a really, really bored person occupied for awhile.
Translation	Instantly translates words or phrases from one language to another.
Unit Converter	Converts units for several different measurements, such as time, length, currency, and pressure.
Weather	Provides the latest weather prognostications for your neck of the woods. Covered in detail later in this chapter.
Web Clip	Lets you create your own widgets. More on this feature later in this chapter.
World Clock	Displays an analog clock that can give you the time of day for hundreds of locations around the world.

Managing widgets

Lion comes fully stocked with a great set of widgets, but there are a lot of them. Those you never use may just take up real estate on your screen. If you install other widgets, as discussed later in this chapter, there are even more icons to browse through in the widget bar. Dashboard provides a handy way to disable the widgets that you rarely use without actually uninstalling them. This comes in handy should you decide to try one of them in the future.

To disable or enable widgets, do the following:

1. **Press F4 (F12 on older keyboards) to open Dashboard.**

2. **Click the plus sign (+) in the lower-left corner of your screen to open the Widget bar.**

3. **Click Manage Widgets to open the Widget manager, as shown in Figure 2.13.**

4. **Deselect the check boxes next to widgets that you want to disable and select those you want to enable.**

5. **Close the Widget manager window when finished.**

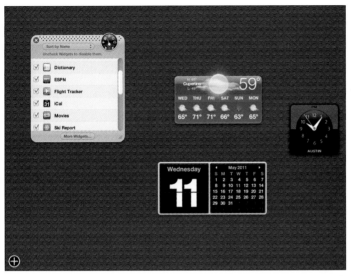

2.13 Use the Widget manager (on the left side of the screen) to organize the Widget bar. Click the plus sign to add one to Dashboard.

Genius

To uninstall widgets that you've added to Dashboard, open the Widget manager and click the remove symbol (the red circle with a horizontal white line in the middle) to the right of the widget name. To uninstall a widget that came with Lion, select Hard Drive ➪ Library ➪ Widgets. Drag the widget you want to remove to the Trash and type your administrator password.

Setting preferences in widgets

Many widgets require a bit of customization to effectively utilize them. For example, Movies doesn't do you much good if you live in Auburn, Alabama, but it's giving you showtimes and theaters in Cupertino, California. Stocks won't be of much assistance either if you want to see what a hot new stock is doing, but all you get are the default stocks set up in the widget.

Let's use Weather to illustrate how to edit the preferences of a widget:

1. **Press F4 (or F12 on an older keyboard) to open Dashboard.**

2. **Position your mouse pointer over the lower-right corner of the Weather widget to see the Information button (i), as shown in Figure 2.14.**

2.14 Click the Information button to open a widget's preferences, if available.

3. **Click the Information button to flip the widget over and see its available preferences.** Make the preference changes you desire and then click Done.

4. **The widget should now reflect the changes you made.**

Note

Not all widgets give you the option of adjusting their preferences, so don't beat yourself up if you can't seem to find the elusive Information button.

Finding more cool widgets

So far, the only widgets you've been privy to are those that come with Lion, but I'm about to change that. There are hundreds of widgets that have been developed, and some of them may be exactly what you're looking for.

One of my favorite places to find new widgets is the Apple website (more on that in a moment), but you can also find widgets by simply performing a search on Google for Mac OS X widgets.

To get new widgets the quick and easy way, do the following:

1. **Press F4 (or F12 on an older keyboard) to open Dashboard.**

2. **Click the plus sign (+) in the lower-left corner of your screen to open the Widget bar.**

3. **Click Manage Widgets to open the Widget manager and then click More Widgets at the bottom of the window.** Safari automatically whisks you away to the Apple Dashboard Widgets website, shown in Figure 2.15. Here you can browse massive amounts of available widgets created by developers and regular users alike.

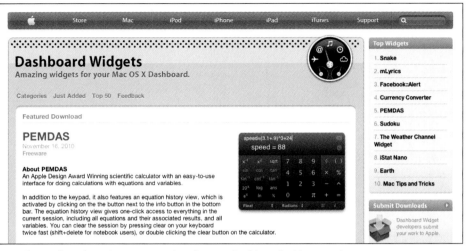

2.15 The Apple website is a one-stop shop for your Dashboard widget needs.

4. **Use the Widget Browser to find one you want to try.** You may need to scroll down slightly on the page to see the browser.

5. **Click Download to have Safari download the widget.**

6. **Click Install when prompted to open your new widget in Dashboard.** If you like what you see, click Keep; if not, click Delete.

Creating your own widgets using Web Clips

A neat feature in Dashboard is the ability to create your own widgets using clips of web pages. This is a great feature for tracking information from a website without having to constantly navigate to it to check its status. For example, you can see the most popular available widgets on the Apple Dashboard Widgets website without browsing to the site. You can simply view the list in Dashboard, as shown in Figure 2.16, by pressing F4 (or F12 on an older keyboard).

To create a widget using Web Clips, do the following:

1. **Press F4 (or F12 on an older keyboard) to open Dashboard.**

2. **Click the plus sign (+) in the lower-left corner of the screen and then click the Web Clip icon in the widget bar.**

3. **Click the Safari icon in the Web Clip Widget window to open Safari.** If Safari doesn't open, simply press F4 to exit Dashboard and select the Safari icon in the Dock.

4. **Type the address of the website you want to use to create your widget.** In this example, I use www.apple.com/downloads/dashboard/.

5. **Choose File ⇨ Open in Dashboard.** The web page darkens and you are presented with a selection box, as shown in Figure 2.16.

6. **Position the selection box over the section of the web page you want to use for your widget and then click to select the area.** You can drag the handles that appear around the selection box to adjust the selected area.

7. **Click Add in the upper-right corner of the Safari window (in the purple bar).** Safari passes the selection on to Dashboard, where your new widget is created.

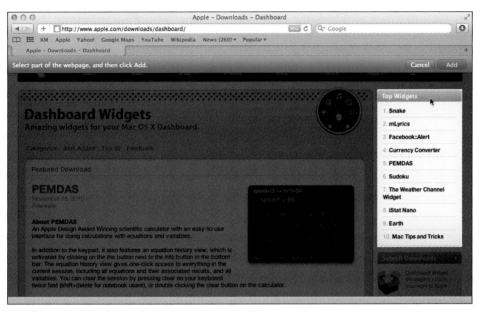

2.16 Select the part of the web page you want to use for your widget.

How Do I Change the Lion System Preferences?

By this point, you are familiar with my affinity for making your Mac behave as you want. No other place in Lion gives you more control over your Mac than System Preferences. This is where you can assert yourself as the alpha user and firmly establish yourself as the ruler of your computing domain. System Preferences is where you can make local and system-wide changes to networking, security, software, hardware, sound, and the appearance of Lion. This chapter explains what preferences are available to help you tame Lion, and how to change them if you need or want to.

Personal

As its name indicates, the Personal section of the System Preferences is where you can customize the way your Mac looks and behaves. I cover only the Language & Text, Security & Privacy, and Universal Access preferences here because the others are covered in detail in Chapters 1 and 2.

Open System Preferences before reading any further in this chapter by choosing Apple menu⇨System Preferences. You are rewarded with the System Preferences window, as shown in Figure 3.1.

3.1 Click the preference you want to view or change from within the System Preferences window.

Language & Text

Lion is quite the international sensation and can speak more languages than I ever knew existed! The Language & Text preferences pane helps your Mac flex its multilingual muscles.

Language

The Language tab (see Figure 3.2) of the Language & Text preferences pane allows you to decide the order in which languages are used for application menus, for sorting items, and for dialog windows.

Genius

Lion is fluent in more than 110 languages, so the list of available languages is quite lengthy. To save yourself from having to hunt for the languages you find useful in the future, click Edit List and deselect the languages you don't need.

3.2 Your Mac can be very cosmopolitan using the Language & Text preferences pane.

Text

The Text tab of the Language & Text preferences (see Figure 3.3) allows you to customize substitution features, spell-checking, and more text magic.

Options available in the Text tab include:

- **Use symbol and text substitution.** Applications in Lion can substitute text you don't want for text you do want. For example, if you select the check box next to (c), when you type (c) it will be replaced by the copyright symbol (©). Click the plus sign (+) in the lower-left corner to add your own custom symbol and text substitutions or click Restore Defaults to return to the original Lion substitutions.

- **Spelling.** Lion can check spelling for you automatically if you select the Correct spelling automatically check box. You can also use the Spelling pop-up menu to customize the languages used.

- **Word Break.** This changes how a word is highlighted when double-clicked. Standard is the typical setting, but those using Japanese as their primary language should select Japanese.

- **Smart Quotes.** Modify how double and single quotes display around your text using the pop-up menus.

59

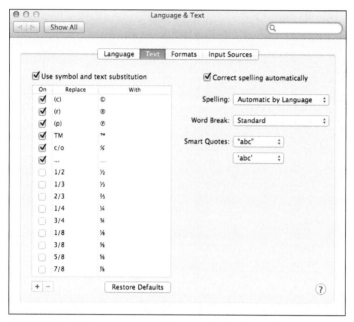

3.3 In the Text tab, you can customize text substitution, and more.

Formats

You can use the Formats tab to decide how items such as dates, time, monetary increments, and measurements display on your Mac by default. Figure 3.4 shows the options that are available for localizing Lion.

Click Customize in the Dates, Times, and Numbers sections to further customize the layout.

Input Sources

Some languages use more characters than there are keys on the keyboard. In these cases, input methods provide a way for you to access those characters. The Input Sources tab, shown in Figure 3.5, allows you to choose from among the multitude of input methods that ship with Lion. Many of these input sources are different keyboard layouts. The keyboard layout used by English speakers is called the Dvorak layout.

For more information, click the Help button (?) in the lower-right corner of the tab.

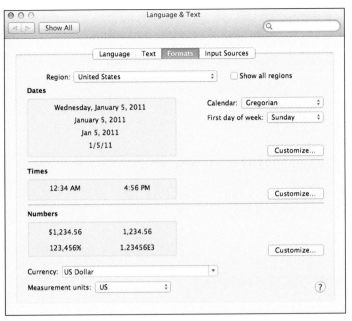

3.4 Choose how best to display regional items with the Formats tab.

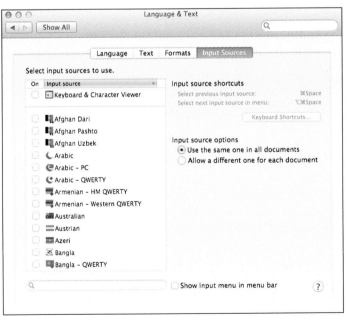

3.5 You can use the Input Sources tab to access characters that aren't available on a standard keyboard.

Security & Privacy

Even a Mac needs to be secured from outside troublemakers, so Lion comes packaged with some very nice security features that you can access through the Security & Privacy preferences pane in System Preferences.

General

Figure 3.6 shows the options available under the General tab.

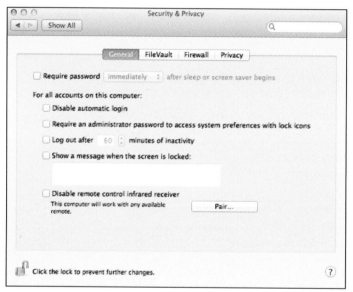

3.6 The General tab of the Security & Privacy preferences.

These are fairly self-explanatory, but some aren't quite as intuitive as others. The General tab options are as follows:

- **Require password after sleep or screen saver begins.** Select this check box to lock your Mac from any user who doesn't know your account password once it goes to sleep or a screen saver activates. Use the pop-up menu to determine when the password is required.

- **Disable automatic login.** If this check box is not selected, your Mac simply boots up into the default account without any prompt for a password.

- **Require an administrator password to access system preferences with lock icons.** There is a lock icon in the bottom-left corner of each preferences pane. If you select this check box, the icon remains in the locked position for every pane in System Preferences and unlocks only with an administrator password.

Note If most of the options in the General tab of the Security & Privacy preferences pane are grayed out, click the lock icon in the lower-left corner of the window and type the username and password of an administrator account on your Mac.

- **Log out after *X* minutes of inactivity.** Select this option to have your Mac automatically log out of your account after the specified time of inactivity.

- **Show a message when the screen is locked.** Select this check box and type your message in the text box. It can be anything you want, from stern warnings to leave your precious Mac untouched, to helpful information for those authorized to log in to the system.

- **Disable remote control infrared receiver.** Some Macs have infrared receivers that they use to receive commands from an Apple remote control for viewing movies, listening to music, and other activities. Select this check box if you want to disable your infrared receiver so that other Mac owners can't control your Mac using their remote.

- **Pair.** You can configure your Mac to respond to a particular remote control by clicking Pair and following the instructions.

Genius I highly recommend that you use both the Require password after sleep or screen saver begins and Disable automatic login options. Not selecting these allows unfettered access to anyone who turns on, restarts, or wakes up your Mac. At that point, the fate of your Mac and all the files it holds is entirely in the hands of the trespasser.

FileVault

The FileVault tab lets you enable the Lion FileVault feature, which I do not recommend unless you are a very savvy and security-minded computer user. FileVault encrypts your entire home folder, which prevents anyone else from seeing its contents. Although this sounds great, the big downfall for someone who is not used to such high security is that if you forget your user account password or recovery key, then all content in the home folder is lost. Yikes!

If you want to turn on FileVault protection for your account, click the FileVault tab in the Security & Privacy preferences pane and click Turn On FileVault. Your Mac must have enough space available on its hard drive to store an encrypted version of your home folder.

Firewall

A firewall prevents unauthorized users from accessing your Mac through the Internet or your net-work. These bothersome folks are up to no good, but a firewall may keep them at bay. To select firewall settings, click the Firewall tab in the Security & Privacy preferences pane. Enable the fire-wall for your Mac by clicking Start. You can then configure the following settings, shown in Figure 3.7, by clicking Advanced in the lower-right corner of the pane:

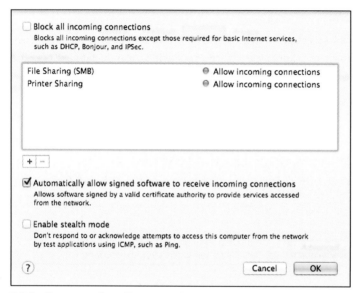

3.7 Configure your firewall to customize incoming connections.

- **Block all incoming connections.** This option prevents all incoming connections from touching your Mac, except the most basic types needed for Internet access, such as DHCP and Bonjour.

- **The allowed applications box lists applications from which you want to receive incoming connections.** Click the plus sign (+) under the lower-left corner of the box to add an application to the list, and then use the pop-up menu to allow or restrict incom-ing connections for it. Click the minus sign (-) to remove applications from the list. This box also shows you other sharing functions you've enabled in the Sharing preferences pane, such as file and printer sharing.

- **Automatically allow signed software to receive incoming connections.** If you select this option, an application or service signed by a valid certificate authority automatically appears in the allowed applications box.

- **Enable stealth mode.** Stealth mode allows your Mac to hide from network probing requests, such as ping.

Note If you are connecting to the Internet through a router, you probably won't need to enable the Lion firewall because the router is most likely running one. Check your router documentation to be certain of its firewall settings. However, if you are on a large network you may want to enable the firewall to prevent uninvited guests from entering your Mac via your network.

Universal Access

Lion implements the Universal Access preferences so that those who have physical difficulties, such as loss of eyesight, can use a Mac with little to no problem. Table 3.1 lists the tabs and options that are available for each preference.

Table 3.1 Universal Access Preferences

Tab	Options
Seeing	VoiceOver tells your Mac to read all text the mouse moves over.
	Zoom turns on the zoom function, which is activated by the keyboard shortcuts listed in the preferences pane.
	Display provides great options for Mac users whose eyesight isn't what it once was.
Hearing	If you have difficulty hearing at normal levels, you can adjust the volume here and have the Mac flash its screen to alert you to incoming information.
Keyboard	This tab provides options for helping Mac users who may have difficulty using the traditional keyboard.
Mouse & Trackpad	Should you have problems using a mouse or trackpad, you can use Mouse Keys, which causes the numeric keypad (available on most Mac keyboards) to act as a temporary mouse.

Hardware

The Hardware section of System Preferences lets Lion know how you want it to interact with the various hardware components of your Mac. For information on the Print & Scan preferences, see Chapter 13.

CDs & DVDs

When you insert a CD or DVD into the Mac disc drive, something's going to happen; what that is, however, is entirely up to you. The CDs & DVDs preferences pane lets you tell Lion how it should behave when you insert a disc, as shown in Figure 3.8.

65

3.8 Tell Lion how to handle CDs and DVDs from here.

Displays

The Displays preferences help you set the resolution of the Mac monitor or screen. The options in both tabs of the pane, Display (see Figure 3.9) and Color, are standard on any computer. There is a third tab called Arrangement that appears if you connect a second display to your Mac. Follow the instructions in the Arrangement tab to set up an extra display.

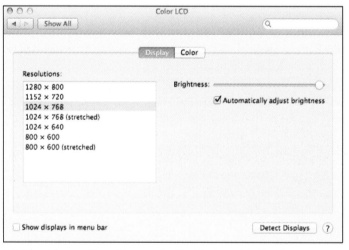

3.9 Adjust the monitor settings under the Display tab in the Displays preferences pane.

The Display tab allows you to change these settings (some settings may not appear, depending on what type of display you are using):

- **Resolutions.** Lets you choose the amount of detail your screen shows. The higher the resolution, the smaller the items on your screen appear; the lower the resolution, the larger they are.

- **Refresh rate.** Determines how often the display is redrawn. If you aren't using a Mac with a built-in display, such as a laptop or an iMac, consult the documentation that came with your monitor for appropriate refresh rates.

- **Detect Displays.** Click this button to have Lion automatically discover newly connected displays and to choose the settings to use with them.

- **Gather windows.** Click this button to move all Displays preferences panes to the display the button is available on. You must be using multiple displays to see this button.

- **Rotate.** This option allows you to rotate the images on your display by the amount you select.

- **Brightness.** Drag the slider to increase or decrease the brightness of your display.

- **Show displays in menu bar.** Select this check box to place a shortcut to the Displays preferences in the menu bar.

- **Overscan.** Should you be using a TV as a display, you may not be able to see the menu bar at the top of the screen. If this is the case, simply enable this option to see the menu bar.

The Color tab is where you can set your display to use color profiles so that it can represent colors more accurately. Deselect the Show profiles for this display only check box to see all profiles installed on your Mac.

Genius

Sometimes the best color is what suits your eye, rather than what Lion automatically chooses for your monitor. You can create a custom profile for your monitor to use by clicking Calibrate and following the instructions. If color matching is old hat to you, select the Expert Mode check box in the Display Calibrator Assistant Introduction screen to gain access to a more finely tuned process.

Energy Saver

Everyone's trying to be a bit greener these days, and Lion is no exception. The Energy Saver preferences provide settings for your computer, hard drive, and display to sleep when they are inactive for the period of time that you set by dragging the sliders, as shown in Figure 3.10.

Note

The Energy Saver preferences differ slightly depending on whether you are on a notebook or desktop. Consult your manual for more specific information.

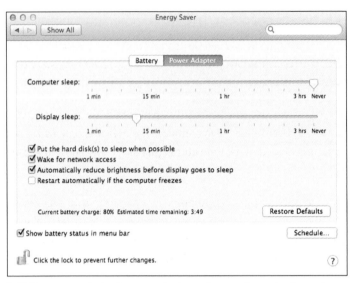

3.10 Save energy by having your display and computer go to sleep when not in use.

Click the Power Adapter tab (or the Options tab on a desktop) in the Energy Saver preferences pane to set these options. The options differ depending on the type of Mac you have, but the basic settings and their functions are as follows:

- **Put the hard disk(s) to sleep when possible.** Puts the hard drive to sleep whenever it's inactive.

- **Slightly dim the display when using this power source.** Lowers the brightness when the power source is switched to the battery.

- **Wake for network access.** Awakens your Mac when a network administrator is trying to access it through the network.

- **Automatically reduce brightness before display goes to sleep.** When not in use, the brightness of your display decreases a couple of minutes before it goes to sleep.

- **Start up automatically after a power failure.** Select this option to have your Mac restart on its own after an interruption in power.

- **Restart automatically if the computer freezes.** Selecting this option causes your Mac to automatically restart if it freezes up (that is, if it becomes stuck).

- **Show battery status in menu bar.** Places a battery icon in the menu bar on a laptop, allowing you to easily monitor the amount of remaining charge.

Keyboard

The Keyboard preferences pane gives you two tabs — Keyboard and Keyboard Shortcuts — to configure how your keyboard interacts with Lion. You can also set up a wireless keyboard using Bluetooth and create your own keyboard shortcuts.

Click the Keyboard tab to modify how quickly the keyboard responds to a key press or whether to automatically illuminate your keyboard in low-light settings. The available options are self-explanatory, but if you need further help, click the Help button (the question mark) in the lower-right corner of the window.

I love the fact that Apple gives you the opportunity to make your own keyboard shortcuts for applications under the Application Shortcuts section of the Keyboard Shortcuts tab, shown in Figure 3.11. Click the plus sign (+) in the lower-left corner to create a new one or highlight a shortcut in the list and click the minus sign (–) to delete it. To disable a shortcut, simply deselect the check box next to it. You can also enable or disable shortcuts for the other sections in the Keyboard Shortcuts tab, such as Services and Spotlight.

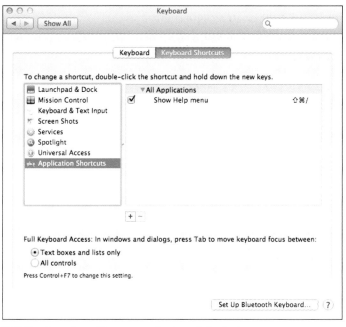

3.11 Create and modify your own keyboard shortcuts.

Mouse

The Mouse preferences pane gives you the ability to configure how your mouse behaves with Lion. You can also set up a wireless mouse using Bluetooth. Lion determines the kind of mouse you have and gives you the options necessary for configuring its operation, but you see something similar to what is shown in Figure 3.12.

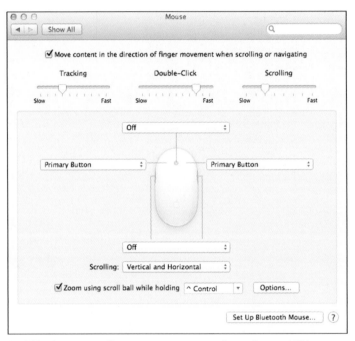

3.12 Lion lets you configure your mouse according to its capabilities.

Trackpad

The Trackpad preferences pane, shown in Figure 3.13, only appears if you are using a laptop or have a Magic Trackpad connected to your desktop Mac.

The Multi-Touch trackpads on Mac laptops provide some amazingly cool features that you can modify to your liking with the options in the Trackpad pane:

- **Adjust tracking, double-click, and scrolling speeds using their respective sliders.**

- **Customize trackpad gestures for scrolling, zooming, dragging, rotating, swiping, pinching, and clicking.** Apple has provided a great visual help with the gestures using short video clips illustrating each type. These can be found by going to Apple menu ⇨ System Preferences ⇨ Trackpad.

3.13 Tweak the Trackpad settings to reflect the way you work.

Sound

Configure the Mac sound in the Sound preferences pane, as shown in Figure 3.14.

3.14 Change your Mac sounds using the Sound preferences.

Table 3.2 gives a brief overview of each tab in the pane.

Table 3.2 Sound Options

Tab	Options
Sound Effects	Select which sounds to use for system alerts, adjust their volume, and set the system-wide output volume.
Output	Choose output devices (such as external speakers) to broadcast Mac sounds and adjust the sound balance.
Input	Select a sound input device (such as an external microphone) and adjust the volume. You can also filter unwanted background noise on devices by selecting the Use ambient noise reduction check box.

Internet and Wireless

The Internet & Wireless preferences are where you tell your Mac how to communicate with the rest of the world through its network connections. Please note that the Bluetooth and Sharing preferences are covered in depth in Chapter 13.

MobileMe

Since July 2008, Apple has offered MobileMe, a service that extends your Mac experience to the Internet. Apple is no longer accepting subscriptions for this service as it is launching a new one called iCloud in late 2011. iCloud will handle the same services as MobileMe, and much more, including the ability to push files to every device. For example, if you take a picture with your iPhone, iCloud automatically copies it to your other devices registered to iCloud, such as a Mac or iPad.

Meanwhile, the MobileMe service is available to those who already have a subscription until June 30, 2012. With MobileMe, you can:

- **Synchronize calendars, contacts, data, and more.**
- **Access your MobileMe e-mail account through any web browser on any computer.**
- **Use an iDisk to store files and synchronize folders.**
- **Create your own website.**
- **Use Back to My Mac to access your home or office Mac from a remote location using any computer connected to the Internet.**

- Organize your family's activities, team meetings, church events, and more using Groups.
- Share photos and movies with incredible ease using Web Gallery.

The MobileMe preferences pane is where you can log in to your MobileMe account and set up how your Mac interacts with the service. To log in to your account, visit www.apple.com/mobileme/.

Mail, Contacts, and Calendars

The Mail, Contacts & Calendars preferences pane is new to Mac OS X, and it greatly simplifies the process of setting up service provider accounts that you might use for e-mail, calendars, and the like, such as Microsoft Exchange or Google accounts. To set up one or more of these accounts, simply click New Account on the left, choose from one of the popular account types listed, and then type the information necessary to access the account. If you don't see what you need, click Other and select an account type from the list provided, as shown in Figure 3.15.

3.15 Manage any accounts you have with service providers for e-mail, calendars, and other items.

73

Network

The Network preferences pane, shown in Figure 3.16, is where you configure settings for your various network connection types.

3.16 The Network preferences pane is where all of your network settings are configured.

The list on the left side of the pane shows the network connections that your Mac supports. The contents of this list vary, depending on the network hardware that is available on your Mac.

- **Wi-Fi.** Settings for using the built-in AirPort card on your Mac or a third-party wireless adapter to access a network wirelessly.

- **Ethernet.** Settings for connecting to a network using the built-in Ethernet port on your Mac.

- **FireWire.** Lion allows you to connect two Macs together with a FireWire cable so that you can share files or Internet connections between them.

- **Bluetooth.** Your Mac can also use its Bluetooth adapter to share your cellular phone's Internet access (assuming the phone has a Bluetooth adapter, as well).

Click one of the network connections to gain access to its innermost workings. Click Advanced in the lower-right corner (see Figure 3.16) to inspect or manually set the network connections for that particular method, as shown for Wi-Fi in Figure 3.17.

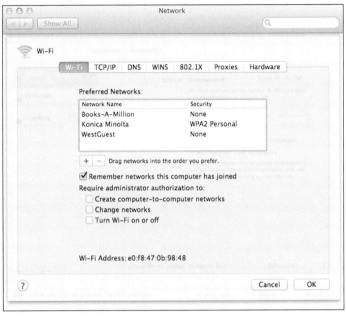

3.17 Advanced settings let you fine-tune the network options.

Detailed information on the options that are available for each of the connection types can be found by clicking the Help button (the question mark).

System

The System section of the System Preferences contains panes for configuring the accounts on your Mac, updating software, choosing a start-up disk, and many more system-wide options. For information about the Users & Groups, and Parental Controls preferences, see Chapter 4. Time Machine is covered in depth in Chapter 14.

Date & Time

Adjust the Mac time settings with the Date & Time preferences pane, shown in Figure 3.18.

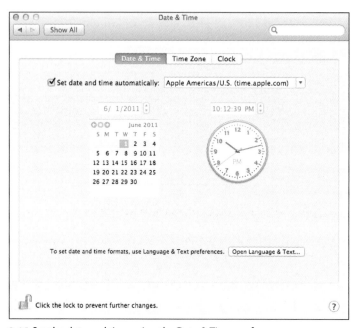

3.18 Set the date and time using the Date & Time preferences pane.

The tabs provide the following options:

● **Date & Time.** Select the Set date and time automatically check box to have your Mac get the correct date and time from an Internet time server, and then select a time server from the list provided. To manually set the date and time, deselect this option and adjust each to your preference.

● **Time Zone.** Select the time zone you are in by choosing an area on the map that appears.

● **Clock.** Decide if and how to display the date and time in the menu bar. You can also set your Mac to speak the time to you at specified intervals.

Software Update

Lion uses the Software Update application to check for updates to the operating system and compatible applications.

The Scheduled Check tab lets you instantly check the Apple servers for new updates by clicking Check Now. You can also schedule update checks by selecting the Check for updates option and specifying how often Software Update should do so.

The Installed Updates tab lists all the updates that have been downloaded and installed on your Mac.

Genius

There are several schools of thought when it comes to upgrading to the latest and greatest software. In my opinion, if there's an update available for your operating system or an application, go ahead and get it. The vast majority of the time, updates don't cause any problems; on the contrary, they usually end up fixing or preventing them.

Speech

Lion is so intelligent that it can talk to you and even respond to spoken commands. Here are the available options.

Speech Recognition

The Settings tab within the Speech Recognition tab, shown in Figure 3.19, lets you turn Speakable Items on or off, as well as select the microphone with which your Mac should listen to your commands. You can also select a listening key, which is the key you press to make your Mac listen for your spoken commands.

3.19 The options available in the Speech settings window under the Speech Recognition tab.

The Commands tab allows you to customize the spoken commands to which your Mac responds. Click Open Speakable Items Folder to see a list of the preconfigured commands your Mac understands. Click Helpful Tips to get great advice on how to successfully use the Speakable Items options and commands.

Text to Speech

This section of the Speech preferences lets you choose which voice your Mac uses when it speaks to you. Select from several pre-installed voices and modify the rate at which your Mac says the words. You can also have Lion announce system alerts, announce when an application needs to be looked after, or speak text that you've highlighted in a document.

Startup Disk

This preference pane allows you to choose to start your Mac from any drive that contains a valid Mac OS X or Windows installation. If you have multiple partitions or external drives containing operating systems on the Mac hard drive, the Startup Disk preferences is where you tell your Mac from which partition or drive you want it to start up. When you first open these preferences, you are presented with a list of drives that are considered to be valid start-up devices. Select the drive with which you want to boot up, and then click Restart.

Adding an Archives preference pane

The most likely reason you would use the Lion Archive Utility is to compress files and folders. This makes them easier to send via e-mail and reduces the amount of space they take up on a drive. From time to time, you may desire to change the way Lion compresses files, depending on the tasks you are trying to perform, but there is no visible way to do so by default. Apple has a hidden preference pane that you can manually add to your System Preferences window. In this pane, you can change the way Archive Utility behaves. Should you need to install it at some point, follow these steps:

1. **Open a new Finder window by pressing ⌘+N from within the Finder.**

2. **Browse to the directory /System/Library/CoreServices and locate the Archive Utility.**

3. **Right-click (or Control+click) the Archive Utility icon and select Show Package Contents.**

4. **Open the Contents folder and then the Resources folder.**

5. **Double-click the Archives.prefPane file.**

6. **Determine whether to install the Archives preference pane only for your user account or for all user accounts on the computer, and then click Install.** Type the name and password of an administrator account when prompted, and then click OK.

7. **The Archives preference pane, shown in Figure 3.20, can be found in the Other section at the bottom of the System Preferences window.**

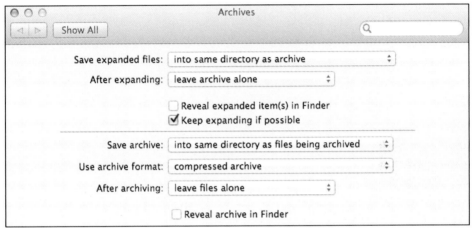

3.20 Determine how Lion compresses files and folders.

How Do I Manage User Accounts?

User accounts are the perfect way to ensure that multiple people can use your Mac without completely goofing up the whole thing. In this chapter, I show you how to create multiple user accounts and the type of accounts you can select. Individual accounts allow all users to configure certain settings to their liking while protecting the other accounts on the Mac. Lion also provides parental controls to help concerned moms and dads keep tabs on their prodigy's computer usage, protecting both their kids and their Mac.

Types of Accounts

Let's face it — some computer users can be trusted more than others. Factors useful for assessing a user's trustworthiness may be age, maturity, responsibility, or prowess with a computer. Lion allows you to create user accounts that have nearly complete access to every component of the operating system, those that have strictly limited access, and anything in between.

Administrator

Administrator accounts are the big dogs of the user accounts world. They are the default account created when you first install Lion. Administrators can handle almost any task on your Mac, including:

- **Creating and removing (deleting) user accounts.**
- **Changing settings for other user accounts.**
- **Changing all system settings, including those that are locked in System Preferences.**
- **Installing software and drivers that any user on the system can utilize (if you allow that, of course).**
- **Deciding whether to rule his Mac kingdom with an iron fist or to be more benevolent, loved, and adored by all of his minions.**

Standard

A standard account is adequate for most users. These accounts allow a user enough freedom to customize without the power to alter other accounts. A standard account user:

- **Can install software in her own account (if she has access to that software, that is).**
- **Can customize her working environment with System Preferences; however, she cannot alter locked System Preferences.**
- **Cannot modify, add, or delete other user accounts.**

Managed with Parental Controls

Parental Controls are used to manage, or limit, these accounts and the privileges they have. I discuss Parental Controls in greater detail later in this chapter, so I won't deal with the particulars here.

Sharing Only

A Sharing Only account restricts a user to accessing the computer only through the network, just as he would a server. Sharing Only accounts are useful for sharing documents with others in your home or office, without giving them access to the rest of your home folder or Mac. The user cannot log on to the Mac with a Sharing Only account.

Creating New User Accounts

Now that I've covered the different account types, you can start to create some. To make a new user account, follow these steps:

1. **Choose Apple menu ⇨ System Preferences and click the Users & Groups icon in the System section to open the Users & Groups preferences window, as shown in Figure 4.1.**

2. **If the lock icon in the bottom-left corner is in the locked position, click to unlock it.** Type an administrator account name and password when prompted.

4.1 The Users & Groups preferences window at your disposal.

3. **After you unlock the Users & Groups preferences, click the plus sign (+) in the lower-left corner of the Users & Groups window to add a new account.**

4. **The new accounts window, shown in Figure 4.2, helps you set up the account.** Table 4.1 lists the new account fields and options, and explains how to configure them.

5. **When the account settings are in order, click Create User.**

4.2 The new accounts window is where you type the username and password information.

Table 4.1 New User Account Settings

Option	Function
New Account	Select the type of account you want to create: Administrator, Standard, Managed with Parental Controls, or Sharing Only.
Full Name	Type the name of the user to whom the account belongs.
Account name	Lion automatically trims the Full Name to provide an Account name, but you can edit it if you prefer.
Password	Create a password to allow access to the account.
Verify	Retype the password you created in the Password field.
Password hint	Type a hint that will help you to remember the password if you are unable to successfully enter it.

Requesting password assistance

If you have difficulty coming up with a secure password, you can ask Lion for a little help. In the new account window, note the icon of a key next to the Password field; click it to open the Password Assistant window, shown in Figure 4.3.

Choose the password type you want to use from these options: Manual, Memorable, Letters & Numbers, Numbers Only, Random, and FIPS-181 compliant. Manual allows you to create your own password, while the other options let Lion choose a password for you, based on the type you select.

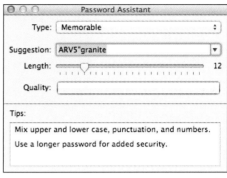

4.3 The Password Assistant can help you out of the password selection rut.

Modifying account settings

The new account (named Victoria in the example shown in Figure 4.1) is in the account list on the left side of the Accounts window.

There are a handful of modifications you can make to the newly created account at this point (see Figure 4.1):

- **Reset Password.** Click to reset the account password. Only an administrator account can perform this action. You would typically only want to use this feature if the user of the account has forgotten his password, but it can obviously be abused by anyone who also has access to an administrator password.

- **Apple ID.** If the user has an Apple ID, enter the username and password here by clicking Set.

- **Allow user to reset password using Apple ID.** Selecting this option allows a user who may have forgotten his password to reset it after he successfully enters his Apple ID username and password.

- **Allow user to administer this computer.** Select this check box if you want to convert a standard account to one with full administrator rights.

85

● **Enable parental controls.** Change the account so that it's managed with Parental Controls by selecting this check box. See later in this chapter for more on Parental Controls.

● **Delete the account.** If you're an administrator, you can remove the account completely by clicking the account to highlight it, and then clicking the minus sign (–) at the bottom of the Accounts window.

● **Change the user account picture.** Click the user account picture to change it. The Edit Picture window opens, as shown in Figure 4.4. You can select one of the available pictures, or click Edit Picture and choose one from the Recent Pictures drop-down list, or click Choose to browse your Mac for a picture. If your Mac has an attached or built-in camera, you can click Take a video snapshot to take a new photo. Drag the slider to alter the size of the picture, and then click and drag it to center it. When finished, click Set.

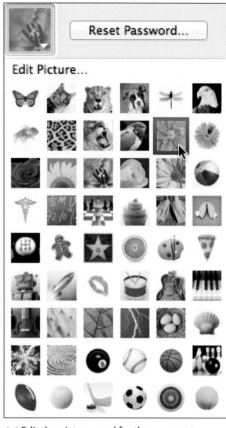

4.4 Edit the picture used for the account to match your preferences.

Caution

Enabling the root account can be bad for the health of your Mac if you aren't careful when logged in to it. As the root user you have complete autonomy and, as such, are given power to cause great good or great harm — especially the latter if you're a more inexperienced user.

The Root Account

Up until now, you thought that administrator accounts were the ultimate power trip, but now meet the real king of the accounts jungle: the root account! The root account is the only account in a UNIX-based operating system (which includes Mac OS X Lion) that truly has full access to any and all files — visible or invisible — on the computer. Administrator accounts are limited in their ability to browse folders on other accounts (although, they can delete the other accounts). The root account isn't hindered from doing or accessing anything on the entire system, and that's why it's disabled by default in Lion. If you are logged in as the root user, one mistake could bring down the entire computer. There are good reasons for using the root account, such as if you need to delete files owned by another user on the system, but I usually don't recommend enabling the root account for the typical user. However, if you want to, here's how (consider yourself duly warned):

1. **Choose Apple menu ⇨ System Preferences, and then click the Users & Groups icon.**

2. **Click the lock in the lower-left corner of the Users & Groups window, and then type an administrator username and password when prompted.**

3. **Select Login Options, and then click Join or Edit next to Network Account Server.**

4. **Click Open Directory Utility.**

5. **When Directory Utility opens, choose Edit ⇨ Enable Root User from the menu.** The root account is turned on at this point. Type a password for the root account when prompted. You certainly want to create a password; otherwise your system is under an enormous security threat. To change the existing password, choose Edit ⇨ Change Root Password, type the current password, and then type the new one.

Logging in to Accounts

When you first start your Mac in the morning, or if you have to restart it at some point during the day, you most likely need to log in to the system using your account name and password. You can also log in to other accounts at the same time without having to restart the Mac or shut down your running applications (now that's cool!).

Login Options

Click Login Options at the bottom of the Accounts window to see what options you have, as shown in Figure 4.5.

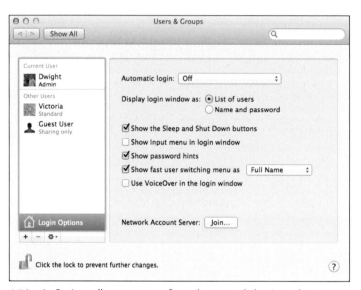

4.5 Login Options allow you to configure how people log in to their accounts on your Mac.

Table 4.2 lists and explains each of these options.

Table 4.2 Login Options

Option	Function
Automatic login	If you enable this option, your Mac logs in to the default administrator account without prompting you for a password, which is most certainly not a good security decision. I recommend that you always set this option to Off.
Display login window as	Determine whether the login window at start-up should show a list of all user accounts on the Mac, or prompt for a username and password. If security is a concern, simply prompting for a username and password may be the best idea.
Show the Sleep and Shut Down buttons	Select this option to have these buttons appear in the login window.
Show Input menu in login window	Displays the input menu in the upper part of the login window. The Input menu is associated with the Input Sources tab of the Language & Text preferences pane, found in System Preferences. If some accounts use a different keyboard layout, they need access to the input menu. Find out more about Input Sources in Chapter 3.

Option	Function
Show password hints	This option allows the password hints that you typed when creating the account to appear in the login window.
Show fast user switching menu as	This option allows multiple users to be logged in at the same time. After selecting the check box, determine how to show the account names in the fast user switching menu with the pop-up menu to the right. The name of the account to which the user is currently logged in is shown in the upper-right corner of the screen; click it to access other accounts.
Use VoiceOver in the login window	Select this option to have the contents of the login window spoken to you by the Mac.
Network Account Server	Click Join and type the name of the server to which you want to automatically connect when you log in to your account.

Login Items

Login Items are applications or utilities that you have slated to automatically start when you log in to your account. You must be logged in to an account to see its Login Items window, as shown in Figure 4.6.

4.6 You can add or remove Login Items here.

To change the Login Items for an account, follow these steps:

1. **Click the account you want to alter in the users list.**

2. **Click the Login Items tab near the top of the Users & Groups window.**

3. **To add items to the login list, click the plus sign (+) in the lower-left corner of the list, and then browse your Mac for the items.**

4. **Remove items from the list by highlighting them and clicking the minus sign (–) in the lower-left corner of the list.**

5. **Select the Hide check box next to any item you want to be automatically hidden after login.** This prevents windows from open applications cluttering your Finder window when you first log in.

6. **Close System Preferences.**

Caution Some applications or utilities may add items to your Login Items list that they need to perform tasks in the background. Be careful about removing Login Items for anti-virus software and other utilities that constantly monitor your Mac's activities.

Setting Up Simple Finder

Simple Finder is a Finder without the frills but with basic functionality for a managed user. Simple Finder only allows the user to access three folders in the Dock: My Applications, Documents, and Shared. Simple Finder doesn't allow access to the remainder of the Mac hard drive or System Preferences. This basic Finder is perfect for children or users who may be a bit uncomfortable with technology.

To use Simple Finder, follow these steps:

1. **Open the Parental Controls preferences by choosing Apple menu ⇨ System Preferences, and then clicking the Parental Controls icon in the System section.** Because all actions in the remainder of this chapter are initiated from the Parental Controls preferences window, I won't mention that they need to be open when I give future instructions.

2. **Choose the account you want to modify in the accounts list.** You may need to click Enable Parental Controls to access the Parental Controls features.

3. **Select the Use Simple Finder check box in the System tab.** The next time you log in to the account, it will use Simple Finder.

Figure 4.7 shows a typical Simple Finder desktop. The three folders in the Dock give the user access to the applications she has permission to use, as well as the Documents and Shared folders. To use the account with a full Finder, deselect the Use Simple Finder check box in the Parental Controls preferences.

4.7 A user account running Simple Finder.

Changing Finder Preferences in Simple Finder

Simple Finder doesn't allow a user to change many settings. This means that if you do need to change settings, you have to use an administrator account. In previous versions of Mac OS X, you have to log out of the account using the Simple Finder, log in to an administrator account, disable Simple Finder in the managed account, and finally log back in to the managed account to change Finder settings. Whew! Thankfully, Lion changes all that. To change Finder settings while in Simple Finder:

1. **Choose Finder⇨Run Full Finder, and then type an administrator's username and password.**

2. **Choose Finder⇨Preferences to make the necessary changes.**

3. **Choose Finder⇨Return to Simple Finder when finished.** The Simple Finder window returns to normal.

Limiting Access with Parental Controls

A few of the most powerful societal influences on youngsters are the Internet, e-mail, and instant messaging. For all the wonderful content that's available on the Internet, there's an equal amount of horrifying content just waiting to be discovered and devoured by young eyes. The Parental Controls help protect our most impressionable citizens from some of the worst the world has to offer.

Take the time to investigate each of these settings to the fullest extent if you have children who use your computer to surf the Internet, receive e-mail, or send instant messages. As a parent, I completely understand the desire to protect your children from things that may be beyond their level of maturity and understanding.

Parental Controls is just as effective with adults as it is with children. If necessary, you can also manage the accounts of users who are inexperienced with computers, or those who, perhaps, haven't quite grown up in other ways.

Enabling Parental Controls

To use Parental Controls, you must either create an account Managed by Parental Controls or enable Parental Controls for an existing Standard account. Follow the instructions earlier in this chapter for creating a new user account. To enable Parental Controls on a current account follow these steps:

1. **Choose Apple menu ⇨ System Preferences, and then click the Users & Groups icon in the System section.**

2. **If it's locked, click the lock icon in the lower-left corner.** To unlock the Users & Groups preferences, type an administrator username and password.

3. **Select the account for which you want to enable Parental Controls in the accounts list.**

4. **Select the Enable Parental Controls check box.**

5. **Click Open Parental Controls to open the Parental Controls window.**

6. **Choose the account you want to manage with Parental Controls in the account list on the left side, as shown in Figure 4.8.** The account is ready for you to take control.

4.8 The Parental Controls window.

Setting application and function restrictions

An alternative to Simple Finder is to run the full Finder with limitations. Parental Controls lets an administrator choose exactly which applications and utilities the managed account can use, and what functions it can perform. To set these kinds of limitations, follow these steps:

1. **In the Apps tab of the Parental Controls window (see Figure 4.8), select the Limit Applications check box.**

2. **Decide whether or not applications downloaded from the App Store can be used with this account by using the Allow App Store Apps pop-up menu.**

3. **In the Allowed Apps window, browse through the list of available applications and utilities.** Click the arrow on the left side of a category to expand it. When you find an application or utility you want the user to be able to access, select the check box to its left.

4. **At the bottom of the window, select the check box next to Allow User to Modify the Dock (see Figure 4.8) if you want to allow this kind of flexibility.**

Applying website restrictions

One of the most useful features in Parental Controls is the ability to control (for the most part) the websites that are accessible to a managed account. To start putting your foot down, click the Web tab in the Parental Controls window. Here, you can decide whether to allow unfettered access to the Internet, to filter websites based on their content, or to restrict access to certain websites.

Allow unrestricted access to websites

This works as advertised. If you don't want to restrict the Internet content that can be accessed through this managed account, select this option.

Try to limit access to adult websites automatically

This option enables website filtering, which scours the contents of a website for buzzwords that might alert the filter that the site is inappropriate for young and curious eyes. Click Customize to modify how the filter works, as shown in Figure 4.9.

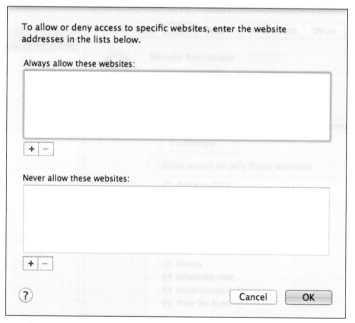

4.9 Allow or restrict certain websites by customizing the website filter.

The website filter isn't perfect. Sometimes it may filter content that you consider safe for your children and allow sites that you would normally curtail.

Click the plus sign (+) under the Always allow these websites section to type the addresses of sites you want the filter to allow, regardless of whether the site content conflicts with the filter or not.

Click the plus sign (+) under the Never allow these websites section to block access to websites that the filter might miss and that you do not want your children to see.

Allow access to only these websites

Select this option to allow access to only the specific sites you enter into the approved list, as shown in Figure 4.10.

4.10 You can determine the specific websites to which the account user has access.

Click the plus sign (+) beneath the list of approved sites to add websites and then choose the Add bookmark option from the pop-up menu that appears. Highlight sites you don't want on the list and click the minus sign (–) to remove them.

95

Setting Mail and iChat limitations

Controlling to whom your kids talk on the Internet is just as important as filtering website content. If you choose to allow the user of the managed account to have access to e-mail and instant messaging, the People tab of the Parental Controls preferences, shown in Figure 4.11, is right where you want to be.

To place restrictions on e-mail and instant messaging, select the check boxes next to Limit Mail and Limit iChat. Doing so allows you to add contacts to the Allowed Contacts list. Click the plus sign (+) under the list to add new names. To remove a name from the list, highlight it and then click the minus sign (–).

4.11 The People tab is where you control e-mails and instant messages for your managed accounts.

Caution

Note that these restrictions apply only to Mail and iChat — not third-party e-mail and instant messaging applications.

One of my favorite features in Parental Controls is the ability to have an e-mail sent to the address of your choice requesting your permission for a person to send e-mails or instant messages to the managed account. Select the Send permission requests to option and then type the preferred e-mail address to which these requests should be sent.

Setting time limits

Another great tool in Parental Controls allows you to limit the amount of time the user of the managed account can access the Mac. This is one that kids hate and parents love! Table 4.3 describes the options available in the Time Limits tab of the Parental Controls window.

Table 4.3 Time Limit Settings

Setting	Operation
Weekday time limits	Select the Limit computer use to check box, and then drag the slider to set the total amount of time the user of the managed account can be logged in for each weekday (Monday through Friday).
Weekend time limits	Again, select the Limit computer use to check box, and then drag the slider to set the total amount of time the user of the managed account can be logged in for a single weekend day (Saturday or Sunday).
Bedtime	Set the times of day for both school nights (Sunday through Thursday) and weekends (Friday and Saturday) that the user of the managed account cannot have access to the computer. This prevents any sneaking around in the middle of the night to check out those websites that you may have forgotten to restrict.

Other limitations

Table 4.4 lists the options found under the Other tab of the Parental Controls preferences pane. These options are functional in nature, and allow or disallow the managed user to perform certain functions in Lion based on how you, the administrator, configure these settings.

Table 4.4 Functional Limitations

Option	Function
Hide profanity in Dictionary	Select this check box if you prefer to hide profane words from prying eyes when your youngster uses the Dictionary application that is part of Lion.
Limit printer administration	Select this option if you want to keep the user from adding or removing printers or managing jobs in the printer queues.
Limit CD and DVD burning	This option prevents the user from burning music and data to CDs or DVDs.
Disable changing the password	Select this option to prevent managed users from changing the account password. This is a good idea if you want to make sure you, as the administrator, can access the managed account at any time.

Keeping account activity logs

When all is said and done, there is simply no way for you to monitor your kid every second of every day. Apple thought of that when it designed Parental Controls. Lion can keep track of which websites your kids have checked out, which websites they are blocked from seeing, the applications they use while logged in, and with whom they are chatting. The Apps, Web, and People tabs of Parental Controls all feature a Logs button in the lower-right corner. This allows you to keep tabs on all of the account activity, as shown in Figure 4.12, so you're informed about what happens, even if you aren't there to see it.

Select the amount of time for which to show account activity in the Show activity for pop-up menu. Determine how the logs should be ordered by using the Group by pop-up menu and choosing either Application (depending on which collection you highlight in the Log Collections pane) or Date. If you find an objectionable site, application, or iChat message, click it to highlight it in the Logs list, and then click Restrict to block access to it. Being diligent in browsing these logs only further protects your child.

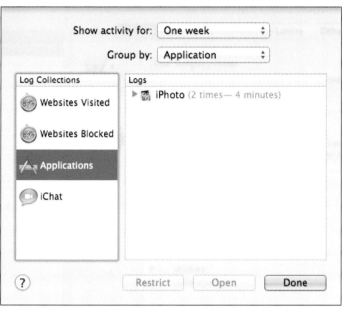

4.12 Some may describe these logs as Big Brother gone awry; I call it responsible parenting.

What Can I Do with Applications?

Lion is more than just an operating system; it's also full of applications designed to make your computing life as productive as possible, while being simple and fun to use. From word processing to buying music online, from surfing the web to taking photos with the Mac camera, Mac OS X 10.7 comes in one flavor: fully loaded! This chapter introduces you to the myriad programs that come with Lion. I show you how to navigate most Mac applications, going in depth with TextEdit and iChat, as well as how to use common keyboard shortcuts.

tasks. With so many applications, you might be wondering what in the world all them can do. I cover the lesser-known (or lesser-used) applications briefly in this chapter, but go more in depth with the Mac word processor, TextEdit. Because I cover some of the more high-profile applications in other chapters, I only give short introductions to them here (see Table 5.3).

To see all the applications at your disposal, open the Applications folder, as shown in Figure 5.1.

5.1 The Applications folder in all its glory.

You can open the Apps folder in any of the following ways:

- **Click the Go menu in the Finder and select Applications.**
- **Click the Launchpad icon in the Dock.**
- **Press ⌘+Shift+A while in the Finder.**

Now, let's take a look at some of the hidden gems in Lion.

Calculator

Calculator, as shown in Figure 5.2, is not a basic run-of-the-mill addition, subtraction, multiplication, and division tool (although it can perform those basic functions with the best of them). Calculator has three modes: Basic, Scientific, and Programmer. Table 5.1 gives a brief description of each.

If you want to see a printout of your calculations, you can use the Paper Tape function. Choose Window ⇨ Show Paper Tape or press ⌘+T to open the Paper Tape window. Choose File ⇨ Print Tape to print your calculations and results.

5.2 Calculator can also convert units of measure such as area, currency, speed, and volume.

Table 5.1 Calculator Modes

Mode	Function
Basic	Performs the traditional tasks of addition, multiplication, subtraction, and division.
Scientific	Expands the Basic mode to perform advanced mathematical calculations, such as trigonometric functions, factorial functions, and square roots.
Programmer	Performs calculations that only a true geek could love (or, most likely, understand), including hexadecimal conversions, binary computations, and logical operations.

Chess

You may have noticed that Mac OS X Lion doesn't come with Minesweeper and Hearts. No, the brainiacs at Apple prefer to include Chess instead, as shown in Figure 5.3. Chess is one of the world's most challenging games, making it ideal to include in such a sophisticated operating system.

To play a game of Chess, simply double-click the icon in the Applications folder. You can play against another person or test your wits against the Mac. To move the board, simply drag any corner of it to the position in which you want it.

5.3 Change the position of the chess board by dragging a corner of it.

Choose Chess ⇨ Preferences to change things, such as the look of the pieces and board, the difficulty level of the computer player, and to allow moves to be spoken aloud. Refer to the Chess Help section (choose Help ⇨ Chess Help) for more information about this great version of a classic game.

Dictionary

Dictionary, like all the other cool applications in Lion, does more than just the obvious.

You can use it as a standard dictionary (the New Oxford American Dictionary, to be exact) or as a thesaurus (the Oxford American Writer's Thesaurus). You can also use it to find terms in the Apple dictionary or to discover articles on Wikipedia. To begin a search, simply type a word or topic in the search field in the upper-right corner of the window (next to the magnifying glass icon), as shown in Figure 5.4. Dictionary displays what it finds in all four sources or only the one you select from the toolbar.

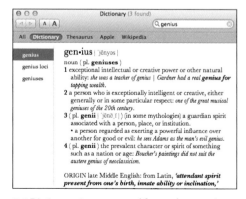

5.4 Dictionary is a great tool for students, writers, business professionals, and anyone else who needs the definition of (or articles on) a word.

DVD Player

DVD Player performs as advertised: it plays DVDs. It can also perform all the basic functions of a regular DVD player. The upside to using this application instead is that you don't have to leave your Mac to catch a flick.

You control the playback of movies with an on-screen remote, shown in Figure 5.5, as opposed to one that is handheld.

5.5 The DVD Player on-screen remote control.

You can also control playback of your DVDs with the Mac keyboard, using the keyboard shortcuts listed in Table 5.2.

Table 5.2 DVD Player Keyboard Shortcuts

Function	Keys
Play/Pause	Space bar
Stop	⌘+.
Scan Forward	⌘+Shift+→
Scan Backward	⌘+Shift+←
Volume Up	⌘+↑
Volume Down	⌘+↓
Mute	⌘+Option+↓
Close Control Drawer	⌘+]
Eject DVD	⌘+E

Font Book

Fonts are very important for creating the look and feel of your Mac, as well as any documents you may create with its applications. Font Book is a fantastic utility that allows you to manage the fonts you have installed on your Mac.

Font Book, shown in Figure 5.6, can install and delete fonts without you having to reboot your Mac. Use it to organize your fonts into collections, enable the fonts you want to use, or disable the fonts you don't want to use rather than completely deleting them from the system.

Refer to the Font Book Help section (choose Help ➪ Font Book Help) to find out more about this exceptional utility.

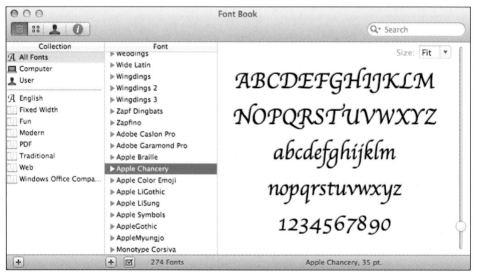

5.6 Font Book helps to organize and manage your font collections.

Stickies

Stickies is a nifty little application for keeping lists, creating reminders, and quickly entering any information you want. It uses the metaphor of the tiny yellow notes that we all have dangling off our computer monitors (except these stickies don't fall off and drift under your desk when you're not looking). Stickies automatically saves your notes, as shown in Figure 5.7.

Make a note of it!

Stickies lets you keep notes (like these) on your desktop. Use a Stickies note to jot down reminders, lists, or other information. You can also use notes to store frequently used text or graphics.

• To close this note, click the close button.

• To collapse this note, double click the title bar.

Your current notes appear when you open Stickies.

5.7 A virtual sticky note.

Additional applications

Table 5.3 lists a brief description of other applications that come with Lion. They are covered in greater detail in other chapters.

Table 5.3 More Lion Applications

Application	Function
Address Book	Keeps contact information in one handy location. See Chapter 8 for more information.
App Store	Your one-stop shop for thousands of Mac apps. Information about using this feature can be found later in this chapter.
Automator	Automates the tasks you find repetitive and mundane. Chapter 14 covers Automator in depth.
Dashboard	Organizes tiny applications called widgets. There is much more on Dashboard and widgets in Chapter 2.
Mission Control	Helps organize your desktop clutter. Chapter 1 covers much more about Mission Control.
FaceTime	Allows you to make video calls to other Mac users, as well as iPhone 4, iPad 2, and iPod touch owners. See Chapter 12 for more information on FaceTime.
iCal	Lets you create calendars to keep up with your hourly, daily, weekly, monthly, and annual tasks and appointments. Chapter 8 goes into much more detail about iCal.
iChat	Send messages instantly to friends, family, and colleagues. iChat is covered later in this chapter.
Image Capture	Capture images from your scanner and/or digital camera with this handy application. Learn much more in Chapter 12.
iTunes	Your Mac entertainment hub. Chapter 11 gives you the inside scoop.
Mail	The Lion e-mail application. Discover how to use Mail in Chapter 10.
Photo Booth	Take pictures and videos using the built-in Mac camera. Read more about it in Chapter 12.
Preview	Capable of opening multiple file types, such as JPEGs, TIFFs, and PDFs. See Chapters 7 and 12 for more about Preview.
QuickTime	Plays video and sound files in a multitude of formats. See Chapter 12 for more info.
Safari	The Mac OS X web browser. Chapter 9 prepares you to cruise the Internet jungle in style.
System Preferences	This is where you make Lion behave the way you want it to. I cover how to tweak settings for your network, change the appearance of your Mac, and much more in Chapter 3.
TextEdit	The Lion word processor. Begin creating documents by perusing the information about TextEdit later in this chapter.
Time Machine	Back up your files and folders to keep them safe, and restore them if necessary. Chapter 14 has the lowdown on this very popular Lion feature.

Navigating Lion Applications

Many of the basic functions and menus of Lion applications and utilities are accessed in the same way. For example, opening a file from within almost any application is done by choosing File ⇨ Open. There are also some keyboard shortcuts universally used in Lion applications.

Opening and closing applications

This one is basic, but necessary, so I'll keep it short and to the point. Use one of these methods to open an application:

- **Click the application icon in the Dock.**
- **Choose Go ⇨ Applications or Go ⇨ Utilities from within the Finder, and double-click the application or utility you need.**
- **Click the Launchpad icon in the Dock and then single-click the application icon.**
- **Choose Apple menu ⇨ Recent Items and select a recently used application from the list.**

You can use one of these techniques to close an application:

- **Choose the application title menu (immediately to the right of the Apple menu) and select Quit.**
- **Press ⌘+Q.**
- **Click and hold the application icon in the Dock, and then select Quit from the resulting pop-up menu (see Figure 5.8).**

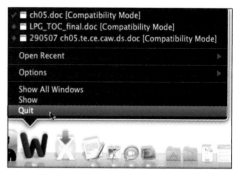

5.8 Easily quit an application from the Dock.

Using commands and keyboard shortcuts

Table 5.4 lists some common commands for Lion applications, as well as the keyboard shortcuts that make issuing those commands even easier.

Table 5.4 Commands and Keyboard Shortcuts

Command	Function	Keyboard Shortcut
Open	Opens a file or document.	⌘+O
Save	Saves the contents of a document.	⌘+S
New	Creates a new blank document.	⌘+N
Close	Closes the active window.	⌘+W
Page Setup	Opens a dialog for selecting the correct paper size and orientation for printing.	⌘+Shift+P
Print	Opens a dialog for printing the current document.	⌘+P
Copy	Copies highlighted text.	⌘+C
Cut	Cuts highlighted text from a document.	⌘+X
Paste	Pastes copied or cut text into a document.	⌘+V
Select All	Highlights all text in a document.	⌘+A
Find	Finds words in the document or window.	⌘+F
Find Next	Finds the next instance of a word in a document or window.	⌘+G
Find Previous	Finds the previous instance of a word in a document or window.	⌘+Shift+G
Force Quit	Opens a window to force an application or utility to quit.	⌘+Option+Esc
Minimize	Minimizes the active window to the Dock.	⌘+M
Preferences	Opens the application preferences.	⌘+,
Hide	Hides the active application.	⌘+H
Quit	Quits the active application.	⌘+Q

Genius

If you are a Windows user who is switching to a Mac, many of the keyboard shortcuts with which you are familiar have Mac equivalents. For example, to print a job in Windows, you would press Ctrl+P and on a Mac you would press ⌘+P. Pressing Ctrl+C copies an item on Windows, while ⌘+C does the same trick on a Mac.

109

Accessing applications with a Stack

If Launchpad isn't your thing, Lion has a neat feature called Stacks that allows you to place folder aliases on the right side of the Dock. You can add a Stack for your Applications folder to the Dock for quick, easy access to all the applications and utilities on your Mac. Follow these steps:

1. **Open the hard drive by doing one of the following:**

   - **Double-click the hard drive icon.**

   - **Press ⌘+N from within the Finder and then select the hard drive icon from the Devices section.**

2. **Drag the Applications folder to the right side of the Dock and drop it.**

3. **Click the Applications folder icon to open the Stack.**

The Stack can display in a fan pattern, as shown in Figure 5.9; a grid, as shown in Figure 5.10; or as a list. As you can see, Fan mode doesn't show all of the items in a folder if it contains a lot. Notice at the top of the fan in Figure 5.9 that it says 19 More in Finder next to the arrow. This means that there are 19 more application icons that can't be shown in the fan due to its configuration; this is where the Grid mode shines.

5.9 A Stack of applications in Fan mode.

5.10 A Stack of applications in Grid mode.

The configuration of the grid allows you to see all of a folder's contents. To select a different view for your stack, simply click and hold the mouse button on the stack icon, and then select the view you want from the View content as section of the contextual menu.

Viewing applications in full-screen mode

Many apps running in Lion can do so in full-screen mode, including Mail, Safari, Terminal, and iCal. This mode allows the app to be the center of your attention, totally hiding anything else on your desktop and changing your workspace to accommodate only the functions of the app.

If the application you are currently running supports full-screen mode, you see a small icon in the upper-right corner of the applications window that looks like two arrows pointing diagonally in different directions, as shown in Figure 5.11. Click this icon to take the app into full-screen mode.

5.11 Click the full-screen mode icon in the upper-right corner to dedicate your screen to one app at a time.

You can move between open windows in full-screen mode by swiping a laptop trackpad, or the Apple Magic Mouse or Magic Trackpad. Exit full-screen mode by clicking the blue box containing two arrows pointing toward one another (this appears when you hold your mouse pointer in the upper-right corner of the screen).

Working with Documents in TextEdit

TextEdit is the Lion built-in word-processing application and it can handle a good deal of your basic document-writing needs. TextEdit is one of those names that advertise just what the application does: it edits text. The TextEdit interface is simplicity itself, as are the functions it provides. Although you don't get all the frills of a full-fledged word processor, like Microsoft Word, Apple Pages, or OpenOffice, TextEdit is surprisingly more capable than it appears at first glance (it can even open documents created by the aforementioned big boys).

Setting TextEdit Preferences

I am a big fan of making things work the way *you* want them to on your computer, rather than the way Apple (or anyone else) says you should. The way I work may do wonders for my production, but cause you to groan with frustration or yawn in tedium. Most applications allow you to change the default behaviors to match your style of working (or playing, as the case may be) and TextEdit is no exception.

To alter the TextEdit default behaviors, choose TextEdit ➪ Preferences from the menu or press ⌘+,. The Preferences window opens and permits access to two tabs: New Document, and Open and Save. The New Document preferences are shown in Figure 5.12.

Figure 5.13 shows the TextEdit Open and Save Preferences.

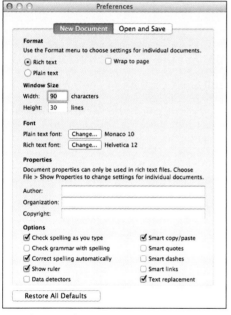

5.12 The TextEdit New Document preferences options.

5.13 The Open and Save preferences options for TextEdit.

Table 5.5 offers a breakdown of each option in the New Document preferences.

Table 5.5 TextEdit New Document Preferences

Preferences	Function
Format	Lets you select Rich text (RTF) or Plain text (TXT) as your default format for new documents. Wrap to page causes text to wrap to document margins instead of window margins.
Window Size	Sets the default window size for new documents by width (measured in characters) and height (measured by line).
Font	Lets you choose the default font for new plain or rich text documents. Click Change to make a different selection.
Properties (RTF only)	Type information you want included with each document you create, such as your name, your company, or any necessary copyright information.
Check spelling as you type/ Check grammar with spelling	Activates the spelling and grammar checkers.
Correct spelling automatically	Corrects spelling mistakes on the fly. Use this option with caution as TextEdit may change something that it mistakenly thinks is misspelled.
Show ruler	Displays a ruler at the top of each window.
Data detectors	TextEdit automatically recognizes dates, locations, contacts, and times, and creates items such as iCal events and Address Book contacts for them.
Smart copy/paste	Automatically adds any necessary spaces when text is added or deleted.
Smart quotes	Uses curly quote marks instead of straight ones.
Smart dashes	Automatically substitutes an em dash (—) when you type double hyphens (--).
Smart links	Automatically turns Internet addresses into links that open the appropriate website when clicked.
Text replacement	TextEdit tries to replace typos with common words it thinks you intended. For example, if you type "arw" TextEdit substitutes "are" instead.
Restore All Defaults	Click this to revert to the TextEdit default preferences.

Table 5.6 covers how the Open and Save preferences can customize your TextEdit experience.

Table 5.6 TextEdit Open and Save Preferences

Preferences	Function
Ignore rich text commands in HTML/RTF files	Opens HTML and RTF files automatically as plain text, retaining no formatting at all. This is beneficial to web developers who need to edit their code.
Add ".txt" extension to plain text files	Automatically tags plain text files with the .txt file extension.

Preferences	Function
Plain Text File Encoding	Lets you decide which text encoding to use by default when opening and saving plain text files. I suggest sticking with Automatic unless you really know what you are doing with these settings.
HTML Saving Options	Lets you choose the default document type, styling, and encoding to use when saving documents as HTML files.
Preserve white space	Select this option to preserve blank areas that are already in your document so they aren't lost during formatting.
Restore All Defaults	Click this to revert to the TextEdit New Document, and Open and Save default settings.

Creating and saving documents

Open TextEdit by choosing Go from within the Finder, selecting Applications, and double-clicking the TextEdit icon. TextEdit automatically opens a new document when you first start it, as shown in Figure 5.14.

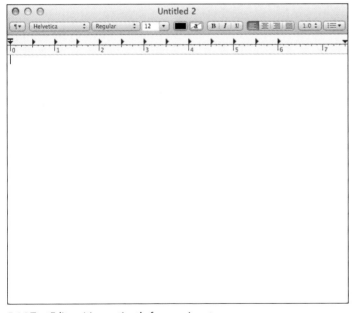

5.14 TextEdit waiting patiently for your input.

Creating a new document doesn't get much easier, but what if TextEdit is already open? Simply do one of the following:

- **Choose File ➪ New.**
- **Press ⌘+N.**

A shiny new document opens. To get started, just begin typing. After you create a document, you typically want to save it so that you can refer to it again later.

To save a document, do the following:

1. **Choose File ➪ Save, or press ⌘+S to open the Save dialog.**
2. **Type a name for your document in the Save As field.**
3. **Navigate to the location on your Mac where you want to save the document.**
4. **Click Save.**

Formatting TextEdit documents

Sometimes, simply typing text into your documents may be good enough for the task at hand, but other situations may call for something nicer, neater, and more polished. The look and feel of a document can be very important — even more so to the reader than the writer — and something as simple as font choice can affect how the reader responds to the text. Because TextEdit uses RTF, tasks like manipulating fonts and adding pictures are almost too easy.

Using fonts

Mac OS X Lion comes with a wide variety of built-in fonts to spice up your word processing world. To manipulate fonts in a document, do the following:

1. **Open an existing file or create a new one in TextEdit by doing one of the following:**
   - **Choose File ➪ Open or File ➪ New.**
   - **Press ⌘+O or ⌘+N.**
2. **Highlight the text you want to change by clicking and dragging the mouse over it.**
   You can highlight all of the text in the document by pressing ⌘+A, or choosing
   Edit ➪ Select All.

3. **Choose Format ⇨ Font to change the fonts used in your document.** You can change the font size, make the letters bold, underline words, change the color of the text, and more, but I cover this a bit later in the chapter.

4. **Choose Format ⇨ Text to manipulate text on the page.** Move the alignment of the text to the left, right, or center. You can also change the spacing between lines, change the direction of your writing from right to left (necessary for text in some languages, such as Hebrew), create tables from existing text, and more.

The Fonts window, shown in Figure 5.15, is the central location in TextEdit for choosing and stylizing fonts. Open the Fonts window by choosing Format ⇨ Font ⇨ Show Fonts.

The toolbar at the top of the window allows you to make changes to the appearance of the text, such as:

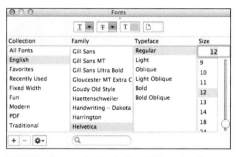

5.15 The Fonts window in TextEdit makes it easy to change the look of your text.

⊙ **Text Underline and Text Strikethrough.** Decide whether to use a single or double line for the underline or strikethrough, as well as what color the line should be.

⊙ **Change the color of the text.**

⊙ **Change the background color of your document.**

Select the font to use in your document by browsing the Collection and Family lists. You can change the size of the font, as well as its typeface characteristics (such as making it bold or italic).

Checking spelling and grammar

No matter who you are or how well educated you may be, at some point, someone catches you in a spelling or grammatical error. Thankfully, writers have brilliant editors who come behind us and clean up our frequent messes, but most folks aren't so blessed. It is to those unlucky enough not to have editors that I dedicate this section of the chapter.

TextEdit may be a simple program, but it's quite a smart one, too. Do you have a problem spelling words like "millennium" or "weird"? Does "I am doing well" come out as "I is doing well"? If so, TextEdit has your back.

To check spelling and grammar in your documents, do the following:

1. **Choose Edit ⇨ Spelling and Grammar ⇨ Show Spelling and Grammar to open the Spelling and Grammar dialog, shown in Figure 5.16.**

2. **Click Find Next, and TextEdit goes through each spelling or grammar violation.** It even makes suggestions for rectifying the problems.

3. **Click Change if you agree to the suggested changes, click Ignore to skip and move to the next violation, or click Learn to teach TextEdit the spelling of a word that may not be in its vocabulary.**

4. **Close the Spelling and Grammar dialog by clicking the red dot in the upper-left corner when finished.**

5.16 You have no more excuses for poor spelling or bad grammar if you use TextEdit.

Genius

TextEdit can check your spelling and grammar on the fly, too. Choose Edit ⇨ Spelling and Grammar, and click Check Spelling While Typing to have TextEdit check each word as you type. Choose Edit ⇨ Spelling and Grammar, and click Check Grammar With Spelling so that TextEdit checks your grammar along with the spelling of your words. To have TextEdit look over your document at any time, press ⌘+;.

Opening an existing document

To open a document from within TextEdit, do the following:

1. **Choose File ⇨ Open to display the Open dialog.**

2. **Navigate the Mac hard drive until you're in the folder containing the file you want to open.**

3. **Select the name of the file and click Open to display the document in TextEdit.**

You can now view, print, or edit your document as needed.

Saving a document in a different format

You may notice that at the bottom of the TextEdit Save As dialog (see Figure 5.17) is a File Format menu. The default TextEdit file format is RTF, which stands for Rich Text Format. Most word processors on any computing platform (including Mac, Windows, and Linux) can open RTF documents, so you don't have to worry whether other computer users can view or edit your TextEdit documents.

| ✓ Rich Text Format |
| Rich Text Format with Attachments |
| Web Page (.html) |
| **Web Archive** |
| OpenDocument Text (.odt) |
| Word 2007 Format (.docx) |
| Word 2003 Format (.xml) |
| Word 97 Format (.doc) |

5.17 Save your TextEdit documents in any of these formats.

RTF allows you to make formatting changes to your document, such as adding some punch to your fonts by changing their size and color.

If you click the File Format pop-up menu, you see the other formats in which TextEdit can save your document (see Figure 5.17). What is the coolest thing about the availability of these formats? Not only can TextEdit save your document in the selected format, but it can also open any document that uses it. This gives you extreme flexibility when it comes to opening and saving files that originate with users of other operating systems, and word processors.

Genius

There is another file format called plain text (.txt). Plain text doesn't allow you to format your documents with fancy fonts or pictures. However, programming is done in this format. It is also a format that all word processors (even those that run in command-line operating systems, like DOS and UNIX) can open, read, and edit. To create a plain text file, choose Format ⇨ Make Plain Text from the menu.

Table 5.7 describes all of the available file formats so that you can decide whether something other than RTF is right for you.

Table 5.7 TextEdit File Formats

Format	Uses
Rich Text Format	Rich Text Format (RTF) is the default file format. This format allows you to make formatting changes to your document, such as changing font size and color.
Rich Text Format with Attachments (RTFD)	This is essentially RTF with graphics included, such as pictures.
Web Page (.html)	HTML stands for HyperText Markup Language, which is a programming language used to create web pages. It allows you to edit web pages or quickly create new ones.

continued

Table 5.7 continued

Format	Uses
Web Archive	This is used primarily as the format in which Safari saves web pages. TextEdit can open, edit, and save these files.
OpenDocument Text (.odt)	OpenDocument is a relatively new standard for word processing files that is native to the OpenOffice.org office suite.
Word 2007 Format (.docx)	Microsoft made a break from the traditional Word file format (.doc) with Office 2007.
Word 2003 Format (.xml)	Open, edit, and save files that were created from Word 2003 using XML (Extensible Markup Language), another programming language used extensively on the web.
Word 97 Format (.doc)	This format should be very familiar to anyone who's used Microsoft Word in the past. It is one of the most widely used formats on the planet.

Getting Started with iChat

Instant messaging is one of the most popular forms of communication today. On the Internet, you can have instant conversations with anyone, anywhere in the world. iChat is a great instant messaging client that can do much more than just send text clips back and forth. You can also exchange files, like pictures, documents, and music. To start using iChat, you need to set up an account and add some contacts to your Buddy List.

Setting up an iChat account

iChat can use several different types of instant messaging accounts, which are laid out for you in Table 5.8.

Table 5.8 iChat Account Types

Account Type	Description
AIM	AIM stands for AOL Instant Messenger. You can use your existing AIM account or sign up for a new one by clicking Get an iChat Account in the second pane of the Welcome to iChat dialog. You can also sign up at www.aim.com by clicking Get a username.
Me.com	If you previously signed up for a me.com account, you can use your username and password to log in to iChat.
Mac.com	If you previously signed up for a .Mac account, you can use your .Mac username and password to log into iChat.
Jabber	Jabber is an open source implementation of instant messaging. Get a login name by going to www.jabber.org/.

Account Type	Description
Google Talk	If you have a Google account, you can log in to chat with Google Talk users with iChat. Learn more about Google Talk at www.google.com/talk/.
Yahoo!	If you prefer Yahoo! as your chat provider, simply type your Yahoo! Messenger account information. If you need an account, simply go to http://messenger.yahoo.com and click the Register link.

After you get your account affiliations in order, it's time to start up iChat. From within the Finder, press ⌘+Shift+A to open the Applications folder, and then double-click the iChat icon. When you open iChat for the first time, you are greeted with a welcome screen. Simply click Continue to move forward and set up an account.

To add your instant messaging account to iChat:

1. **Select iChat and choose Preferences from the menu.**

2. **Click the Accounts tab and then click the plus sign (+) in the lower-left corner.**

3. **In the Account Setup window, shown in Figure 5.18, choose the account type you want to use, type the necessary information, and then click Done.** Your new account is now added to the list.

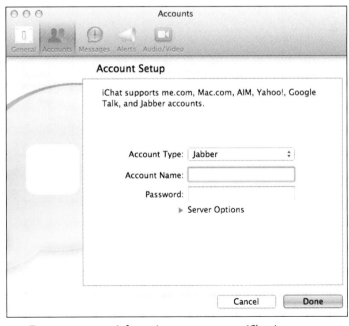

5.18 Type your account information so you can start iChatting.

Note

Some account types can only chat with people who are using the same account type. For example, if you have a .Mac account but your friend is using Jabber, you can't instant message that person unless one of you signs up for an account with the service the other is using.

Adding buddies to your Buddy List

After you add an account, you are logged in to it automatically and a Buddy List window appears, as shown in Figure 5.19.

To add buddies to your list, click the plus sign (+) in the lower-left corner of your Buddy List and choose Add Buddy. Type your buddy's account information in the window, similar to the one shown in Figure 5.20, and click Add.

Your newly added buddy should show up in your Buddy List, ready and waiting to chat with you. You may have the ability to do everything with iChat: text, audio, and video. However, if your buddy is on an older version of iChat, has a slower Internet connection or computer, or uses a different chat client altogether, he may not be able to join you in one form of chat or another. You can check his iChat abilities quite easily with the following steps:

1. **Select your buddy's name in the Buddy List.**
2. **Choose Buddies ⇨ Show Profile from the menu.**
3. **Your buddy's iChat capabilities are listed in the Profile tab of the Info window, as shown in Figure 5.21.**

Different ways to chat

You have your iChat account and you've added some buddies to your Buddy List. The only thing left to do is start chatting. As I mentioned earlier, there are three ways in iChat to converse with someone: text, audio, and video. I show you how to get started with each method in the following section.

5.19 Check the status of your buddies in the Buddies list.

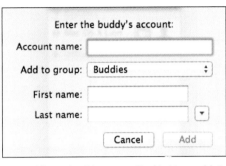

5.20 Adding a buddy to your Buddy List couldn't be much easier.

5.21 A typical Info window for someone in your Buddy List showing his iChat capabilities.

Text chats

Text chats are the most common method of instant messaging, but as more and more people get broadband Internet connections (such as cable and DSL), the trend will most likely be toward video.

To start a Text chat:

1. **Select the buddy you want to chat with from your Buddy List.**

2. **Click A in the bottom of the Buddy List window to initiate the chat session.**

3. **Start typing away, and soon you'll be chatting like there's no tomorrow, as shown in Figure 5.22.** After you finish typing a response, press Return to send it.

Audio chats

You may wonder why you would want to audio chat when you have a phone. In some cases (when traveling internationally, for example), phone conversations may not be free, but audio chats are always free.

To begin an audio chat:

1. **Select the buddy you want to chat with from your Buddy List.**

2. **Click the phone in the bottom of the Buddy List window to initiate the audio chat session.**

3. **Your buddy receives an invitation like the one shown in Figure 5.23.** He can choose to send a text reply instead of speaking with you, decline the invitation altogether and bruise your ego, or accept.

5.22 iChatting with my newest buddy.

5.23 Accept an invitation to begin audio chatting.

Video chats

Video chats are where it's at! The ability to see and speak to one another across the miles (for free, no less) is the dream of every displaced parent and grandparent. It was a godsend when I had to be away from my wife and kids for two weeks on business.

Note To video chat via the Internet, you must have a broadband connection — no ifs, ands, or buts about it. Dial-up simply doesn't have the ability to stream video.

To initiate a video chat:

1. **Select the buddy you want to chat with from your Buddy List.**

2. **Click the video camera at the bottom of the Buddy List window to initiate a video chat.**

3. **Your buddy receives an invitation like the one sent for an audio chat.** Again, she can choose to send a text reply, decline, or accept the invitation. It may take a few seconds to connect to one another, depending on the speed of your Internet connections.

4. **Once you establish a connection, you can see one another and talk, just as if you were in the same room.** You see your buddy in the large window and yourself in a smaller preview window (so you can see how goofy you look to your friend).

Genius To add special effects (and some pizzazz) to your snapshots, click Effects in the lower-left corner of the video chat window. Choose from any of the effects on the list to make you appear in the video chat window using those effects. There are filter effects (like Glow), distortion effects (such as Dent), or you can use video backdrops.

Acquiring New Applications in the App Store

The App Store is Apple's way of saying "boxed software is so 1980s." In the App Store, you can download literally thousands of applications and utilities for your Mac (some are free, some are not). The great thing about the App Store is that you can browse for the application you want, download it instantly, and fire it right up. There are no order forms to fill out, no waiting for the software to be delivered by a courier, and no boxes or discs to store. The App Store, shown in Figure 5.24, even keeps a running record of the software you download and alerts you when updates are available. It's truly the one-stop shop for Mac applications.

5.24 Thousands of apps are ready for download in the App Store.

 Note This may seem rather obvious to some, but you must have an Internet connection in order to use the App Store. No Internet, no App Store.

Signing in and viewing your account

If you have an iTunes Store or MobileMe account, or any type of account that requires an Apple ID, you are ready to sign in and begin using the App Store. If you don't have an Apple ID, you need to get one before you can purchase and download items.

To create an Apple ID:

1. **Open the App Store by clicking its icon in the Dock.**

2. **Choose Store ⇨ Create Account from the menu.**

3. **Follow the instructions in the Welcome to the App Store window to create your Apple ID.**

Now that you have an Apple ID, you can sign in to the App Store and start browsing the virtual shelves. To sign in to your Apple ID, choose Store ⇨ Sign In from the menu, or click Sign In under the Quick Links section on the right side of the window. Type your Apple ID and password in the appropriate fields, and then click Sign In.

You can also view and edit your Apple ID account. To do so:

1. **Choose Store ⇨ View My Account from the menu or click Account in the Quick Links section on the right side of the window.**

2. **Type your Apple ID and password in the appropriate fields, and then click View Account.**

3. **Inspect and edit your information if you wish, and then click Done to return to the App Store.**

Browsing for applications

The App Store makes it simple to find the application you've been looking for. You can search for apps in one of three ways:

- **Click the Featured tab at the top of the window to see the latest and greatest apps to come to the App Store.** Apple gives some of the more well-known apps the lion's share (pun intended) of the headlines at the top of the Featured page.

- **You can see lists of the best-selling and most popular apps by clicking Top Charts at the top of the window.** The apps are broken down into three categories: Top Paid, Top Free, and Top Grossing.

● **Click Categories to see a wide array of app categories, as illustrated in Figure 5.25.**
If you know the kind of app you want, but aren't sure which particular one to get, this is
the place to start.

5.25 Search categories of apps when you only have an idea of what you seek.

Viewing apps you've purchased

Pretty soon you may begin to lose track of everything you've purchased from the App Store.
Thankfully, unlike the clerk behind the counter at your local software haunt, the App Store remembers everything you purchase, and even shows you the status of the app on your Mac.

Simply click Purchased at the top of the App Store window to see a list of the apps you've bought.
The button to the right of the app name alerts you to its status. For example, if you previously
installed an app, the button says Installed. If not, simply click Install to do so.

Keeping your apps up to date

From time to time developers release updates to their software to iron out a few bugs or add some cool new features, and you want to know when this happens. The App Store makes it simple: just click Updates at the top of the window and a list of available updates displays, as shown in Figure 5.26.

5.26 Click Update to retrieve the latest version of your app.

To update your apps:

1. **Click Update next to the name of the app you want to update.**

2. **Type your Apple ID and password, and then click Sign In to download the latest and greatest version of your app.**

3. **The App Store provides you with a progress bar to keep track of how much longer it will take to retrieve the update.** You can pause if you have to take a break and click Resume when you're ready to continue the download.

4. **Once the download is complete, the update automatically installs.**

What Can I Do with Utilities?

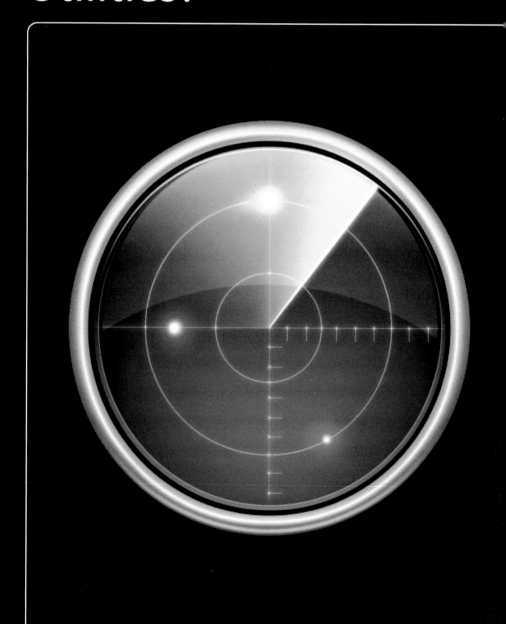

Utilities do a lot of the dirty work for your Mac. They diagnose problems with your network, help you partition or format drives, take screenshots, manage passwords, and much more. Some utilities are more specialized than others, but there's a little something for everyone in Lion's utilities. In this chapter, I explore the Lion utility offerings and the basics on how they can be used to enhance your Mac experience. I also delve a bit into Terminal as homage to the Lion UNIX underpinnings. These utilities can all be found in the Applications ➪ Utilities directory on your Mac.

Working with Software Utilities

Software utilities help you with matters related to software functions, such as monitoring color profiles and taking screenshots. Even though some of these utilities may touch hardware from time to time, typically their work is software-centric.

Note
All of the utilities in this chapter have Help systems that can teach you much more about those that interest you the most. To access the Help system for any application, simply click Help in the menu bar.

Using AppleScript Editor

AppleScript Editor is a tool that helps you write and edit AppleScripts. "Great," I can hear you say, "but what are AppleScripts?" AppleScript is a scripting language built in to Mac OS X. The scripts you can produce with it are called AppleScripts. You have most likely already used an AppleScript without being aware of it. This is because they are generally used by applications (and other utilities) to perform tasks and commands behind the scenes. AppleScript Editor is typically used by application developers, but some savvy Lion users may find it useful to write their own AppleScripts to automate repetitive tasks. For much more about AppleScript and AppleScript Editor, go to the AppleScript Help by clicking the Help menu and making a selection, or visit some (or all) of the following websites:

- **www.macosxautomation.com/applescript/**

- **http://mac.appstorm.net/how-to/applescript/
  the-ultimate-beginners-guide-to-applescript/**

- **http://macscripter.net/**

Managing color profiles with ColorSync Utility

This utility manages the Mac color profiles for devices such as monitors and printers. If you have to ask what a color profile is, you probably don't want to mess with this one. However, if you do, you can open ColorSync by choosing Applications ➪ Utilities and double-clicking its icon.

Repairing color profiles

Sometimes your color profiles may catch a bug or need other repairs, and ColorSync Utility is up to the role of color profile doctor. To find problem profiles and repair them, follow these steps:

1. **Click the Profile First Aid tab at the top of the ColorSync Utility window.**

2. **Click Verify in the lower-right corner and ColorSync Utility finds any profiles with health issues, as shown in Figure 6.1.**

3. **Click Repair to have ColorSync Utility provide proper care to the sickly profiles.**

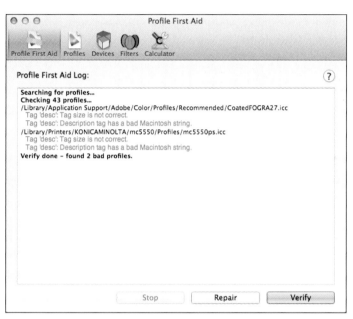

6.1 ColorSync Utility finds profiles with problems and resolves their issues.

Viewing installed color profiles

It's simple to view all of the color profiles installed on your Mac. To do so, follow these steps:

1. **Click the Profiles tab at the top of the ColorSync Utility window.**

2. **Decide which profile category you need: System, Computer, User, or Other.** Click the arrow to the left of the category to see its profiles.

- **System profiles are those installed and used by Lion itself.** They are located in the System ⇨ Library ⇨ ColorSync ⇨ Profiles directory.

- **Computer profiles are those installed by you or another administrator for use by all account holders on the Mac.** They are located in the Library ⇨ ColorSync ⇨ Profiles directory.

- **User profiles are those installed by you or another administrator for use by an individual account holder on the Mac.** They are located in the accounts Home folder ⇨ Library ⇨ ColorSync ⇨ Profiles directory.

- **Profiles in the Other category are those installed by third-parties in directories other than those mentioned above.**

3. **Select a profile to see all of its attributes, as shown in Figure 6.2.** Click Open in the upper right to see even more detailed information it.

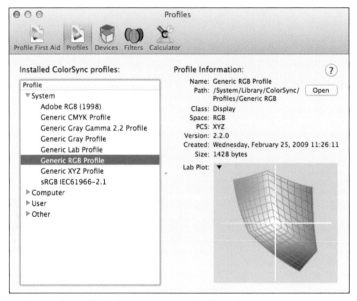

6.2 View color profile information in the Profiles tab.

 Genius You can see a really neat 3-D rendering of the profile color gamut in the graph that appears in the lower right of the window. Click and drag your mouse anywhere in the graph and the color gamut rotates for you.

Assigning profiles to devices

A nice feature, especially when it comes to high-end printing and color matching, is the ability to assign a profile to a device, such as a printer or display. To assign a profile to a device, follow these steps:

1. **Click the Devices tab at the top of the ColorSync Utility window.**

2. **Browse the list of devices to find the one to which you want to assign the profile and then select it, as shown in Figure 6.3.**

3. **Click the arrow next to Current Profile and choose Other from the pop-up menu.**

4. **Browse your Mac for the profile to which you want to assign the device and then click Open.**

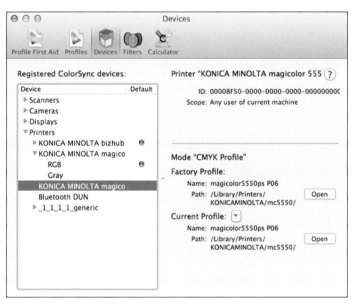

6.3 You can assign profiles to a device for more precise color management.

Editing Quartz filters

Quartz filters can be used when printing to customize the color of a file, among many other things. ColorSync Utility affords the ability to edit these Quartz filters and even create new ones.

To edit existing Quartz filters or create new ones, follow these steps:

1. **Click the Filters tab in the toolbar.**

2. **Click the disclosure triangle next to the filter that you want to edit or click the plus sign (+) at the bottom left of the filter list to create a new one.**

3. **Adjust the settings for each part of the filter by clicking the disclosure triangles next to each part and using the pop-up menus to change the settings as required.**

Calculating colors on your screen

If you really like one of the colors you see on your display, you can use the ColorSync Utility Calculator to calculate its color percentages. Follow these steps:

1. **Click the Calculator tab in the toolbar.**

2. **Click the magnifying glass at the bottom of the window.**

3. **Drag your mouse pointer (which now looks like a circle with a cross hair in the center) over the pixel on your screen with the color values you want to see.**

4. **Click the pixel to see the color values represented, as shown in Figure 6.4.**

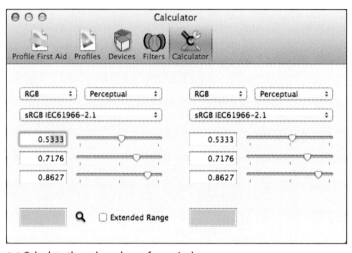

6.4 Calculate the color values of any pixel on your screen.

Measuring color values with DigitalColor Meter

DigitalColor Meter measures the color values on your display so that you can enter them into other programs, such as graphics applications.

To see the values associated with a particular pixel on your screen, simply hold your mouse pointer over the pixel. DigitalColor Meter shows you the color and the values represented.

Using Grab

This utility takes screenshots of items on your Mac. In fact, Grab was used extensively in the creation of art files for this book. For more in-depth information about Grab, see Chapter 12.

Working with Grapher

Grapher is an algebra geek's dream come true, and it's also a neat utility that graphs equations, visualizing them in two or three dimensions. You can even animate your graphs with this baby and share them as QuickTime movies. For more information about Grapher, please go to its help center by clicking the Help menu.

Setting the Java Preferences

The Java Preferences, shown in Figure 6.5, allow you to determine which Java Virtual Machine to use with your browser, and Java and web applications. You can also set up any necessary security settings for using certain Java applications. A Java runtime is essential if you plan to run Java-based applications on your Mac; whether this is a need for you is something that only you (or your IT administrator) can answer.

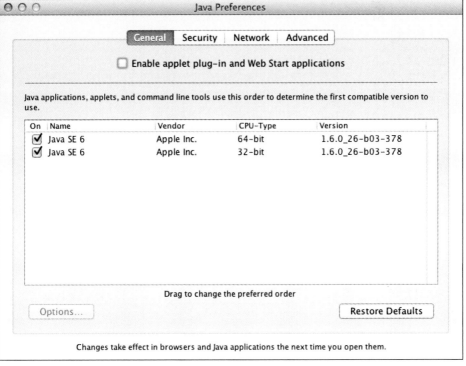

6.5 Determine which Java runtime environment to use with Lion.

When you first launch Java Preferences you are asked if you want to install a Java runtime. In order to use Java Preferences you must click Install to continue. When you click Install, Software Update finds and downloads a Java runtime environment. Once the installation is complete you can open Java Preferences and tell your Mac how it should function.

Storing passwords with Keychain Access

Keychain Access manages your plethora of passwords in one convenient location. Keychain Access can store passwords of any type (including those used for accessing servers and websites), as well as other sensitive information, such as bank accounts and credit card numbers. The purpose of Keychain Access (along with securely storing private information) is to remember your passwords for you, which is very helpful given the crazy amount the typical Internet user is required to have these days.

When you first log in to Lion a default login keychain is created. This keychain uses the same password as your user account. I highly suggest perusing the Help feature of Keychain Access if you want to get more familiar with its functionality.

Using Podcast Capture and Podcast Publisher

Podcast Capture allows you to record and distribute podcasts as long as you have access to a Mac OS X server running Podcast Producer.

Podcast Publisher is new to Mac OS X with the advent of Lion. This application allows you to create an audio or video podcast and share it from your Mac. You can share your podcasts via iTunes, e-mail, or you can use a Mac OS X Lion server using a Podcast Library.

Setting up VoiceOver

VoiceOver allows your Mac to describe the contents on your screen verbally. Your Mac literally speaks to you and reads the contents of your open documents and windows. This is obviously a fantastic utility for anyone who has difficulty seeing what is on the screen.

You can configure VoiceOver to your specific needs by customizing its many options, including:

- **Have your Mac speak a greeting to you upon login.** Among other uses, this is helpful if some instructions need to be provided for a user before they get started working with the computer.

- **Configure Lion to tell you when the Caps Lock key is pressed.** This can wreak havoc for someone trying to enter a case-sensitive password.

- **Adjust the rate, pitch, volume, and intonation of the Mac voice.** This is helpful for adjusting to compensate for various hearing difficulties.

- **Configure the layout of a connected braille display.**

Working with Terminal

Terminal is your gateway to entering the command-line world of UNIX. In my opinion, in order to even think of yourself as a Mac OS X aficionado, you must have at least attempted some basic UNIX commands using the old-fashioned way. To take a step back in computing time, open Terminal by choosing Go menu ⇨ Utilities (or press ⌘+Shift+U). Next, double-click the Terminal icon to open a new window, as shown in Figure 6.6.

6.6 This is what computing looked like before the advent of the graphical user interface.

Terminal, like other applications, can be modified to work the way you want it to. Click the Terminal menu and select Preferences (or press ⌘+,) to open the Preferences window.

Startup

When you first open Terminal, it automatically opens a new Terminal window. The Startup options in the preferences window, shown in Figure 6.7, allow you to define the state in which Terminal starts up.

Choose one of the following:

- **On startup, open:** Choose what settings to use for the new window or to open a series of windows called a window group (more on window groups a little later in this chapter).

- **Shells open with:** Determine whether to open Terminal in its default shell (called bash) or in a different shell. A shell is software that allows a user to interact with the UNIX services, and provides the commands that can be executed by the user. You can download and install other UNIX shells from the Internet. To use a shell other than bash, select the Command (complete path) radio button and type the path to the directory in which the shell is located.

● **New windows open with and New tabs open with:** Determine what settings to use when opening new windows or new tabs.

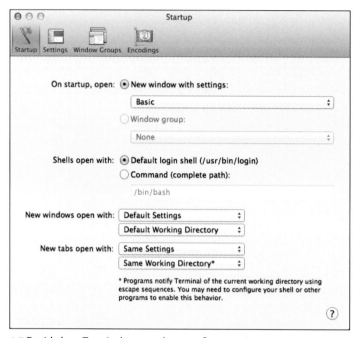

6.7 Decide how Terminal reacts when you first start it.

Genius

If you are someone who uses Terminal quite a lot (and you're an official card-carrying geek, if you do), it's a good idea to keep a shortcut to it in your Dock. That way, the comfort of the command line is within easy reach. I've used Mac OS X for years and I like to keep the Terminal feature close by my side. You never know when the uncontrollable urge to chmod, mkdir, or ping might strike you.

Settings

The Settings section, shown in Figure 6.8, lets you adjust the look and behavior of your Terminal windows.

The list on the left side of the Settings window contains preformatted window settings that you can choose. Set one as your default by highlighting the desired setting and clicking Default. Add or delete saved settings by clicking the plus (+) or minus (–) signs.

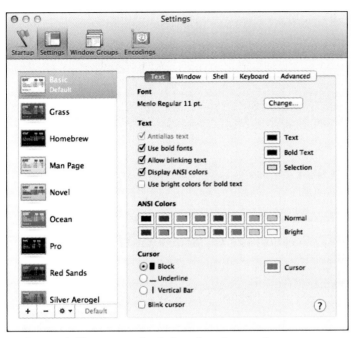

6.8 Even geeks like to customize their work environment!

Table 6.1 gives a brief description of what each tab in the Settings section allows you to modify.

Table 6.1 Options Available in the Settings Tabs

Tab	Options
Text	Change the appearance of text, including the font and the colors designated for certain types of text. You can also control how the cursor is displayed.
Window	Set the default title of windows, as well as what other information appears in the title bar, such as the dimensions of the window or the name of the currently active process. Choose the default background color of windows, the default size of new windows, and how far back a user can scroll.
Shell	Have the shell issue a command by default as soon as a new window is opened; tell Terminal how to behave when a user exits a shell, and whether it should prompt the user before closing the window.
Keyboard	Assign commands to shortcut keys to make entering commands even faster.
Advanced	Settings allow you to change the Terminal emulation, alarms, and character encodings.

Window Groups

In the Window Groups window, you can delete, import, and export your window groups. Window groups are useful for users who utilize several windows, allowing them to run multiple tasks during their Terminal sessions.

Creating window groups causes Terminal to keep each window's individual settings intact, so that they are in the same state when you reopen them as they were when you closed them. To create a window group, follow these steps:

1. **Open the windows with which you want to work.** Make sure they are set up in the format that you need.

2. **Choose the Window menu and select Save Windows as Group.**

3. **Give the window group a descriptive name, like Network diagnostics, and click Save.** Select the check box in the Save window to have this window group open automatically when you first open Terminal.

Encodings

The options in the Encodings window allow you to enable and disable international character encodings so that Terminal can display international characters.

Tabbed windows

Some users may prefer to have several Terminal windows open at once, but I like the simplicity of having one window running multiple tabs, as shown in Figure 6.9.

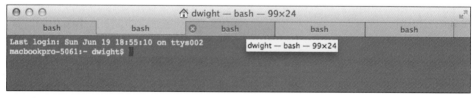

6.9 Tabbed Terminal windows are the way to go for me.

To create a new tab, choose Shell ➪ New Tab and select the setting for the new tab. For example, choose Basic to select a default shell interface. Close tabs by clicking the X in the upper-left corner of the tab. You can also save tabbed windows as a window group by choosing Window ➪ Save Windows as Group and giving the group a descriptive name.

Entering UNIX Commands

To effectively navigate in a CLI (command-line interface), you need to understand how UNIX views the structure of your files and folders on the hard drive. UNIX calls each folder on your Mac a directory, and recognizes the drives as volumes. The beginning — or top — level of your start-up drive is known as the root directory, which is represented by a slash (/).

Let's begin learning how to get around in UNIX by opening a new window. To do so, choose Shell ⇨ New Window and select the setting for the new window.

When you first bring up a Terminal window, it opens in your home directory, which is represented by a tilde (~). To move to another directory, type its path on the command line. For example, to move to the root directory of your hard drive, simply type cd / and press Return (cd stands for change directory). To move back from the root directory to your home directory, simply type cd ~ and press Return.

Moving to a subdirectory can be a little trickier; however, knowing where directories are located on your drive helps immensely. Directories are separated by slashes when typing their path. For example, type the following to move to the Utilities folder on your hard drive and press Return:

```
cd/Applications/Utilities
```

Common commands

You can bend Lion to your will using the Terminal just as you can with the mouse. Typing commands in the CLI executes functions that range from listing items in a directory to performing diagnostics on your network. As I covered in the previous section, entering and executing a command is as simple as typing it and pressing Return — that's it!

Table 6.2 lists some of the most commonly used UNIX commands and gives a brief explanation of the functions they perform.

Table 6.2 Common UNIX Commands

Command	Function
ls	Lists files in the current directory.
ls –a	Lists all files (including hidden files) in the current directory.
cd	Changes directories. Type this command, followed by the path of the directory to which you want to change.
man	Displays the manual page for a command.

continued

143

Table 6.2 continued

Command	Function
su	Stands for superuser. Temporarily enables the root user account, discussed in Chapter 4. Type su followed by the command you want to invoke as the superuser and then press Return. Type the password for the root account when prompted.
mv	Moves or renames a file. Type mv followed by the name of the file (and in some cases, the path to the file) you want to move, and then type the path and name of the file to which you want to move it. This action creates a new file in the new location and deletes the original.
rm	Deletes a file. Type the command followed by the path and name of the file you want to delete.
rm −r	Deletes a directory and all of its contents. To use this command, type rm −r *directory name* (where *directory name* is the name of the directory you want to delete) and press Return.
pwd	Displays the path to the directory in which you are currently working.
cp	Copies a file. Type cp followed by the path and name of the file you want to copy, and then type the path and name of the file to which you want to copy it. This creates a new file in the new location, but also retains the original.
mkdir	Creates a new directory. Type mkdir, and then type the path and name of the new directory.

X11

Also known as the X Window System, X11 allows you to run UNIX applications alongside those in Mac OS X. Because the Lion version of UNIX, Darwin, is a fully compliant and certified UNIX variant, it can compile and run the full gamut of your UNIX applications. There are thousands of applications, many of which use graphical user interfaces.

Finding Additional UNIX Information

UNIX adds a whole other dimension to Lion that many regular users may never discover. However, there are hidden treasures in UNIX that you may find are well worth learning about. Here are some additional resources on UNIX:

- **www.apple.com/opensource/**
- **http://developer.apple.com/opensource/**
- **www.unix.org**

All of these links are accurate at the time of this writing. The Internet is chock-full of more UNIX goodness, so feel free to scour it for all the command-line enlightenment you can stand.

What's Up, Man?

There are literally hundreds of UNIX commands at your disposal in Lion and each of them might have several options that further expand its abilities. Needless to say, there's simply no way for me to explain the functions of all of those commands, but fear not; there's a UNIX command that can tell you everything you need to know: the man command. In a Terminal window, type man followed by the name of the command about which you need more information and press Return. The man (or manual) page for that command then appears. The man page describes what that command can do and what options are available for it.

When you first open the man page for a command, you see only a few lines of it. To navigate through the man page, follow these steps:

1. **To scroll up or down one line at a time, press the Up and Down arrows on your keyboard.**
2. **Press the spacebar to move to the next page.**
3. **Press Q to exit the man page.**

Administering System Utilities

System Utilities help you manage, monitor, and configure items related to the internal system functions of Mac OS X. These include things like the load on your processor and general information about the computer.

Tracking your Mac with Activity Monitor

Activity Monitor keeps track of all the goings-on in Lion, such as what applications are running and how much processor capacity is being used, as shown in Figure 6.10.

Select an activity or process from the list to quit, inspect, or sample it using the buttons in the toolbar. You can also monitor the CPU and hard drive using the tabs at the bottom of the Activity Monitor window: CPU, System Memory, Disk Activity, Disk Usage, and Network.

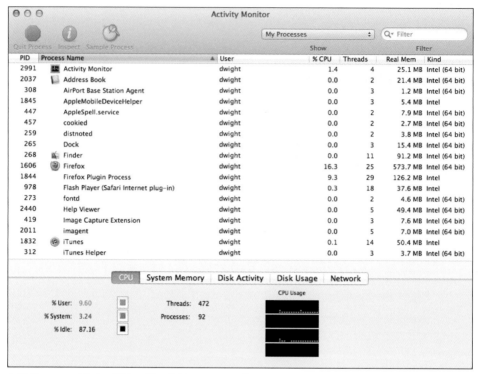

6.10 Keep up with the CPU and hard drive activity of your Mac.

Discovering errors with Console

Console displays messages generated by your Mac or its applications when an error occurs. This utility is great for tracking down problems with Mac OS X. For instance, if you are having an issue with a certain app crashing, the log for that application (found in Console) could be useful to the technical support representative when you call the developer of the app for help.

Moving information with Migration Assistant

Migration Assistant moves all the user account information from one Mac to another using a FireWire cable. You can bring over your network information, passwords, the contents of your user account folders, and so on in one fell swoop. Migration Assistant also helps you restore information from a Time Machine backup.

Using Remote Install Mac OS X

Remote Install Mac OS X helps install Mac OS X on a Mac that doesn't have an optical drive. For example, the MacBook Air doesn't have an internal optical drive of its own, so it relies on optical drives in other computers or an external optical drive.

Using System Information

System Information gives you all the information you could ever want about your Mac hardware, software, and network functionality. Select an option from the list on the left, as shown in Figure 6.11, and System Information gives you more information than you bargained for.

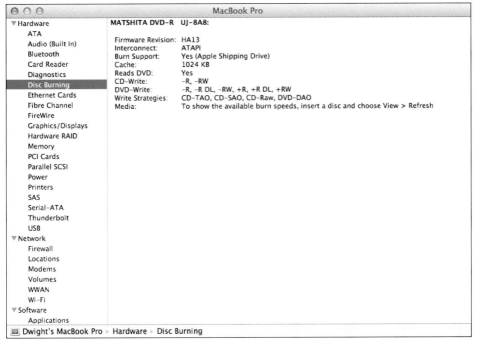

6.11 System Information is loaded with everything you could ever want to know about your Mac.

Using Hardware Utilities

Utilities of the hardware variety concentrate on helping you configure and use the various types of hardware you may want to connect to your Mac.

Configuring devices with Audio MIDI Setup

Audio MIDI Setup helps set up audio and MIDI devices that you connect to your Mac, including those that are built in, such as the speakers shown in Figure 6.12.

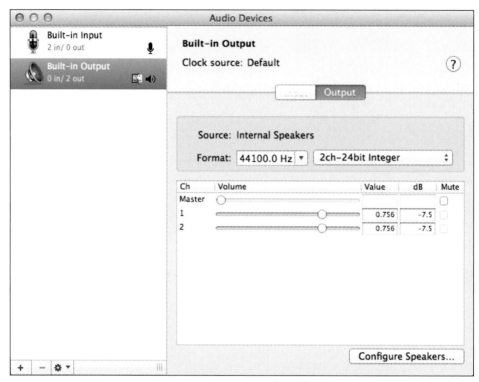

6.12 Audio MIDI Setup helps you set up audio devices, such as speakers, on your Mac.

Format and manage drives with Disk Utility

Disk Utility formats and manages hard drives, removable media (such as CDs and DVDs), and disk images. You can also create new disk images from folders, CDs, or DVDs. Chapter 16 contains more information on using Disk Utility to repair permissions on your hard drive and explains what symptoms to look for to see if a repair is necessary.

Configure multiple drives with RAID Utility

The RAID (Redundant Array of Inexpensive Disks) Utility allows you to configure multiple hard drives to act as one contiguous drive. This is good if you have a massive amount of information to store. For example, if you have a server utilized by many users who create very large files (an advertising agency would be a good example), this utility would come in handy. You must have a RAID card installed on your Mac to use the RAID Utility, which means that (at the time of this writing) only a Mac Pro can use it as it's the only Mac that can accept a RAID card.

Managing Network Utilities

The two network utilities in Lion allow you to manage, configure, and diagnose issues with your network.

AirPort Utility

AirPort Utility helps you manage your AirPort Base Station or Time Capsule. You can use it to do all of the following (and more):

- **Discover and install new firmware updates for your AirPort Base Station or Time Capsule.**
- **Share your Internet connection.**
- **Control who can access your wireless network.**
- **Monitor and diagnose any problems with your AirPort Base Station or Time Capsule.**
- **Restore your AirPort Base Station or Time Capsule to its factory defaults.**
- **Set up a password to protect your AirPort Base Station or Time Capsule settings.**

Please consult the AirPort Utility help for more information about how to utilize this great tool.

Network Utility

Network Utility monitors network traffic and diagnoses any issues that may creep up. This is a great utility, but you almost have to be a network administrator to understand and utilize some of its diagnostic tools.

The Info tab, shown in Figure 6.13, can provide invaluable information about your connection to the network, which can come in handy when troubleshooting networking issues.

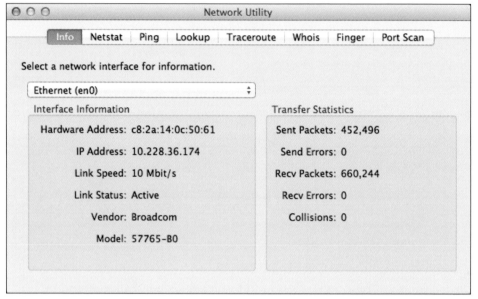

6.13 Network Utility provides you with vital information about your Mac network connections.

Genius

If you're trying to see if a certain device responds to you using its IP address, then the Ping section of Network Utility is for you. Just type the IP address of the device with which you are trying to communicate and click Ping to see if it responds over the network.

If you're looking at your Utilities folder right now, you might notice that I don't touch on Boot Camp or Bluetooth File Exchange. That's because they are discussed elsewhere in this book: Boot Camp is covered in Chapter 15 and Bluetooth File Exchange is discussed in Chapter 13.

How Do I Work with PDFs in Preview?

PDF

Portable Document Format files (PDFs) are the de facto standard for disseminating documents over the Internet and throughout many corporations. This is due largely to their portability across multiple operating systems, their relatively small file sizes, and the availability of security options for sensitive information. Lion includes an application called Preview that can open, edit, and save PDFs (most of the graphics on your screen are created with PDF technology anyway). In this chapter, I show you how to work with PDF files using Preview.

Opening and Saving PDFs in Preview

PDF files have become a standard document format that almost anyone who uses a computer has seen at some point. Most documents on the Internet are PDF files. Anyone on any computer can open PDFs, whether the computer runs Mac OS X, Windows, or Linux, as long as a PDF reader application, such as Preview or Adobe Reader, is installed.

Preview can open many types of files (see Chapter 12 for a comprehensive list), but this chapter maintains a laser-like focus on PDFs. To open a PDF file in Preview, do the following:

1. **From within Finder, choose Go ➪ Applications, and then double-click the Preview icon to open the application.**

2. **Choose File ➪ Open, or press ⌘+O to display the Open dialog.**

3. **Browse to the file you want to open, click its icon to highlight it, and then click Open, as shown in Figure 7.1.**

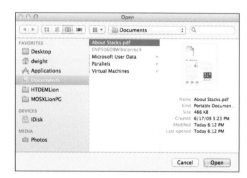

7.1 Choose the file you want to open in Preview.

Genius

If the Preview icon is in your Dock (either because it's already open or because you keep an alias for it there), you can simply drag and drop a PDF file onto the Preview icon to open it.

If you make changes to an open PDF, Preview automatically saves them as versions of the document. This allows you to view the file as it has appeared throughout the time you worked with it. It also eliminates the need to repeatedly save your documents as you make changes.

Preview automatically saves versions of a document you are editing once an hour, but does so more often if you make frequent changes. Preview also saves versions of documents when you open, save, duplicate, lock or rename them, or revert to previous versions. Preview trims the number of saved versions to make them easier to browse and also deletes all saved versions when you delete a document.

While this process is automatic, you can also save versions of PDFs on your own. If you make changes to a PDF in Preview and want to save those changes, press ⌘+S. You can also choose File ➪ Save a Version.

If you make changes to a file but you want to save the changed version under a different name and/or in a different location, follow these steps:

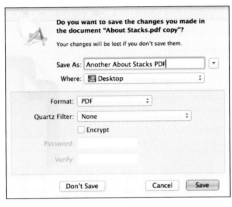

1. **Choose File ➪ Duplicate from the menu to create an exact copy of your original document.**

7.2 You can duplicate files and save them under a new name, or in a new location.

2. **Press ⌘+S or click the red Close button in the upper-left corner of the document window to open the Save As dialog, shown in Figure 7.2.**

3. **Type a new name for the file, choose a location in which to save it, and then click Save.**

Genius

If you can't find the location in which you want to save your file in the Where pop-up menu, click the square containing the black arrow. This expands the Save As window, allowing you to browse your entire hard drive.

Preview has a really cool way of browsing through the versions of a document. It is very reminiscent of the way Time Machine lets you browse through backed-up files (see Chapter 14 for more info).

To browse through the many different versions of a document and possibly revert to one of them:

1. **Open the document with the versions you want to browse.**

2. **Choose File ⇨ Revert to Saved from the menu and your screen is transformed into something resembling the latest sci-fi blockbuster, as shown in Figure 7.3.**

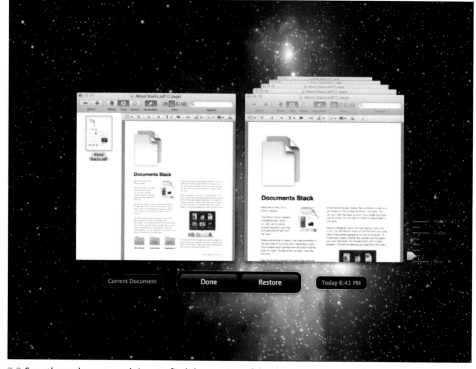

7.3 Soar through space and time to find the version of the document you need.

3. **Click the gray tick marks on the right side of the window or drag the slider to find the version you want to see.**

4. **Perform one of the following tasks:**

   - **To restore the document to a previous state, select the version and click Restore.**

   - **To delete a version, click the pop-up menu in the upper-right corner of its window and select Delete.**

   - **To create a new document from a version of a previous one, select the version, hold down the Option key, and then click Restore a Copy.**

   - **To return to your document without reverting to any previous versions, click Done.**

If you've ever double-clicked a file to open it, only to have it open in an application you didn't expect, you'll love this little nugget. To make a certain file type open only in an application you designate, do the following:

1. **Click the file one time to highlight it, and then press ⌘+I to open its Info window, as shown in Figure 7.4.** You can also Control+click (or right-click) the file and select Get Info from the pop-up menu.

2. **If the gray triangle to the left of the Open with section is pointing to the right, click it to expand that section.**

3. **Click the pop-up menu to choose the application you want to set as the default for opening this file.**

4. **To make the selected application the system-wide default for opening all files of this type, click Change All.**

5. **Close the Info window by clicking the red button in the upper-left corner.**

7.4 Get Info on any file by highlighting it and pressing ⌘+I.

Setting the Preview Preferences for PDFs

The way you set the preferences for Preview affects how you use the application. I'm a big advocate for making Lion and all of its applications work the way you want them to. It's very important that your application preferences fit your work style.

The Preview preferences are divided into five categories: General, Images, PDF, Bookmarks, and Signatures. However, the only three covered in this chapter are PDF, Bookmarks, and Signatures (the other two are discussed in Chapter 12). Open Preview, and then press ⌘+, to open the Preferences window.

PDF

The options under the PDF tab in the Preview preferences are shown in Figure 7.5.

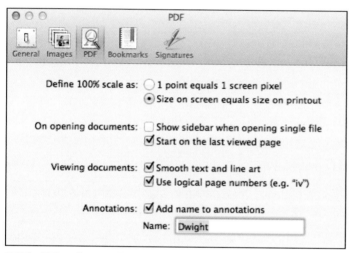

7.5 The PDF preferences for Preview.

Table 7.1 covers the functions of the different options under the PDF tab.

Table 7.1 PDF Preferences

Preference	Function
Define 100% scale as	Determine whether 100 percent scale of a PDF is based on screen pixels or the actual printout.
On opening documents	Select the first check box to open the window sidebar even when opening a single PDF file; select the second check box to begin viewing a PDF from the last page you viewed the previous time it was open.
Viewing documents	Select these check boxes to smooth lines in text and line art, or to use logical page numbers when viewing PDFs.
Annotations	Select this check box to assign a name to annotations you make in a PDF, and then type that name in the Name field.

Bookmarks

Preview allows you to bookmark images and PDFs so that you can zip right to them when needed. This is very much like using bookmarks in a web browser. To add a bookmark, open the file you want and press ⌘+D, or choose Bookmarks ➪ Add Bookmark from the menu.

The Bookmarks tab lists all the bookmarks you create. You can rename them or delete them from the list by clicking Remove.

Signatures

How cool would it be if you could add your own John Hancock to your PDF files? You're about to find out, because that is exactly what Preview lets you do with one of its latest options.

To add a signature to your arsenal of PDF tricks, follow these steps:

1. **Open the Signatures pane of the Preview preferences window and click Create Signature.**
2. **Sign your name (in black ink) on a white piece of paper.**
3. **Hold the paper up to the Mac camera.** Be sure that the signature on the paper is resting on the blue line in the preview window, as shown in Figure 7.6.

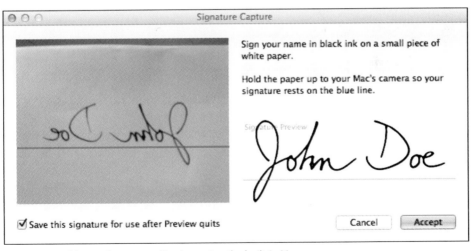

7.6 You can add your signature to Preview using the built-in Mac camera.

4. **Click Accept and your signature is added to the list in the Signatures preferences pane.**

You can add or remove signatures from the list by using the plus (+) and minus (–) signs in the lower-left corner of the Signatures preferences pane. Read on to find out how to insert signatures into your PDFs.

Viewing and Editing PDFs

Lion is a whiz at opening, viewing, editing, and creating PDF files. As I covered opening files earlier in this chapter, I concentrate on viewing and editing them in this section. The creation of PDFs is covered later in this chapter.

To get started, you need to open a PDF, as described earlier.

Annotating PDFs

To *annotate* a PDF is to highlight, strike through, or underline text that needs to be edited or removed. Annotation also means to add notes or links to a document, or to spotlight an area of the page with an oval, arrow, line, or rectangle. Figure 7.7 shows an example of annotations in a PDF.

To annotate a PDF, do the following:

1. **Click and drag the mouse cursor over the text you want to mark up to highlight it.**
2. **Choose Tools ⇨ Annotate.**
3. **Select which type of annotation to use:**
   - Highlight Text (⌘+Control+H)
   - Strike Through Text (⌘+Control+S)
   - Underline Text (⌘+Control+U)
   - Add Oval (⌘+Control+O)
   - Add Rectangle (⌘+Control+R)
   - Add Line (⌘+Control+I)
   - Add Arrow (⌘+Control+A)
   - Add Note (⌘+Control+N)
   - Add Link (⌘+Control+L)
   - Add Text (⌘+Control+T)
   - Add Outlined Text
   - Add Boxed Text

- Add Speech Bubble

- Add Thought Bubble

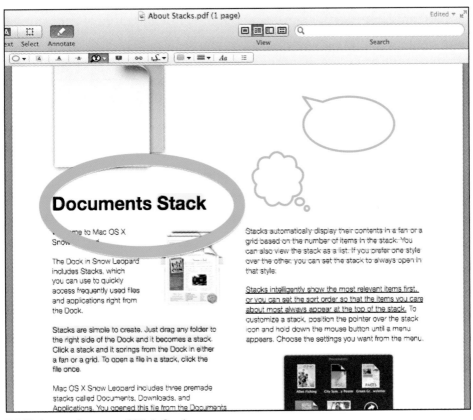

7.7 Mark up and annotate PDFs in Preview.

Genius

If annotating PDFs is something you do often, memorize the keyboard shortcuts for them. Keyboard shortcuts can save you much more time than you realize. It's worth taking the time to learn them if you work in a fast-paced environment.

Adding your signature to a PDF

Some PDFs may require your signature and Lion has added this really cool tool to Preview. As covered earlier in this chapter, you can create a signature in Preview via the Preferences pane. To add a created signature to your PDF, do the following:

1. **Open the PDF to which you want to add the signature.**

2. **In the Annotations toolbar, click the Signature button and select the signature you want to place in your PDF, as shown in Figure 7.8.** If you don't see the Annotations toolbar, choose View ➪ Show Annotations Toolbar.

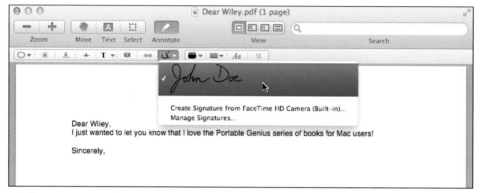

7.8 Choose a signature from the Annotations toolbar.

3. **Click and drag the signature to the location in the document you prefer.**

4. **Resize the signature if necessary by dragging the handles (gray dots) found on each side and in each corner of the signature window, as shown in Figure 7.9.**

7.9 Signatures can be resized by dragging the size handles.

Deleting pages from a PDF

Just a couple of years ago, the only way to delete or rearrange PDF pages was to pay through the nose for a third-party program. Thanks to Apple, Preview now has these capabilities, which means you can provide a professional level of service without having to shell out a professional level of money.

To delete a page from a multipage document, do the following:

1. **If you are unable to see all the pages of the PDF in the sidebar, choose View ➪ Contact Sheet, and then choose View ➪ Sidebar ➪ Expand All.**

2. **Find the page you want to delete in the sidebar and click to select it.** You can select multiple pages by holding down the ⌘ key while clicking the individual pages. The sidebar must be displaying thumbnails, not Table of Contents. To set the sidebar to display

thumbnails, click the Thumbnails button in the View section of the toolbar at the top of the PDFs window.

3. **Choose Edit ➪ Delete to remove the page from your PDF.**

4. **Save your PDF (⌘+S) to keep the changes or press ⌘+Z to undo a change.**

Note If you try to make changes to a locked PDF, Preview gives you three options to continue working with the document. To automatically save the changes to your document, click Unlock. To create a new document that retains the changes you made, click Duplicate. If neither of those sounds appealing, click Cancel to just forget the whole affair.

Rearranging pages in a PDF

As mentioned in the previous section, rearranging pages in a PDF is a treat for anyone who doesn't have an expensive third-party application. To shuffle your PDF pages, do the following:

1. **If you are unable to see all the pages of the PDF in the sidebar, choose View ➪ Contact Sheet, and then choose View ➪ Sidebar ➪ Expand All.**

2. **Search the sidebar for the page you want to move.** The sidebar must be displaying thumbnails, not Table of Contents. To set the sidebar to display thumbnails, click the Thumbnails button in the View section of the toolbar at the top of the PDF window.

3. **Click and drag the page to the location in the sidebar you prefer, and then drop it in place, as shown in Figure 7.10.**

4. **Save the changes by pressing ⌘+S or undo them by pressing ⌘+Z.**

Magnifying the contents of a PDF

Sometimes the fonts in a PDF may be too small to view, or you may simply want to read a section of the document without having to zoom in on the entire page. Preview has a nifty tool called the Magnifier (catchy name) that can accommodate you. Here's how to zoom in on a specific section of a page:

1. **Open a PDF and go to the page you want to view.**

2. **Choose Tools ➪ Show Magnifier from the menu and the Magnifier window appears in your PDF window, as illustrated in Figure 7.11.**

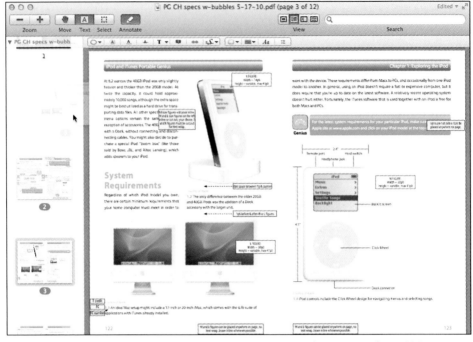

7.10 Drag pages from their old location to a new one to rearrange the contents of your PDF.

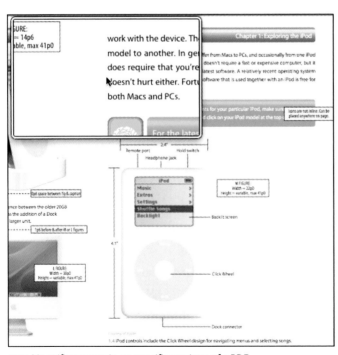

7.11 Magnifier zooms in on specific sections of a PDF.

3. **Click and drag the Magnifier to the location of the PDF on which you want to zoom in.**

4. **When finished, choose Tools ⇨ Hide Magnifier to go back to normal viewing.**

Changing the page view

If your PDF contains multiple pages it may behoove you to view the contents of the document in its entirety so you can jump from one page to another rather quickly. The View section of the toolbar can be found just to the left of the Search field (if the toolbar isn't visible at the top of the PDF window, press ⌘+B). It contains four buttons for selecting a specific type of view. Preview provides multiple page-viewing options from which to choose:

- **Content Only shows only the currently selected page in your PDF.**

- **Thumbnails opens the sidebar on the left side of the PDF window and displays thumbnail images of each page in your PDF.**

- **Table of Contents view displays the PDF table of contents (assuming it contains one) in the sidebar.**

- **Contact Sheet displays every page of the PDF in a single window, as shown in Figure 7.12.**

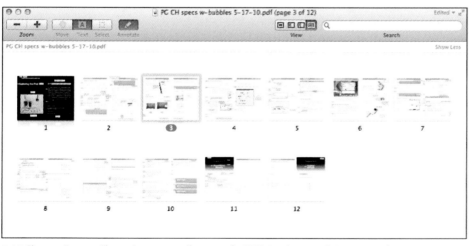

7.12 Choose Contact Sheet view to see all pages of a PDF simultaneously in one window.

Creating Your Own PDFs

Once upon a time, PDFs could only be generated by expensive software. Mac OS X has changed that due to its extensive use of the PDF file format throughout the operating system. Lion affords you the ability to create PDFs from any document you please, for free!

To create a PDF using Lion, do the following:

1. **Open a document in an application.** If you want to follow along, I'm using TextEdit.

2. **Choose File ⇨ Print.**

3. **Click PDF in the lower-left corner of the window to see the options you have at your beck and call (see Figure 7.13).**

4. **Select Save As PDF from the menu to open the Save dialog, shown in Figure 7.14.**

5. **Give the PDF an appropriate name, decide where on your Mac to save it, and click Save.**

The ability to create PDFs with any document on your Mac without expensive third-party software is a huge boon, no doubt about it. However, that third-party software (specifically Adobe Acrobat) has always had the ability to make PDF files secure from prying eyes.

This is a great feature and is required by some corporations when disseminating sensitive information. Previous versions of Mac OS X were lacking in this department, but Lion has come to the rescue of the security-obsessed among us. To secure your PDFs, refer back to Step 5 of the previous section. Prior to clicking Save, click Security Options to see the PDF Security Options window, as shown in Figure 7.15. Table 7.2 spells out the available security options. Click OK to assign those you have chosen for a file.

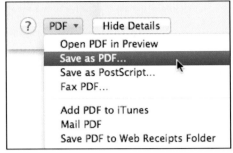

7.13 Lion gives you several options for creating PDF files from any document.

7.14 The options available in the PDF Save dialog.

7.15 Secure your PDFs from anyone not authorized to view them.

Table 7.2 PDF Security Options

Option	Function
Require password to open document	Select this check box to enable the password feature. Type a secure password in the Password field and then retype it in the Verify field.
Require password to copy text, images, and other content	Check this box to prevent someone from copying elements of the PDF and pasting them into an unsecured document without knowing the password to do so. Type a secure password in the Password field and then retype it in the Verify field.
Require password to print document	If this check box is selected, a user must know the password in order to print this document. Type a secure password in the Password field and then retype it in the Verify field.

How Do I Organize My Life with iCal and Address Book?

f your life is anything like mine, you need as much organization as you can get. Enter iCal and Address Book. With iCal, you can create calendars for family or work events while Address Book keeps all of your contacts in one location. You can create events in iCal with reminders for important dates (no more excuses if you forget your anniversary, guys). Address Book allows access to your contacts through any application programmed to use it, including Mail or iChat. In this chapter, I show you how to make iCal and Address Book work for you.

Creating Calendars

Open iCal to get started; choose Go ⇨ Applications in the menu and double-click the iCal icon, or use Launchpad to find and start iCal.

You can create calendars that reflect the different areas of your everyday life, such as your work schedule, bill due dates, or school events. Having a separate calendar for each makes it easier to organize your time.

There are two ways to create a new calendar:

- **Choose File ⇨ New Calendar.**
- **Press ⌘+Option+N.**

Performing either of these opens the Calendars list and displays an untitled calendar. Next, simply type a name for the calendar. Create as many as you need before proceeding.

Your calendars are now ready to be put to work. There are a number of ways in which you can manage them:

- **Arrange calendars in the list by clicking and dragging them into the order you prefer, as shown in Figure 8.1.**

- **Rename a calendar by right-clicking (or Control+clicking) it in the Calendars list and selecting Get Info from the pop-up menu.** Type a new name for the calendar in the Name field.

8.1 Click and drag calendars into the order you prefer.

- **The events you enter (more on that a bit later in this chapter) are represented by the color of their respective calendars.** You can change the color of a calendar by right-clicking (or Control+clicking) it in the Calendars list and then selecting Get Info. Click the color button in the upper-right corner of the window and select a color from the list.

- **Notice the check box to the left of each calendar you create.** It indicates whether events are displayed for the calendar in question. Deselecting some of these check boxes can help make sense of a particularly busy schedule.

● **Create groups to arrange similar calendars together in the calendar list.** Choose File ⇨ New Calendar Group or press ⌘+Shift+N, and then give the new group a descriptive name. Arrange calendars into groups by simply dragging and dropping them underneath the desired group.

Note   You can change the way your calendars are displayed in the iCal window by clicking the Day, Week, Month, and Year tabs at the top. Click the arrows in the upper-right area of the iCal window to scroll to the previous or next day, week, or month. The Full Screen button is the one with two opposite-pointing arrows in the upper-right corner of the iCal window. To exit Full Screen, press ESC.

Adding events to calendars

A calendar without an event is about as useful as a car without tires, and it probably won't even get you as far. Events are the items that you add to your calendars to make them come alive; they are your life, only organized.

To create a new event:

1. **Select the day the event begins.**

2. **Press ⌘+N or choose File ⇨ New Event to create a new event for that day.**

3. **Type a descriptive name for the event and press Return.** The event information window then opens automatically.

You now have your first event, but you most likely want to edit the contents of it before considering it a done deal.

Editing calendar events

After you create an event, some tweaking may be in order. To edit your event, follow these steps:

1. **Open the event information window (if it isn't open already) by double-clicking it, or click to highlight it and then choose Edit⇨Show Event.** If this is not a new event, but a previously created one, double-clicking only displays its basic information. Press ⌘+E or click Edit to gain access to the details shown in Figure 8.2.

2. **Click to the right of each item in the event information window to edit it.** Table 8.1 lists the available items and their functions.

3. **Click Done.**

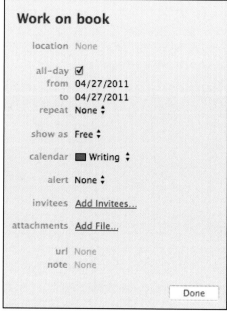

8.2 An event ready for editing.

Table 8.1 Editing Events

Item	Function
location	Where the event is to be held.
all-day	Select this check box if the event lasts an entire day, as opposed to an hour or two. All-day events are highlighted in the calendar.
from and to	Select the begin and end dates and times for your event.
repeat	Click the options menu next to this item if you want the event to be repeated (such would be the case with a recurring event, like a birthday or weekly meeting).
show as	Decide whether to show yourself as free or busy during this event.
calendar	Choose the calendar to which this event belongs.
alert	Select from several alert types, such as e-mail, on-screen messages, and sound. You can set multiple alerts for each event.

Item	Function
invitees	Invite others to add this event to their calendars.
attachments	You can attach documents and other files to your events. For example, you could attach a grocery list to a scheduled shopping trip.
url	Include a relevant website or shared calendar address.
note	Type any additional information you may need for the event.

Setting iCal Preferences

You can change the iCal preferences to customize how it works. Choose iCal ⇨ Preferences to see what options are available (see Figure 8.3).

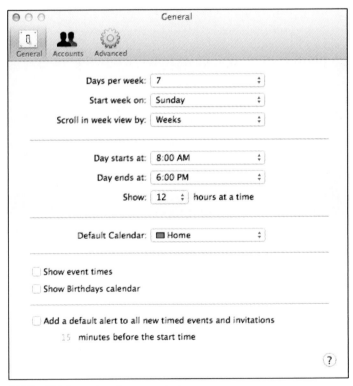

8.3 The iCal General preferences window.

The General tab allows you to make the most basic of setting adjustments. The settings are listed in Table 8.2.

Table 8.2 The iCal General Preferences Tab

Setting	Function
Days per week	Set the number of days for your normal week. For example, you might change this to 5 to reflect a five-day workweek.
Start week on	Choose on which day to start your week.
Scroll in week view by	Select to view either weeks or days when in week view.
Day starts at	Decide at what time your typical day begins.
Day ends at	Set the time your typical day ends.
Show X hours at a time	Choose how many hours to display when in Day and Week viewing modes.
Default Calendar	Select the calendar to which new events are automatically added.
Show event times	Select this option to show appointment times when in Week or Month view. These are hidden by default due to space restrictions.
Show Birthdays calendar	Select this option to display a calendar that lists birthdays from your Address Book.
Add a default alert to all new timed events and invitations	Every new event or invitation is assigned an alert that goes off in the amount of time you specify prior to the event.

The Accounts tab allows you to subscribe to CalDAV and Exchange servers, which some companies and organizations use to share calendars among several users. To subscribe to your company or organization's CalDAV server, click the plus sign (+) in the lower-left corner, and then type the server information (if you don't have this information, contact your IT department).

The Advanced tab, shown in Figure 8.4, helps you set preferences for time zone support, to-do's, events, alarms, and invitations.

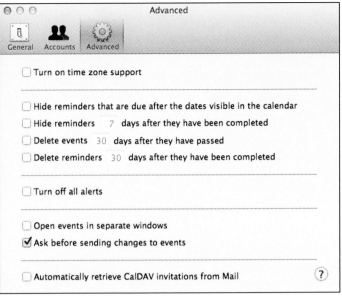

8.4 The Advanced preferences tab for iCal.

Table 8.3 lists the Advanced preferences available for iCal.

Table 8.3 The iCal Advanced Preferences Tab

Setting	Function
Turn on time zone support	Allows you to view your schedule as it would be in a time zone other than your default. When you select this check box, select the appropriate time zone from the pop-up menu that appears. This option is great for those who travel or work with others in different time zones.
Hide reminders that are due after the dates visible in the calendar	Reminders that you create won't appear in the reminder list (displayed by pressing ⌘+Option+T) if their dates are after the current view being used for your calendar.
Hide reminders X days after they have been completed	Select the number of days after an event for a reminder to be hidden from view.
Delete events X days after they have passed	Automatically removes events from your calendars after the number of days you specify past their completion.
Delete reminders X days after they have been completed	Automatically removes reminders from the reminders list after the number of days you specify past their completion.
Turn off all alerts	Prevents any alerts from occurring.
Open events in separate windows	Causes events to open in a separate window when double-clicked. This is a good trick for comparing two or more events.

continued

175

Table 8.3 continued

Setting	Function
Ask before sending changes to events	Check this box to have iCal alert you and make certain you want to send changes you've made to events.
Automatically retrieve CalDAV invitations from Mail	Select this check box to have event invitations shown in iCal instead of just Mail.

Sharing Calendars

Life is much easier when everyone is on the same page — be it your company or your family. iCal offers two ways to share your calendars with others: Publishing and exporting.

Publishing a calendar

When you publish a calendar, you place a copy of it on the Internet or a local WebDAV server. Other users can then access it through iCal, another third-party calendar application, or a standard web browser using any computing platform. To publish a calendar:

1. **Open the calendar list, and then click the calendar or calendar group to which you want to publish.**

2. **Choose Calendar ⇨ Publish from the menu.** The Publish calendar window, as shown in Figure 8.5, appears.

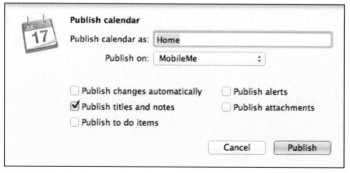

8.5 Publish calendars to share them over a network or via the Internet.

3. **When the window opens, type a name for your calendar if you don't want to use the default.**

4. **Select where to publish your calendar (your MobileMe account or a private server) using the Publish on pop-up menu.** If you select Private Server, type the server information, along with a login name and password to gain access.

5. **When the options are set to your liking, click Publish.**

Exporting a calendar

Exporting a calendar is a good way to move calendars from one computer to another. You can also edit calendars that you've exported, although you cannot edit calendars that you've published from another computer.

To export a calendar, follow these steps:

1. **Open the calendar list, and then click to select the calendar (or calendar group) from which you want to export.**

2. **Choose File ⇨ Export ⇨ Export to open the Save As window, as shown in Figure 8.6.**

3. **Give a descriptive name to the file, choose a location to save it, and then click Export.**

4. **Share the exported calendar by e-mailing it, placing it on a shared server, or any other way you can think of.**

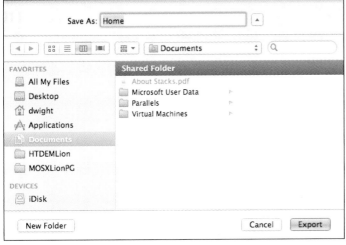

8.6 You can export calendars from iCal and import them onto other computers.

Genius

The default format of exported calendars in iCal is ICS. ICS files can be imported into almost any third-party calendar application, so you don't have to worry about your Windows or Linux pals not being able to view your calendar. Likewise, you can use your friends' calendars in iCal if they export them from their applications using the ICS format.

Backing up a calendar

It's always a good idea to back up your calendars in case you need to restore them sometime in the future. The iCal Archive feature is just the tool for such a task; all of your calendars are backed up in this single file.

Here's how to create an archive:

1. **Choose File ⇨ Export ⇨ iCal Archive to open the Save As window.**
2. **Give a descriptive name to the file.**
3. **Choose the location to which you want to save the file and then click Save.**

Note There's no need to perform this procedure if your calendars are stored on an external server, such as MobileMe or Google. Those calendars are automatically backed up.

Subscribing to calendars

It stands to reason that if some people are publishing their calendars, then there must be others subscribing to them. There are two ways to subscribe to calendars. This is the easy way:

1. **Choose Calendar ⇨ Subscribe from the menu.**
2. **Type the URL of the calendar to which you want to subscribe in the Calendar URL field.**
3. **Click Subscribe to see the information window for the calendar, as shown in Figure 8.7.**

8.7 Subscribing to calendars is a snap with iCal.

There are tons of calendars on the web just begging you to subscribe. To find some, visit www.apple.com/downloads/macosx/calendars/ or http://icalshare.com/.

4. **Decide whether to remove Alerts, Attachments, or To Do items (which I recommend if you don't know the person who created the calendar).** You can also choose how often the calendar automatically refreshes in case there are any changes made by its creator.

5. **Click OK to complete the subscription process.**

This is the even easier way:

1. **If someone sends you the link to his or her calendar in an e-mail, or if you click the link to a calendar from a web page, iCal automatically begins the subscription process.**

2. **Click Subscribe to see the information window for the calendar.**

3. **Decide whether to remove Alerts, Attachments, or To Do items (which I recommend if you don't know the person who created the calendar).** You can also choose how often the calendar automatically refreshes in case there are any changes made by its creator.

4. **Click OK to complete the subscription process.**

Printing calendars

If you're like me, you understand that, while the concept of a paperless office sounded pretty cool in the 1980s, it most certainly — and to some degree, thankfully — hasn't come to fruition. Sometimes I just like to have a printed page in hand as opposed to being tied to my desk or lugging around a laptop. I love my Mac, but we're not permanently attached at the hip. iCal can provide you with great printed calendars to use for yourself or to give to others. This is a great tool for offices and schools, or any other organization or team, for that matter. Another plus — printed calendars are much easier to hang on your fridge than your computer screen.

To print your calendars, follow these steps:

1. **Choose File ➪ Print.**

2. **Select from among the myriad options shown in Figure 8.8 and then click Continue.**

   Table 8.4 lists the printing options and gives brief explanations of them.

3. **Click Print in the Print window.**

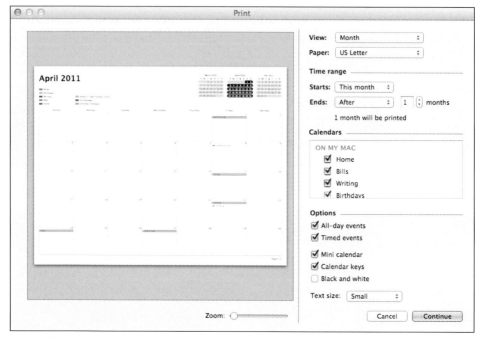

8.8 The iCal printing options.

Table 8.4 The iCal Printing Options

Option	Function
View	Choose what view to use for your printed calendar from the pop-up menu.
Paper	Select a paper size on which to print your calendar.
Time range	Decide when the printed calendar (or calendars) should begin and end using the Starts and Ends pop-up menus.
Calendars	Select the check boxes next to the calendars with events you want to include.
Options	Determine whether to print all-day events, timed events, mini-calendars, calendar keys, or if you want to print only in black and white.
Text size	Choose what size font to use when printing your calendars.
Zoom	Drag the slider to enlarge the preview image.

Working with Contacts in Address Book

Have you ever needed to find an elusive phone number or address for a prospective client, and had to thumb through ten devices and books to find it? Apple created Address Book just for you. Creating contacts in Address Book can sure make rounding up all those Christmas card addresses a lot easier.

Contacts are files that contain information for people in your life, such as street addresses, e-mail addresses, birthdays, and even their pictures. To get started, open Address Book by clicking Go ⇨ Applications and then double-clicking the Address Book icon. You can also enter Launchpad and single-click the Address Book icon.

Address Book is fairly useless without contacts, so let's start adding a few.

Creating a contact card

A contact card contains all of a person's information, so to get started you need to create a new one. There are a few ways to begin creating a new card:

- **Choose File ⇨ New Card from the menu.**
- **Press ⌘+N.**
- **Click the plus sign (+) at the bottom of the All Contacts page in the Address Book window.**

Genius

You can add new contact cards quite easily when you receive a vCard in an e-mail. A vCard is a digital business card that some people attach to e-mails so others can easily save their contact information. In Mail, simply double-click a vCard in an e-mail to create a new card in Address Book.

181

Any of these actions creates a new blank card awaiting your input, as shown in Figure 8.9.

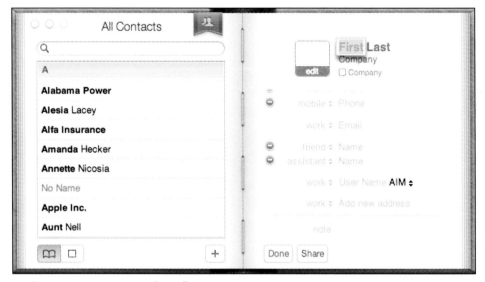

8.9 Creating a new contact card is really easy.

After you finish typing in the necessary info, press Tab on your keyboard to move to the next available field. If there's a field that you don't need to use, leave it blank and it won't appear on the card after you save it. If the contact is a company, check the Company check box. This enables the company to be found in your contacts list alphabetically by the first letter of its first name. For example, Alabama Power appears in the A section, rather than under the P's (for Power). To add a new field, choose Card ⇨ Add Field and select one from the list.

After you finish typing the information, press ⌘+S or click Edit below the card window to save it. You can always edit the information in the card by clicking to highlight it in the Name column of the Address Book window and then clicking Edit beneath the card window. The Edit button turns blue when in editing mode.

Creating a contact group

A great feature that I use quite a bit in Address Book is groups. Using groups, you can create different categories of contacts, such as Family, Work, and Church. As with contact cards, there are several techniques you can use to create new groups:

- **Press ⌘+Shift+N.**
- **Choose File ⇨ New Group from the menu.**

- **Click the red Groups ribbon with the two embossed silhouettes at the top of the Address Book window.** After the page turns (how cool is that?), click the plus sign (+) at the bottom left of the page.

Be sure to give your group a descriptive name referencing the items it contains. To add cards to the groups, drag and drop them from the Name column onto the preferred group in the Group column, as shown in Figure 8.10. This action doesn't remove the card from the Name column — it just associates it with the selected group.

Genius

> There's an even faster way to create a group. Select multiple cards from the Name column by holding the ⌘ key while you click the names, and then choose File➪New Group from Selection.

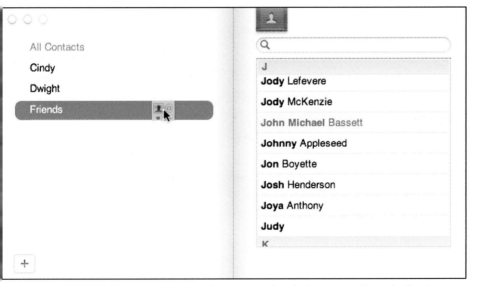

8.10 Drag and drop the contact's name onto the group under which you want him to be listed.

Creating a Smart Group

Smart Groups are groups to which contact cards are automatically added if they meet certain specified criteria. For example, if you create a Smart Group to look for contact cards with certain last names, a new card created using that last name is automatically added to the Smart Group. To create a Smart Group, follow these steps:

1. **Press ⌘+Option+N, or choose File ⇨ New Smart Group from the menu.** The Smart Group window appears, as shown in Figure 8.11.

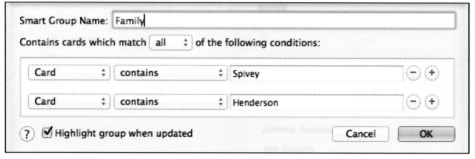

8.11 Add some intelligence to your Smart Group.

2. **Give the Smart Group a descriptive name.**

3. **Decide whether the Smart Group should contain cards that match any or all of the conditions you are about to set.**

4. **Remove or add conditions by clicking the minus (-) or plus (+) signs on the right.**

5. **Select the Highlight group when updated check box if you want Address Book to notify you when a new contact card is added to the Smart Group.**

6. **Click OK to save the new Smart Group or click Cancel to delete it.**

You can change a Smart Group's criteria at any time by Control+clicking its name in the Group column and selecting Edit Smart Group.

Genius

If your contact list is a mile long, you can quickly find a contact with just a smidgen of information. Simply type something about the contact (such as her name, e-mail address, or the city in which she lives) in the search field, which is denoted by the magnifying glass at the top of the All Contacts page. As you type, the closest matches appear in the contacts list.

Importing contacts

Address Book can import files from other applications when created in the following formats:

- **vCard**
- **LDIF (LDAP Interchange Format)**
- **Tab-delimited**
- **Comma-separated (CSV), which is usually the most compatible with other applications**

Caution

When you import an Address Book Archive, your existing Address Book database is replaced. This causes you to lose all existing contact cards in Address Book. You are prompted by Address Book to be sure that you want to continue this action. Make sure that you have a backup archive before continuing (see the export instructions in the next section).

Consult each application to find out how to export contacts from it in one of these formats. To import contacts to Address Book, follow these steps:

1. **Choose File ⇨ Import, and then select the format of the file you want to import.**

2. **Browse to the file you want to import and click to highlight it.**

3. **Click Open in the bottom-right corner.**

   - **If importing a tab-delimited or comma-separated file, choose the Text File format.**

   - **If you import a vCard with a contact already in Address Book, you must choose how to handle the conflict by clicking Review Duplicate.** As shown in Figure 8.12, you can choose to keep the old card, keep only the new card, keep both cards, or update the old card with the new information.

Exporting contacts

The file format preferred by Address Book for exporting contacts is vCard. vCard is a standard format common to most applications that have functionality similar to Address Book.

To export vCards from Address Book, follow these steps:

1. **Select the contacts you want to export.**

2. **Choose File ⇨ Export and then select Export vCard.**

8.12 Decide the ultimate fate of a vCard.

3. **Give the exported vCard a name.**

4. **Browse to the destination on the Mac hard drive to which you want to save the exported file, and then click Save.**

Genius

Notice in the File ⇨ Export menu that there is another selection called Address Book Archive. Choose this format if you want to make a complete backup file of your Address Book database. I highly recommend doing this after importing a large number of files to make sure you don't lose all the work you've just done. At the very least, I suggest performing one of these backups once a month.

Eliminating duplicate contacts

While populating your Address Book, you may inadvertently enter the same contact multiple times or you may find that you have duplicate contacts, with slightly different information. Address Book is quite adept at handling these situations.

To search for and resolve duplicate contacts:

1. **Open Address Book.**

2. **Choose Card from the menu and select Look for Duplicates.**

3. **Address Book searches for duplicates.** If it finds any, it lets you decide if you want to merge the information, as shown in Figure 8.13. If so, click Merge; otherwise, click Cancel.

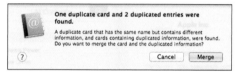

8.13 You can easily merge duplicate contacts in Address Book.

Setting Address Book Preferences

As with most other applications, Address Book has many preferences to help you customize your experience. Open the preferences by choosing Address Book ⇨ Preferences from the menu or pressing ⌘+,.

General

The General preferences allow you to make several basic appearance and behavior modifications, as shown in Figure 8.14.

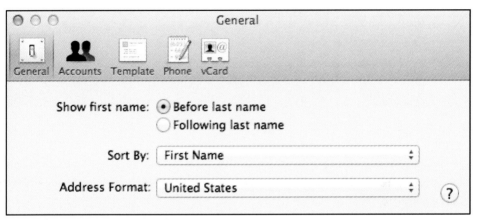

8.14 The Address Book General preferences, at your service.

While these options are fairly self-explanatory, Table 8.5 gives a brief description of each.

Table 8.5 Address Book General Preferences

Option	Function
Show first name	Display a contact's first name before or after the last name.
Sort By	Decide to sort contacts by first or last name.
Address Format	Select the country that uses the address format you want to use.

Accounts

The Accounts preferences, shown in Figure 8.15, allow you to synchronize contacts with other accounts (such as MobileMe) or share your Address Book with others.

Select the check box next to the type of account with which you want to synchronize your contacts. Next, click Configure beside the account you selected.

Template

Use the Template preferences shown in Figure 8.16 to modify the fields automatically displayed when creating new contact cards. Remove fields by clicking the minus sign (–) to the left. To add fields, click the plus sign (+) or choose a field type from the Add Field pop-up menu.

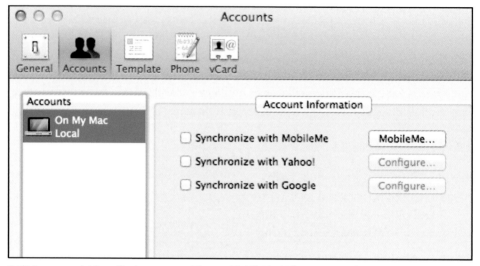

8.15 Sync your Address Book contacts with your MobileMe, Yahoo!, or Google account.

8.16 I love the Address Book Template preferences because they allow customization of the fields on contact cards.

Phone

Phone simply allows you to modify the format in which Address Book displays phone numbers. You may want to change this to reflect the country in which you or your contact is. Check the Automatically format phone numbers box and then choose the preferred format from the Formats pop-up menu. You can also create your own by clicking the triangle next to the Formats pop-up menu and then clicking the plus sign (+) in the bottom-left corner of the window.

vCard

The vCard options, shown in Figure 8.17, allow you to change the default vCard format version in Address Book and to specify how much information you want to share when sending others your vCard.

Table 8.6 explains the vCard options.

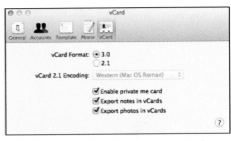

8.17 The vCard options in the Address Book preferences.

Table 8.6 vCard Options for Address Book

Option	Function
vCard Format	Choose between versions 3.0 and 2.1. Version 3.0 is the default; choose 2.1 if others have problems importing your vCards.
vCard 2.1 Encoding	Select the appropriate encoding for your language. English speakers generally want to stick with Western (Mac OS Roman). This option is only available if you select 2.1 for the vCard format.
Enable private me card	When this check box is selected, you can deselect the items you don't want exported with your contact card. For example, you may want to share everything except your personal e-mail or home address.
Export notes in vCards	Select this check box to include notes you have typed in your contacts' vCards.
Export photos in vCards	Select this check box to include any photos that you associate with the contact card (or cards) being exported.

Getting Maps for Addresses

A great feature included in Address Book is the ability to see maps of the addresses in your contact cards. This functionality really shines when you need to get to a client's location but aren't sure where it is. Here's how to use this cool feature:

1. **Click the card you need so that you can see the contact information.**

2. **Highlight and then Control+click (or right-click) the address in the contact information window, and then choose Show Map, as shown in Figure 8.18.**

3. **Safari automatically opens the Google Maps page, displaying a map of the location.** From here, you can get directions from your current location to the address.

Address Book and Google Maps work well together to give you accurate information — this feature is a pleasure to use.

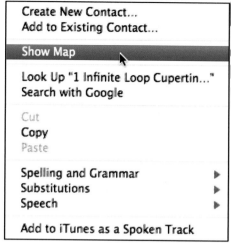

Create New Contact...
Add to Existing Contact...

Show Map

Look Up "1 Infinite Loop Cupertin..."
Search with Google

Cut
Copy
Paste

Spelling and Grammar ▶
Substitutions ▶
Speech ▶

Add to iTunes as a Spoken Track

8.18 Choose Show Map from this contextual menu to get a detailed map of a location.

Syncing Contacts and Calendars with Devices

Lion can connect to and synchronize contacts and calendar information with the iPhone and iPod touch using iTunes, making it very easy to keep contact information and calendar data consistent across multiple devices.

To synchronize, follow these steps:

1. **Connect your iPhone or iPod touch to your Mac.**

2. **Open iTunes.**

3. **Click the name of your iPhone or iPod touch in the source list under Devices to highlight it.**

4. **Click the Info tab to see the sync settings for Contacts and Calendars, as shown in Figure 8.19.**

5. **Select the check boxes next to Sync Address Book contacts and Sync iCal calendars.**

6. **Click Apply in the lower-right corner (you may need to scroll down to see it) and then click Sync.**

iTunes informs you when the synchronization process is complete.

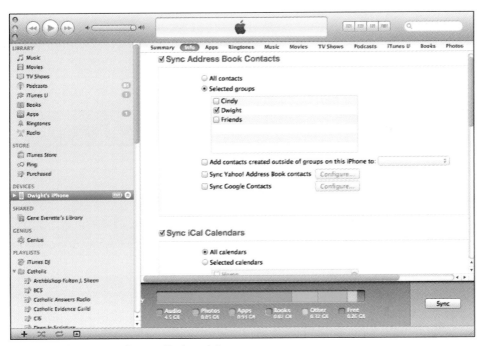

8.19 iTunes keeps your iPhone or iPod touch in sync.

How Do I Master the Web with Safari?

Since the advent of television, nothing has impacted our daily activities quite like the Internet. Checking e-mail and surfing the web have become as routine as waking up in the morning. Lion comes loaded with the fifth version of one of the web's best surfboards: Safari. Safari is a lightning-fast and standards-compliant browser that has even the most demanding of browser critics smiling. Most computer users are quite familiar with the bare basics of web browsing so in this chapter, I jump right into the meat and potatoes of using and customizing Safari.

Setting Safari Preferences

The heart of Safari is its preferences. They tell Safari how you want it to behave in both everyday browsing and special circumstances. In this section, I discuss preferences in some detail so that you can use them to streamline and customize your surfing experience. To open the Safari preferences, hold down the ⌘ key and press the comma key (,) or select Safari ⇨ Preferences from the menu.

General

The General pane of the Safari preferences is shown in Figure 9.1.

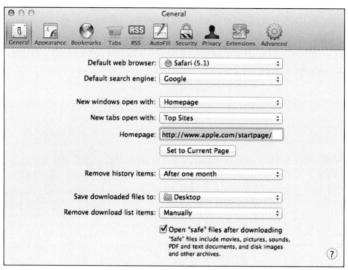

9.1 The options in the Safari General preferences pane.

Table 9.1 gives the scoop on all of the available options.

Table 9.1 Safari General Preferences

Option	Description
Default web browser	If you've installed web browsers other than Safari, such as Firefox or Opera, choose one to be the default for your Mac.
Default search engine	Set Google, Yahoo!, or Bing as your default search engine for Safari.
New windows open with	Select whether new windows should open with your homepage, a blank page, your bookmarks, or the same page as the previous window.

Option	Description
New tabs open with	Choose to open new tabs in Top Sites (more on Top Sites later in this chapter), your homepage, an empty page, the same page as the current tab, or display your bookmarks.
Homepage	Type (or paste) the URL of the Internet site you want to be your homepage. Click Set to Current Page to make the website you are currently viewing your homepage.
Remove history items	Delete items from your browsing history after the prescribed length of time you choose from the pop-up menu.
Save downloaded files to	Select in which folder your downloaded files are to be saved.
Remove download list items	Safari keeps a history of files you've downloaded. This option lets you choose from the pop-up menu how often items on that list should be purged.
Open "safe" files after downloading	Select this option to have Safari automatically open certain types of files, such as disk images and zipped archives, when they finish downloading.

Appearance

The Appearance pane, shown in Figure 9.2, displays all of the available options.

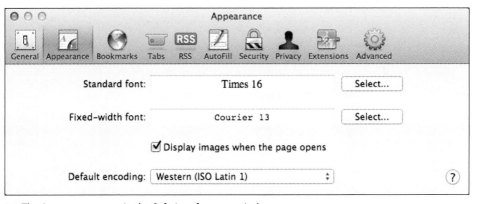

9.2 The Appearance pane in the Safari preferences window.

If you are a speed freak (or conversely, are using a dial-up connection) and don't care about the pictures and graphics that adorn most websites, deselect the Display images when the page opens check box. This causes web pages to zip open, displaying text but no images.

195

Bookmarks

The selections in the Bookmarks pane (see Figure 9.3) allow you to include links stored in your Reading List, Top Sites, and Address Book, as well as those on the home pages of devices running the Bonjour network protocol in your Bookmarks bar, Bookmarks menu, or your Collections.

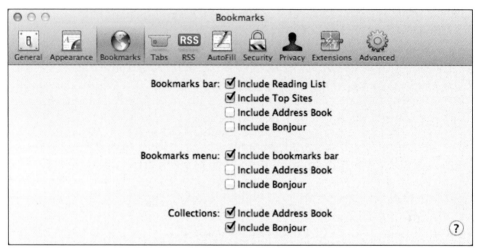

9.3 The Bookmarks preferences pane can help manage your bookmarks.

Tabs

Tabs allow you to have multiple sites open at once, but within one window, as opposed to having a window open for each site you're visiting. The Tabs pane (see Figure 9.4) lets you tell Safari how it should handle new tabs when they are opened, as well as whether it can close multiple tabs at once without prompting you. There are also keyboard shortcuts listed to help you easily open and navigate to new tabs and windows.

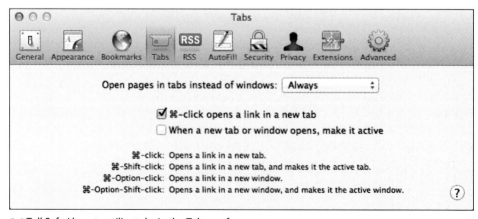

9.4 Tell Safari how to utilize tabs in the Tabs preferences pane.

RSS

RSS (Really Simple Syndication) is used by websites that update their information on a frequent basis, such as news sites. The site uses an RSS feed to broadcast when updates to the website have been posted. Figure 9.5 shows the Safari RSS preferences pane.

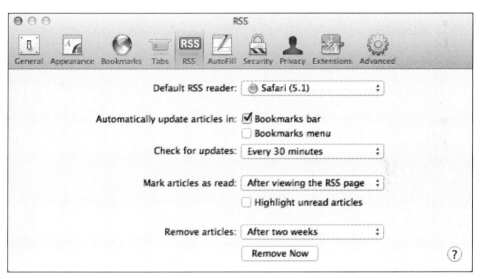

9.5 Options for viewing RSS feeds in Safari.

Table 9.2 describes the available options.

Table 9.2 RSS Feed Preferences

Option	Description
Default RSS reader	If you've downloaded other RSS readers, you can designate one of them to be the default for your Mac using this drop-down menu.
Automatically update articles in	Safari can let you know when a site has updated its contents by displaying the number of new articles in the Bookmarks bar, the Bookmarks menu, or both.
Check for updates	Determine how often Safari should check your subscribed RSS feeds for content updates.
Mark articles as read	Choose whether to mark articles as having been read after you view the page or click its link. The Highlight unread articles option causes unread feeds to be more visible.
Remove articles	Select how often to delete old articles in the pop-up menu. Click Remove Now to instantly clear out all of the articles.

AutoFill

Safari uses AutoFill to remember the information you type into forms on websites. This way, it can automatically enter that information for you in the future. The following options, shown in Figure 9.6, are available:

- **Using info from my Address Book card.** This option lets Safari use the information you've entered about yourself in the Address Book application. Click Edit to open Address Book and change your information.

9.6 AutoFill helps you quickly enter information on web pages with fields.

- **User names and passwords.** Select this option to have Safari save the usernames and passwords that you use to log on to secure websites. I do not recommend this option if security is of any importance to you. Click Edit to see a list of websites and their corresponding usernames.

- **Other forms.** Safari remembers the information you type into fields of websites, such as online application forms or addresses for driving directions. Clicking Edit allows you to see all the sites in which you've entered information in the past.

Security

The Security settings for Safari are shown in Figure 9.7.

Note

One of my few gripes with Safari is the inability to allow some websites to open pop-up windows while blocking others. With Safari, it's all or nothing: you either enable pop-up blocking, or you don't. Some sites have legitimate uses for pop-ups and, when visiting them, you have to temporarily turn off pop-up blocking and remember to turn it back on after leaving.

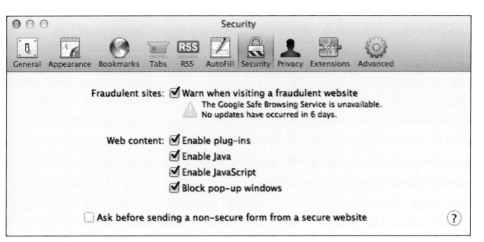

9.7 Choose how best to secure your browsing expeditions.

Table 9.3 covers the options available in the Security pane.

Table 9.3 Safari Security Options

Option	Description
Fraudulent sites	Select the check box to have Safari warn you when you visit a site that may be fraudulent.
Web content	Plug-ins help Safari view or play certain types of content on websites, such as movies and sound files. Java and JavaScript are also used for interactive elements on many web pages. Select the check boxes next to these options to enable them in Safari. Select the Block pop-up windows option to avoid those pesky ads that infest some websites.
Ask before sending a non-secure form from a secure website	When you select this check box, Safari prompts you if you are about to send sensitive information in a form that has little (or no) security on what is supposed to be a secure site.

Privacy

The Privacy preferences pane, shown in Figure 9.8, affords options to keep your browsing habits from being known all over the free world. Some websites can be a bit too intrusive and others can be downright sly in how they wantonly share your personal information.

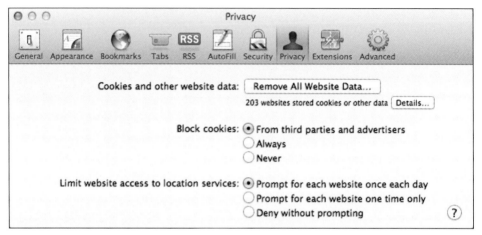

9.8 Protect your personal information while browsing the web.

The Privacy pane can protect you in three areas:

- **Cookies and other website data.** This section allows you a bird's-eye view of the cookies and other information websites have stored on your system. Click Remove All Website Data to remove all cookies and stored information. Click Details to see a list of all the websites that have stored tracking info and cookies on your Mac.

- **Block cookies.** These options allow you to determine which sites (if any) can store cookies on your Mac. However, be aware that choosing the Always option may cause some problems — some sites require cookies to function properly.

- **Limit website access to location services.** Some sites use your current location to help you find services and places of interest in your local surroundings. The Location services section lets you decide whether and how these sites gather your location information.

Extensions

Finally! It only took Apple five versions to do so, but it has finally included the use of third-party extensions in its browser (which other browsers have done for quite some time). Third-party extensions provide even more functionality to Safari, allowing you to do anything from getting the latest weather report, to being notified of new e-mail right in your browser. The Extensions pane of the Safari preferences, shown in Figure 9.9, allows you to find and manage extensions.

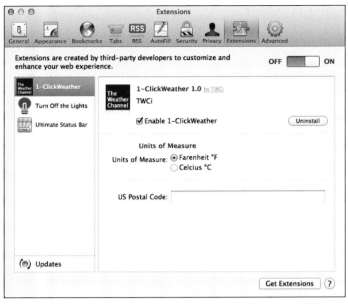

9.9 Expand your Safari capabilities using Extensions.

Toggle the Off/On button to enable or disable the use of extensions, and then click Get Extensions in the lower-right corner of the window to be whisked away to the official Apple Safari Extensions Gallery website (or go to: https://extensions.apple.com).

Once extensions are installed, they display on the left side of the Extensions pane. Select each extension to view its information, adjust its settings, or uninstall it if you're not particularly impressed with it.

Advanced

The Universal Access options in the Advanced pane (see Figure 9.10) allows you to make small text display with a larger font for easier reading. You can also press the Tab key to highlight and navigate items on a web page without using a mouse.

The Style sheet drop-down menu lets you choose a Cascading Style Sheet of your own to use when browsing the web.

Click Change Settings next to the Proxies option to allow your Mac to access the Internet when using a firewall. You may want to ask your IT department what proxy settings to use if you are on a corporate network.

Some sites allow you to create and edit documents online, using space on your hard drive to store those documents. Use the Database storage drop-down menu to allocate the amount of hard drive space you want available for such tasks.

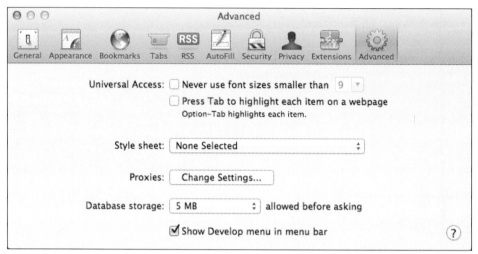

9.10 The Advanced preferences pane in Safari.

Selecting the Show Develop menu in menu bar option displays the Develop menu, which is used mainly by programmers for testing their web pages. You may need to use this menu to access websites designed for other browsers, as described in the sidebar.

This Website Won't Open in Safari!

Sometimes web developers put (usually) superficial limitations on which browsers can access their websites; for example, the developer may harbor a personal preference for Internet Explorer. Thankfully, this practice is beginning to rapidly decline with the increased use of browsers such as Safari and Firefox. However, you can bypass these contrived limitations with the following steps:

1. **Enable the Develop menu by selecting the Show Develop menu option in the Advanced Preferences pane of Safari.**

2. **Choose Develop ⇨ User Agent.**

3. **Select the browser version you want Safari to emulate from the list.** Safari can even pretend it's a browser on a Microsoft Windows PC.

4. **Refresh the offending web page and (usually) this bypasses the bogus limitation.**

Using Bookmarks

Bookmarks are links that you create for your favorite websites so that you can easily and quickly visit them. To bookmark a website, follow these steps:

1. **Choose Bookmarks ⇨ Add Bookmark, or press ⌘+D.**

2. **Give the bookmark an appropriate name.**

3. **Select a location for the bookmark to reside.**

4. **Click Add, as shown in Figure 9.11, to create the bookmark.**

Organizing bookmarks

Like toys in a child's room, bookmarks can quickly get out of hand if they aren't organized. To open the Bookmarks window, as shown in Figure 9.12, choose Bookmarks ⇨ Show All Bookmarks, press ⌘+Option+B, or simply click the icon in the Bookmarks bar that looks like an opened book.

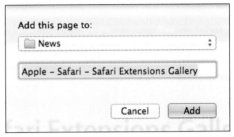

9.11 Create bookmarks so that you can quickly access your favorite locations on the web.

9.12 Bookmarks waiting to be whipped into shape.

Genius Safari has an even easier way to create a bookmark. Simply click and drag the address of the page in the Address field to the Bookmarks bar, give it a name, and then click OK.

The bookmarks list is on the left side of the window (under Bookmarks Bar) and houses your bookmark collections. Each collection can contain subfolders as well as bookmarks.

You can organize bookmarks in the Bookmarks window by doing the following:

- **Arrange bookmarks in a collection.** Select the collection you want to organize, and drag and drop the bookmarks in the order you want them to appear.

- **Arrange bookmark folders in the order you want them to be listed.** Click and drag the bookmark folder you want to move to its new position in the bookmarks list.

- **Create new collections.** Click the plus sign (+) under the left column to create a new bookmark collection, and then give the collection a descriptive name.

- **Create subfolders in collections.** Select the collection to which you want to add a subfolder. Click the plus sign (+) under the right column and give the subfolder a descriptive name.

- **Change the name or address of a bookmark.** Select the collection that contains the bookmark you want to change. Right-click (or Control+click) the bookmark, and select either Edit Name or Edit Address to make your changes.

- **Delete a bookmark or collection.** Right-click (or Control+click) the item you want to remove, and select Delete from the list.

Genius You can keep bookmark folders in the Bookmarks bar to provide fast access to multiple sites. Apple provides a News and Popular folder in the Bookmarks bar — experiment with them to see how beneficial they are.

Importing and exporting bookmarks

Most browsers can export a list of their bookmarks so that you can easily back them up or use them in another browser. To import bookmarks into Safari, follow these steps:

1. **Choose File ⇨ Import Bookmarks.**

2. **Browse your Mac using the Import Bookmarks window, and find the bookmarks file you want to import.**

3. **Highlight the file and click Import**. The Bookmarks window automatically opens and reveals the list of imported bookmarks so that you can organize them.

To export bookmarks from Safari, follow these steps:

1. **Choose File ⇨ Export Bookmarks.**

2. **Name your bookmarks file in the Export Bookmarks window.**

3. **Browse your Mac for a location to save the bookmarks and click Save.**

Customizing the Main Safari Window

You can personalize your browsing experience by making some custom changes to the main window in Safari. There are several options for making Safari more efficient for you:

● **Hide or show the status bar at the bottom of the Safari window.** This area displays the address for links (see Figure 9.13), how many elements of a page have been loaded, and more. Choose View ⇨ Hide Status Bar, or View ⇨ Show Status Bar (depending on its current state).

9.13 Viewing the URL for a link using the status bar at the bottom of the Safari window.

● **Choose whether to display the Bookmarks bar.** Choose View ⇨ Hide Bookmarks Bar or View ⇨ Show Bookmarks Bar.

● **Hide the URL field so that it doesn't clutter your browser window.** Choose View ⇨ Hide Toolbar or resurrect it by choosing View ⇨ Show Toolbar.

Genius

You can rearrange the items in your toolbar with typical Mac OS X ease. Hold down the ⌘ key, and then click and drag an item in the toolbar to move it to a better location. Other items in the toolbar shift automatically to accommodate the item being moved.

● **Add or remove items from the toolbar.** Choose View⇨Customize Toolbar. In the resulting dialog (see Figure 9.14), click and drag items you want to add from the window to the
toolbar, and then drop them in place. To remove items from the toolbar, drag them out
and drop them outside of the Safari window where they disappear in a puff of smoke.

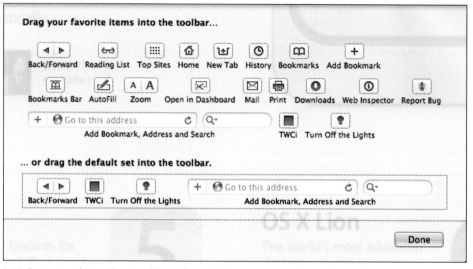

9.14 Customize the toolbar to add your favorite items or remove those that are in your way.

Viewing Your Favorite Pages with Top Sites

Top Sites shows you a preview of the websites you frequent most often, and it works in typical
Apple fashion: really cool and really easy. To view your Top Sites, as shown in Figure 9.15, click Top
Sites on the left side of the Bookmarks bar. Next, simply click a site's page in the Top Sites window
to visit it.

Here are a few tips to maximize your Top Sites experience:

● **Click History at the top of the window to get a really cool look at the list of sites
you've recently visited in Cover Flow (see Figure 9.16).**

  ● **Type part of a site name in the Search field to instantly find it.**

  ● **Click Clear History to erase the list of sites you've previously visited.**

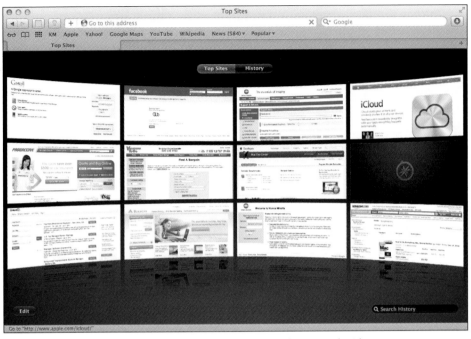

9.15 Top Sites displays your favorite websites in a neat, three-dimensional grid.

9.16 Cover Flow shows the sites you've visited recently.

● **Click Edit to organize sites on the Top Sites page, as shown in Figure 9.17.**

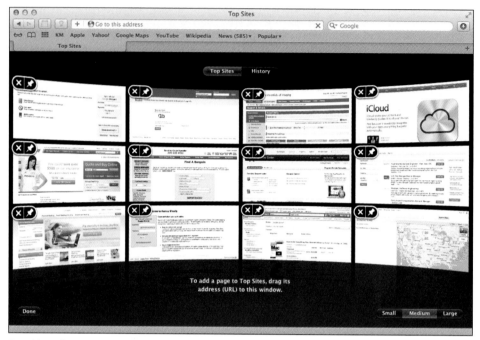

9.17 It's really easy to organize your Top Sites using the Edit button.

● **Click the X in the upper-left corner of a site to remove it from Top Sites.**

● **Select the pin to keep a site on the Top Sites page permanently.**

● **Determine a size for the sites by clicking Small, Medium, or Large on the lower-right side of the window.**

● **Rearrange the placement of sites on the Top Sites page by dragging and dropping them into a new position.**

● **Click Done when finished.**

Private Browsing

Are you the type who doesn't like the world knowing your business? Do you value your privacy when surfing the web? Are you a super spy who doesn't want your evil arch nemesis to know what websites you've been visiting? You're in luck if you use Safari as your browser. Private Browsing prevents anyone else using your Mac from ever knowing what pages you've viewed during your browsing session.

Genius To quit Private Browsing, choose it from the Safari menu again, and make sure you close any windows you had open (not tabs, but the actual window). If you don't close the window, someone else could use the Forward and Back buttons to view the sites you were visiting.

To enable Private Browsing, choose Safari ⇨ Private Browsing and then click OK, as shown in Figure 9.18.

Do you want to turn on Private Browsing?

Safari can keep your browsing history private. When you turn on private browsing, Safari doesn't remember the pages you visit, your search history, or your AutoFill information.

Cancel   OK

Viewing RSS Feeds

9.18 Enable Private Browsing for additional privacy.

As covered earlier, many sites that change their content frequently offer an alternative method for viewing the site called RSS (Really Simple Syndication). RSS pages show you the titles of the most recent articles on a website along with the first few lines to give you an idea of the topic. Clicking the title should open the site containing the complete article if you are interested.

Whenever Safari detects a site that uses RSS, it displays a blue RSS icon on the right side of the address bar. Click the RSS icon to view the RSS page for the site, as shown in Figure 9.19.

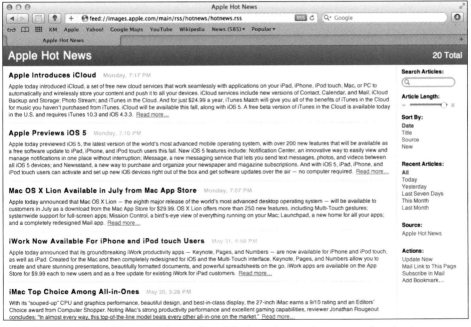

9.19 RSS is a good way to get a quick overview of the latest happenings on your favorite sites.

209

Viewing Windows Media Files

Watching videos on the web is becoming more and more common, and two of the most popular formats for doing so are QuickTime and Windows Media. Lion has QuickTime built in, but it has no way for you to view Windows Media files out of the box. Don't worry: Windows Media Components for QuickTime by Flip4Mac makes this a nonissue. To get the WMV (Windows Media) components, follow these steps:

1. **Go to www.microsoft.com/mac/products/flip4mac.mspx, and click the appropriate links to download the WMV Components disk image.** Safari automatically opens the installer program, as shown in Figure 9.20.

2. **Click Continue and accept the license agreements.**

3. **Select the hard drive on which to install the necessary files and then click Continue.**

4. **Click Install, and type the username and password of an Administrator account to begin the installation.** When you see the Install Succeeded prompt, you are finished and can now view Windows Media files on your Mac.

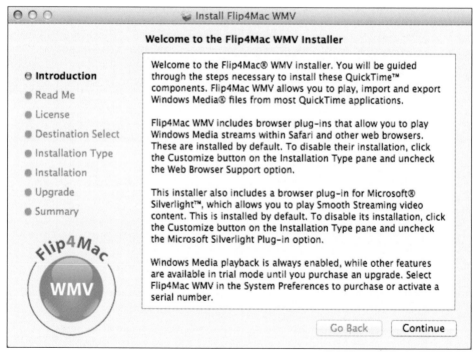

9.20 You are just a few steps away from viewing Windows Media files in Lion.

Note The WMV components work with any browser on your Mac, not just Safari. Nothing further needs to be done in your other browsers to view Windows Media files.

Using the Reading List

The Reading List is a new feature in Safari 5 that allows you to save links to pages you want to come back to and read later. Accompanying the Reading List is the Reader, which enables you to read the articles in your Reading List (as well as many that aren't) without the annoyance of ads and other distractions typical to most web pages.

To add a site to your Reading List, follow these steps:

1. **Open the website you want to add to your Reading List.**

2. **Click the Reading List icon (the pair of glasses) on the left side of the Bookmarks bar.** This opens the Reading List sidebar.

3. **In the Reading List sidebar, click Add Page to add the site to the list.**

Genius You can quickly add a site to your reading list by clicking its link while holding down the Shift key.

When you're ready to read your article using Reader, follow these steps:

1. **Click the Reading List icon to open the Reading List sidebar.**

2. **Select the article you want to view.** Once the site loads, a Reader icon displays on the right side of the address field (if the article is text based).

3. **Click the Reader icon to view the article free of distractions, as shown in Figure 9.21.**

It's a final: Auburn wins national championship on Wes Byrum's kick as time expires | al.com

It's a final: Auburn wins national championship on Wes Byrum's kick as time expires

GLENDALE, Ariz. - A quarterback with skills like none other this season, the school's all-time leading scorer and a defense that had just enough presented Auburn the ultimate prize in college football Monday night in the Arizona desert.

Wes Byrum kicked at the game-winning field goal as time expired to give Auburn a 22-19 victory in the BCS national championship game.

Auburn freshman running back Mike Dyer, the offensive MVP of the BCS National Championship Game, stiff-arms Oregon linebacker Casey Matthews. (The Birmingham News / Hal Yeager)

Thriller.

Cam Newton threw two touchdown passes and the Tigers' defense came up with

9.21 Reader cuts out all the extraneous info so you can simply read your article.

Finding Text on a Website

Sometimes you may be looking for a specific word or phrase on a web page, but it's so packed with information, it could take you half the day to find it. Safari provides a great mechanism for finding text on a web page that can quickly point you to what you need. To search for text on a web page, follow these steps:

1. **Press ⌘+F to open the Find field near the upper-right corner of the window.**

2. **Type the search term or phrase in the Find field (in this example, Auburn) and Safari immediately begins searching as you type, as shown in Figure 9.22.**

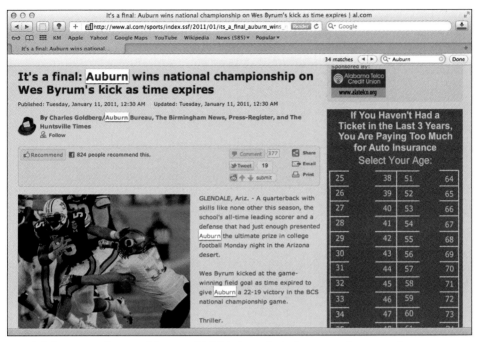

9.22 Safari grays out the rest of the page, highlighting only the instances of your search term.

3. **Safari displays the number of matches it finds for your search term to the left of the Find field.** The page is grayed out and the instances of the search term are highlighted.

4. **Click the left and right arrows to cycle through the matches.**

5. **Click Done next to the Find field when you finish.**

Troubleshooting

Safari can make web surfing a joy, but nothing is perfect. Just like anything else, Safari sometimes doesn't behave. The following sections provide a quick look at some of the most common problems experienced when surfing the web with Safari, what causes them, and suggestions for how to fix the situation.

A web page won't open

There could be a lot of reasons why a web page doesn't open, such as:

- **The page may be temporarily down.** If so, try accessing it later.

- **You may not have an Internet connection.** Even if you were cruising the web seconds before, something may have caused you to lose connectivity.

- **The cached site is corrupt.** If this is the case, your browser keeps trying to open the corrupt cache site instead of refreshing it. To fix this, try emptying the cache and reloading the website. Choose Safari ➪ Empty Cache from the menu, and then select Empty.

- **Be sure that you are typing the correct website address.** This one has bitten me more than once!

A file won't download

Sometimes when you click a link on a site, the file may appear not to download (for example, you can't find it on your Mac) or it may, indeed, not be downloading. You can view the files being downloaded or files that have previously been downloaded by clicking the Downloads button, which is found in the upper-right corner of the Safari window and looks like a square containing a downward-pointing arrow. The Downloads window displays a list of downloaded files, as shown in Figure 9.23.

9.23 A list of my recently downloaded files.

Here are a few things to check when this problem occurs:

- **See if the file is in the list in the Downloads window to find out if Safari tried to download it, but failed.**

- **If you see the file in the Downloads window but can't find it on your Mac, click the magnifying glass to the right of the filename.**

- **Should a link simply not download the promised file, contact the proprietors of the site.** Perhaps there is a missing or broken link to the file.

A downloaded file won't open

Sometimes that file you're downloading just won't cooperate and open. What to do? Here are a few suggestions:

- **Is the file completely downloaded?** If not, resume the download or start over.

- **Try downloading the file again.** It may have been corrupted during the download process.

- **Some files may not be supported by Mac OS X.** Find out what type of file it is (the extension on the end of the file is a dead giveaway) and search Google for software that opens that type of file on a Mac.

AutoFill isn't working

I think AutoFill is pretty convenient. When it's not working, I'm not a happy camper. If it's not working on your Mac:

- **Be sure that AutoFill is turned on.** Choose Safari ⇨ Preferences and click the AutoFill tab. Select the check box next to each of the options you want to use.

- **The information needed may not have been entered before.** If that's the case, type the info again.

Images aren't displaying correctly

One day, you might be surfing along when suddenly a page that should be chock-full of images has none. In some cases this may not be a big deal, but in others it may be a huge issue (how can you properly shop for a new Mac if you can't see what it looks like?). Here are a couple of ideas:

- **Try reloading (a.k.a. refreshing) the page by pressing ⌘+R on the keyboard.**

- **Safari may not know it should be displaying images.** Choose Safari ⇨ Preferences and click the Appearance tab. Select the Display images when the page opens check box.

- **The links to the images on the site may be missing or broken.** Contact the webmaster of the site.

How Do I Stay Connected with Mail?

Mail is the easy-to-use Lion e-mail application, and it is head and shoulders above most e-mail programs that I've used. Mail was already a great e-mail client in its previous incarnation, but it takes a big leap forward with Lion. The ease with which you can set up several popular e-mail accounts, including Gmail and Microsoft Exchange Server, along with its new widescreen, two-column view, makes the newest version of Mail an instant hit.

Getting Around in Mail

Mail is a very straightforward application — most of its tools are in plain view for easy clicking capability. Figure 10.1 shows the Mail main window so that you can get familiar with its features.

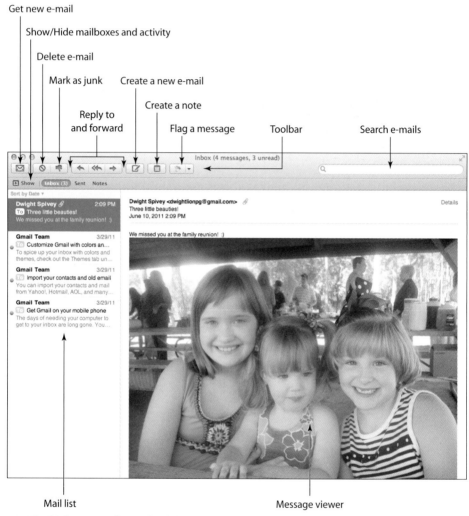

Get new e-mail

Show/Hide mailboxes and activity

Delete e-mail

Mark as junk   Create a new e-mail

Create a note

Reply to
and forward   Flag a message   Toolbar   Search e-mails

Mail list   Message viewer

10.1 The Mail main window in the default layout.

Table 10.1 explains a few of the features that are available in the main window. All others are discussed in further detail throughout this chapter.

Table 10.1 The Mail Main Window Features

Feature	Description
Junk	Junk e-mail is anything you don't want, whether it's unsolicited advertising or messages from your long-lost cousin who just found out you won the lottery. Highlight the offending message in the Mail list and click the Junk button to permanently mark an e-mail as junk. This filters future e-mails like it automatically into the Junk folder.
Search	Type a search term into the Search field, and Mail finds all e-mails that contain the term.
Show or Hide	Click to show or hide the Mailbox pane (which shows you all of the Mailboxes you have configured) and Mail activity window (which displays a progress mail activity bar when sending or receiving mail).

Customizing the Toolbar

The toolbar is where the main Mail controls reside, but you aren't limited to just the default set of controls. You can quite easily modify them to your liking by following these steps:

1. **Choose View ⇨ Customize Toolbar.**

2. **From the huge list of available controls, shown in Figure 10.2, select those you want to add to the toolbar.**

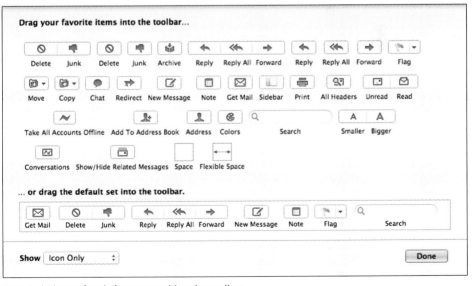

10.2 A plethora of tools for you to add to the toolbar.

3. **Click and drag the controls you want to add to the toolbar, and drop them where you want them.** You may also want to rearrange the controls using the same drag-and-drop technique. The neat thing is how the other controls move out of the way of the one you are moving.

4. **Delete controls from the toolbar by clicking and dragging them out of the window, and then dropping them.** They disappear from the toolbar in a puff of smoke.

5. **Click Done when you're finished.**

Managing E-mail Accounts

Mail won't do much more than take up space on your hard drive if you don't have an e-mail account. When you sign on with an Internet service provider (ISP), it should provide you with all the information you need to add an e-mail account to Mail. Be sure to get all the e-mail information from your ISP before you begin to use Mail.

Automatic setup

The first time you start Mail, in the Welcome to Mail screen you are asked to set up an account, as shown in Figure 10.3.

10.3 The Welcome to Mail screen.

To set up the account, follow these steps:

1. **Type a name for the account.** Keep in mind that this is the way your name appears when you send e-mail.

2. **Type the e-mail address to use for the account.**

3. **Type the password for your e-mail account and click Continue.**

4. **Decide whether to set up iCal (Calendars) and iChat with the same account, and then click Create.** Mail does the rest for you!

You can set up additional accounts automatically. Follow these steps:

1. **Choose Mail ⇨ Preferences or press ⌘+,.**

2. **Click Accounts in the Preferences window to open the Accounts pane, as shown in Figure 10.4.**

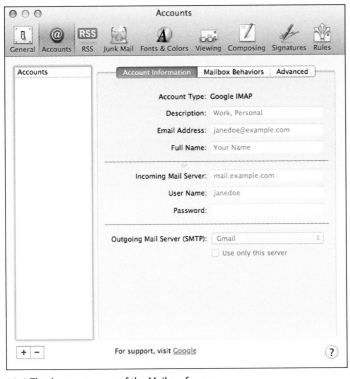

10.4 The Accounts pane of the Mail preferences.

3. **Click the plus sign (+) in the lower-left corner to add an account.**

4. **Type the required information in the Add Account window and click Create.**

Manual setup

Mail supports POP, IMAP, and Exchange e-mail accounts, and you can add any of these types manually if you prefer this to an automatic setup. Ask your ISP or network administrator what type of account you have and what settings you need to create your account.

To manually create a new account, follow these steps:

1. **Choose Mail ➪ Preferences or press ⌘+,.**

2. **Click Accounts in the Preferences window to open the Accounts pane.**

3. **Click the plus sign (+) in the lower-left corner to add an account.**

4. **Type the correct information in the Full Name and Email Address fields of the Add Account window (leave the Password field blank), and then click Continue.**

5. **You receive an error dialog; simply click Continue to set up the account manually.**

6. **In the Incoming Mail Server window, shown in Figure 10.5, choose your Account Type (in my case, IMAP), and type the required information as provided by your ISP or network administrator.** Click Continue.

10.5 This information is required to receive e-mail.

7. **Consult your ISP or network admin regarding the options in the Incoming Mail Security window, set them as needed, and then click Continue.**

8. **In the Outgoing Mail Server window, shown in Figure 10.6, type a Description for your SMTP server and choose an Outgoing Mail Server.** This is required to send e-mail to other people. Select the Use Authentication check box if a username and password are required by your e-mail provider or ISP, and type the information in the appropriate fields. Click Continue to proceed.

10.6 Type this information and you're almost done configuring your Mail account.

9. **Consult your ISP or network admin regarding the options in the Outgoing Mail Security window, set them as needed, and then click Continue.**

10. **Select the Take account online check box to instantly begin using your account and then click Create.**

Setting Preferences in Mail

Just like any other app, Mail works best when it works best for you. Because only you know what works best for you, Mail provides the ability to change its default behavior to suit your needs using Preferences. Press ⌘+, to open the Mail preferences window.

General

The options in the General pane are shown in Figure 10.7.

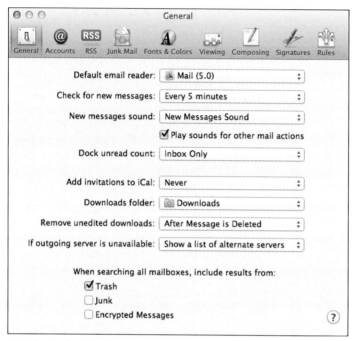

10.7 The Mail General options.

Table 10.2 gives the scoop on each of these options.

Table 10.2 Mail General Preferences

Option	Description
Default email reader	Choose an e-mail app to be the default for your Mac if you've installed others in addition to Mail, such as Thunderbird or Outlook.
Check for new messages	Determine how often Mail automatically taps your e-mail provider on the shoulder to see if any new messages have arrived in your inbox.
New messages sound	Select an alert sound for Mail to use to notify you when new messages arrive. Select the Play sounds for other mail actions check box to sound alerts when you send messages or when Mail wants you to be aware of other activities, such as when new messages are sent or when an error occurs.

Option	Description
Dock unread count	The Mail icon in the Dock shows you how many unread messages you have. It also tells Mail where to look to find those unread messages.
Add invitations to iCal	You can set Mail to automatically add any invitations you may receive in an e-mail to iCal.
Downloads folder	Choose where Mail saves attachments by default.
Remove unedited downloads	Mail temporarily saves attachments in the Mail Downloads folder unless you specify that it save them elsewhere. These are deleted once you delete the e-mail to which they were attached unless you change that behavior here.
If outgoing server is unavailable	If you send an e-mail and Mail tells you it is unable to reach the outgoing mail server for your account, you can use the pop-up menu here to have Mail either show you a list of alternative outgoing servers to use, or to hold the message until your original outgoing server is available.
When searching all mailboxes, include results from	Select any or all three (Trash, Junk, and Encrypted Messages) of the available options for Mail to include when searching other mailboxes.

Accounts

The Accounts pane lets you see and edit your account information, and decide how Mail handles certain behaviors for your accounts. Earlier in this chapter, I discussed adding and removing accounts from this pane. Now, let's take a look at the other options available for your accounts. The Accounts pane is separated into three tabs: Account Information, Mailbox Behaviors, and Advanced.

Account Information

The Account Information tab, shown in Figure 10.8, allows you to set up the information necessary to receive e-mail from any one account. This information is available from your e-mail provider or your company's IT administrator.

The Outgoing Mail Server pop-up menu lets you specify an SMTP server to send mail from this particular account. If you haven't set up an outgoing server, click the pop-up and select Edit SMTP Server list to enter the information as provided by your e-mail provider or IT admin.

Select the Use only this server check box to prevent Mail from using a different SMTP server should the one assigned to this account be unavailable for any reason.

225

10.8 Account Information is where you tell Mail the settings for your e-mail account.

Mailbox Behaviors

The options in the Mailbox Behaviors tab (see Figure 10.9) differ depending on whether the account type is IMAP or POP.

The options include:

10.9 Tell Mail how to handle items in your mailboxes with the Mailbox Behaviors tab.

- **Drafts.** Decide whether to keep copies of drafts on your e-mail provider's servers or not. I advise you to select this check box so that if something happens to your Mac, your draft messages can still be accessed from another computer. This option is only available for IMAP accounts.

- **Notes.** Choose whether to store your notes in your Inbox for quick access.

- **Sent and Junk.** Choose whether Mail should erase Sent or Junk mail from their respective mailboxes, and choose how to handle deleted sent and junk messages.

- **Trash.** Tell Mail how to handle messages that you delete. Moving deleted messages to the Trash mailbox gives you the opportunity to find them again should you find they are needed. Storing deleted messages on the e-mail server is a good idea. This way, you can get to those messages if you need them, but they won't take up extra space on your Mac (if you uncheck the first option, that is).

Advanced

The Advanced tab allows you to enable or disable the account you've selected. You can also tell Mail to automatically check for new messages, automatically erase deleted messages from an IMAP account in which you don't move deleted messages to the Trash, and keep copies of e-mails on your e-mail provider's server. You can also specify the IMAP Path Prefix, port number, and the authentication type necessary to communicate with your e-mail provider's SMTP server.

Caution The Remove copy from server after retrieving a message option should be deselected if your e-mail account uses POP. Selecting this check box prevents you from retrieving e-mails from your e-mail provider should you have problems with your Mac. Deselecting this check box keeps copies of e-mails on your e-mail provider's server as a backup.

RSS

The options in the RSS pane, shown in Figure 10.10, are self-explanatory:

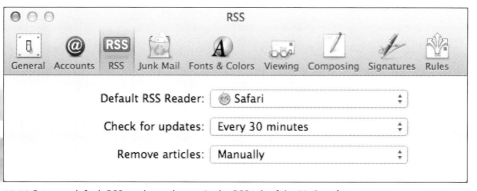

10.10 Set your default RSS reader and more in the RSS tab of the Mail preferences.

- **Default RSS Reader.** Set the application you prefer as your default RSS reader. If you don't see the app you want in the pop-up menu, click Select and browse your Mac to find it.

- **Check for updates.** Determine how often Mail checks your RSS feeds for updates.

227

● **Remove articles.** Tell Mail when to delete articles from your RSS feeds.

Junk Mail

Everyone gets junk e-mail from time to time, and the Junk Mail pane, shown in Figure 10.11, helps you kick those unwanted messages to the curb. It also tells Mail which e-mails are not junk.

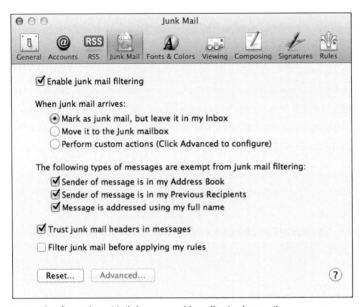

10.11 Configure how Mail detects and handles junk e-mail messages.

The available options are:

● **Enable junk mail filtering.** Select this check box to turn on the junk mail filters.

● **When junk mail arrives.** Tell Mail how to handle junk e-mails that arrive. You can mark them as junk but still keep them in your Inbox so that you can inspect them, move them automatically to a Junk mailbox so you can peruse them at your leisure, or you can customize how they are handled.

● **The following types of messages are exempt from junk mail filtering.** This option is invaluable as it lets Mail know which messages it should never mark as junk. If your messages are from senders in your Address Book, senders from previous e-mails, or if they are addressed to your full name, you can instruct Mail not to filter them as junk.

● **Trust junk mail headers in messages.** Some e-mails already contain indicators that they are junk. Selecting this option lets Mail rely on those indicators to filter the messages out as junk.

- **Filter junk mail before applying my rules.** Later in this chapter, I cover how to set rules for Mail. Selecting this option lets the junk mail filter run on all e-mails before your rules are carried out.

- **Reset.** Click Reset to return Mail to its default junk filtering options. Use this one with caution; once you reset the junk filter it forgets any settings and rules you applied to it.

- **Advanced.** Click Advanced to set your own custom rules for what Mail should do with junk e-mails. Select the Perform custom actions radio button in the When junk mail arrives section to access the Advanced button.

Fonts & Colors

This one doesn't get much simpler. Use the Fonts & Colors pane to set the default font for your Message List, messages, notes, and fixed-width fonts. If you are sending a plain text message (as opposed to the default HTML), you can choose to use a fixed-width font. You can also set the default colors for quoted text, which is the text that is included when you reply to or forward an e-mail.

Viewing

The Viewing pane, as shown in Figure 10.12, is where you tell Mail how to display your e-mails.

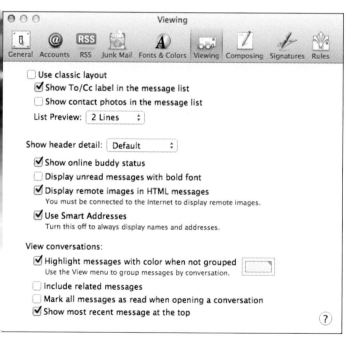

10.12 You can customize how your messages are displayed in Mail with these options.

The available options include:

- **Use classic layout.** Select this option to have your messages appear in a list on top of the preview pane as in earlier versions of Mail.

- **Show header detail.** The pop-up menu and check boxes below it let Mail know how you want the header information to appear in your e-mails. To clarify, headers are items that are commonly seen at the top of e-mails, such as From and To. The four boxes under the pop-up menu perform the following tasks:

  - **Show online buddy status.** Selecting this option shows the status of your iChat buddies in your e-mails.

  - **Display unread messages with bold font.**

  - **Display remote images in HTML messages.** Select this option to include pictures and graphics.

  - **Use Smart Addresses.** You can decide to have Mail display the name of the recipient in the address field, as opposed to their actual e-mail address, by selecting this option.

- **View conversations.** Mail allows you to view related e-mails as a group, which is called a conversation. The self-explanatory options in this section let you determine how these messages are displayed in conversation view.

Composing

There are many options in the Composing pane, as shown in Figure 10.13, and they are divided into three sections: Composing, Addressing, and Responding.

Composing

The following options (see Figure 10.13) help you when creating a new e-mail or when replying to one:

- **Message Format.** Determine the default format to use when creating new e-mail. If you choose plain text, you can't use the advanced graphics features of Mail, such as Stationery.

- **Check spelling.**

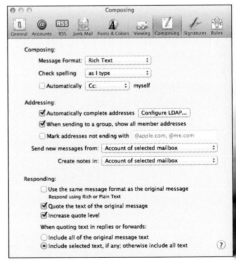

10.13 The options in the Composing pane configure how Mail puts together an e-mail.

- **Automatically Cc myself.** Select this check box to send a copy of e-mails you send to others to yourself. However, note that Mail automatically puts a copy of your sent messages in the Sent folder.

Addressing

The Addressing section (see Figure 10.13) helps configure how Mail works with e-mail addresses in new e-mails and notes:

- **Automatically complete addresses.** This option allows Mail to complete e-mail addresses as you type them, saving you tons of keystrokes over time. LDAP (Lightweight Directory Access Protocol) is used by many businesses to access company-wide telephone and e-mail directories. Your IT administrator can tell you if your company uses LDAP servers. If it does, click Configure LDAP and type the information needed to connect to the LDAP server.

- **When sending to a group, show all member addresses.** If you send e-mail to groups, selecting this option displays the e-mail address for each individual in the group.

- **Mark addresses not ending with.** This option helps prevent you from sending unintentional e-mails to folks by marking e-mail addresses that don't end with a particular domain name.

- **Send new messages from.** Choose which e-mail address to show in the From field when sending messages to others.

- **Create notes in.** Choose the default account for storing and e-mailing notes.

Responding

The Responding options in the Composing pane (see Figure 10.13) let Mail know how it should reply to those who have been courteous enough to send you messages:

- **Use the same message format as the original message.** It's a good idea to reply to someone using the same format as her original e-mail. For example, if you reply to a plain text e-mail with rich text the recipient may not be able to read it.

- **Quote the text of the original message.** Select this option to display the original message and subsequent exchanges under your reply.

- **Increase quote level.** Select this option to distinguish individual quotes using colors and indentions.

- **When quoting text in replies or forwards.** To include all text from the original e-mail in a reply or forward, select the first radio button. To include only text you've selected in the original e-mail, select the second radio button.

Signatures

The Signatures pane, shown in Figure 10.14, allows you to create and edit personal e-mail signatures. A signature can contain any information you like, such as your address, phone number, fax number, and so on. You can create as many signatures as needed, which comes in handy if you have multiple accounts because you can assign specific signatures to each one.

10.14 Signatures give your e-mails a personal touch, much like signing a handwritten letter.

To create a signature:

1. **Select the account to which you want to assign the signature or choose All Signatures to allow all accounts to use it.**

2. **Click the plus sign (+) to add a new signature.**

3. **Give the signature a descriptive name and type the signature information in the large text field on the right.**

4. **To edit the fonts and colors in the signature, highlight the text you want to change and then right-click (or Control+click) it.** Next, choose Font ⇨ Show Fonts or Font ⇨ Show Colors, and then make the changes you desire.

5. **If you want to keep uniformity throughout the message and signature, select the Always match my default message font check box.**

6. **Select the Place signature above quoted text check box to situate your signature after your message but before the quoted text.**

Rules

Under the Rules tab, Mail allows you to create your own rules and dictate how it distributes and marks certain messages. These rules can be based on criteria that you set, allowing a high level of customization.

Using the four plus and minus sign buttons on the right side of the pane, as shown in Figure 10.15, you can add, edit, duplicate, and delete rules.

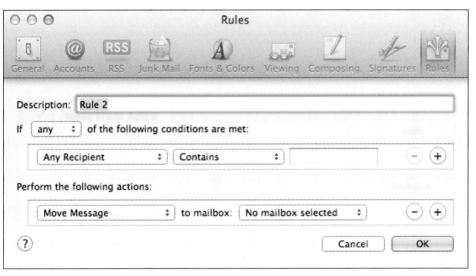

10.15 Create your own rules to customize how Mail distributes your messages.

To add a new rule to the Rules List, follow these steps:

1. **Click Add Rule in the Rules preferences pane.** The rule specification window appears.

2. **Type a descriptive name for your new rule.**

3. **A rule tells Mail that if a certain condition exists, it should perform a certain task or action.** To create a rule:

   a. **Determine if any or all conditions must be met using the pop-up menu.**

   b. **Select the conditions using the appropriate pop-up menus.** To add more conditions, click the plus sign (+). To remove conditions, click the minus sign (–).

   c. **Select the task to be performed using the pop-up menus in the Perform the following actions section.** Click the plus sign (+) to add more actions or the minus sign (–) to remove them.

4. **Click OK to create the new rule.**

Composing E-mail

Composing and sending e-mail is a snap with Mail. To begin sending that world-changing memorandum, do the following:

1. **Click the New Message button in the toolbar.** It's the one with the piece of paper and a pencil.

2. **In the New Message window, type the e-mail address of the person you want to receive your message in the To field, as shown in Figure 10.16.** To send a copy of the e-mail to other folks, type their addresses in the Cc field.

10.16 Putting together the perfect e-mail.

3. **Type the topic of your e-mail in the Subject field.**

4. **If you like, click the Customize button (the small rectangle on the left with three lines and a downward-pointing arrow), and choose whether any other fields, such as Priority, should appear in the New Message window.**

5. **Type the content of your e-mail and click the Send button (the paper airplane in the upper-left corner).**

6. **Congratulate yourself for being a full-blown member of Internet society.** Just like the toolbar in the main Mail window, the toolbar in the New Message window can be modified to suit your style. With a New Message window open, choose View ⇨ Customize Toolbar to arrange, remove, or add items to enhance your productivity.

Using Stationery

One of the coolest features in Mail for Lion is the ability to customize e-mails with Stationery. Stationery is preformatted e-mails that Apple provides with Mail. This feature can transform any ordinary e-mail into a stunning creation. To use Stationery, follow these steps:

234

1. **Open a New Message window.**

2. **Click the Show Stationery button (the small rectangle containing a piece of paper) in the upper-right corner of the toolbar.**

3. **Browse the topics listed on the left of the Stationery field (underneath the Subject field and immediately above the e-mail content window), as shown in Figure 10.17.** Select the Stationery that is appropriate for your message.

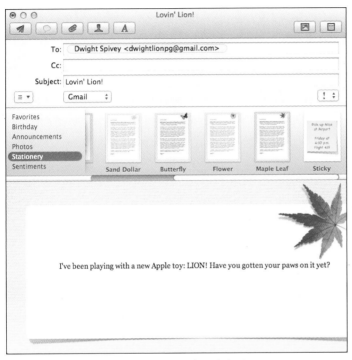

10.17 Create beautifully formatted e-mails with Stationery.

4. **Customize the content of your e-mail by dragging and dropping your own images into the image placeholders (if any), and type your own text in the preformatted text fields.**

Adding attachments

Sometimes you want to e-mail a picture or send along an accompanying document with your message; these additions are called attachments. To add an attachment to your e-mail, follow these steps:

1. **Open a New Message window and type the addresses of your recipients.**

2. **Click the Attachment button (the one with the paper clip) in the toolbar.**

3. **Browse your trusty Mac for the file you want to attach, select it, and then click Choose File.** If you're sending a picture from your iPhoto or Photo Booth libraries, click the Photo Browser button (the one with a mountain and a moon) in the toolbar. Click and drag a picture from the Photo Browser window, and drop it into the body of the e-mail, as shown in Figure 10.18.

10.18 Drag and drop your picture into an e-mail.

4. **Send your e-mail on its merry way by clicking the Send button in the toolbar.**

Keep Your Recipients Anonymous

Sometimes when sending an e-mail to multiple recipients you may need to hide their names and e-mail addresses. This technique is called Blind Carbon Copy (Bcc for short) and Mail makes it a snap to do:

1. **Open a new message window.**

2. **Click the Customize button and select Bcc Address Field.**

3. **Type the addresses of the recipients in the Bcc field and this conceals their identities from the other recipients.**

Formatting content

Add a little pizzazz to your message by customizing its fonts and colors. To format an e-mail, follow these steps:

1. **Open a New Message window.**

2. **Type the text of your e-mail.**

3. **Highlight the text you want to format.**

4. **Click the Show formats bar button (the icon looks like the letter A) in the toolbar, and then select the font you want to use.** You can alter the font typeface and size, underline the text, change the font color, add a shadow to the text and modify it, and even rotate the text.

Receiving, Replying to, and Forwarding E-mail

Your Inbox typically attempts to receive e-mails automatically every few minutes, but you can also have Mail check the server for new e-mails manually in one of the following ways:

- **Click the Get new messages in all accounts button (the envelope) on the left side of the toolbar.**

- **Press ⌘+Shift+N.**

- **Choose Mailbox ⇨ Get New Mail, and then select the account you want to check.**

Note

You don't have to be working in Mail to see when new e-mail arrives, but Mail does have to be running, of course. The Mail icon in the Dock displays a red circle containing the number of unread e-mails in your Inbox so that you can easily tell when you have new mail.

When someone sends you an e-mail, it shows up in your Inbox for the account the e-mail was sent to. It appears in the Mail list in bold letters and has a blue dot to the left of the From field. The Inbox button in the toolbar also displays the number of unread e-mails it contains in parentheses. Simply click the e-mail in the Mail list to read it in the Message Viewer.

To reply to or forward an e-mail you've received, follow these steps:

1. **Highlight the e-mail to which you want to respond in the Mail list.**

237

2. **Click the Reply button to respond to the person who sent you the e-mail.** The Reply All button sends a message to all recipients of an e-mail and the Forward button sends the e-mail to other parties.

3. **Type text or add attachments to your message.**

4. **Click the Send button in the toolbar.**

Organizing Mailboxes

In this section, I show you how to use mailboxes to keep your e-mail organized, type Notes to keep your thoughts straight, and create To Do's to keep that list of tasks in tip-top shape.

Using standard mailboxes

Standard mailboxes keep your e-mail organized, and each account can have several. Table 10.3 lists some of the types of standard mailboxes that accounts can have.

Table 10.3 Functions of Standard Mailboxes

Mailbox	Description
Inbox	Incoming messages to your e-mail account are stored here.
Drafts	Sometimes you may want to save an e-mail you've typed so that you can send it at a later time. The Drafts folder is where those saved e-mails reside until you are ready to send them.
Sent	Copies of messages you have sent to people are kept here.
Trash	This is where your deleted messages reside until you are ready to completely erase them from your Mac.
Junk	Messages that are flagged as junk mail are deposited into this mailbox. This way, they don't intrude with your normal activities but can be sifted through later at your convenience.

Creating custom and Smart Mailboxes

Mail lets you create your own mailboxes to suit your individual needs. You can make custom mailboxes that are named for different items or topics (such as Bills), or you can use Smart Mailboxes. A Smart Mailbox allows you to create rules that the Smart Mailbox follows. For example, you could set up a Smart Mailbox that automatically grabs and stores any e-mail that comes from a particular person.

To create a new custom mailbox, follow these steps:

1. **Click the plus sign (+) in the bottom-left corner of the Mail window and select New Mailbox.**

2. **In the New Mailbox dialog, shown in Figure 10.19, select a location where the new mailbox can be saved.**

10.19 Creating a new mailbox.

3. **Give the new mailbox a descriptive name and then click OK.** The new mailbox appears in the Mailbox pane on the left side of the Mail window.

Back Up Those Mailboxes!

It is always a great idea to keep a backup of your e-mails in case something happens to Mail, Lion, or worse, your Mac. You can restore your lost e-mails to their proper places if you've been making consistent backups of your mailboxes.

To back up a mailbox:

1. **Select the mailbox you want to archive.**
2. **Choose Mailbox ⇨ Export Mailbox.**
3. **Select the folder in which you want to save the mailbox archive, and click Choose.**
4. **An archive of the mailbox is created in the appropriate folder using the MBOX format.**

To restore a mailbox, follow these steps:

1. **Choose File ⇨ Import Mailboxes.**
2. **Select the Apple Mail radio button and click Continue.**
3. **Browse your Mac to find the archived mailbox you want to restore, select it, and then click Choose.**

To set up a Smart Mailbox (I love these things), follow these steps:

1. **Click the plus sign (+) in the lower-left corner of the Mail window and select New Smart Mailbox.**

2. **In the sheet that appears (see Figure 10.20), give the mailbox a descriptive name.**

Smart Mailbox Name: Smart Mailbox 1

Contains messages that match [all ‡] of the following conditions:

| Any Recipient ‡ | Contains ‡ | mosxlionpg@gmail.com | – + |
| Contains Attachments ‡ | | | – + |

☐ Include messages from Trash
☐ Include messages from Sent   Cancel   OK

10.20 Create a Smart Mailbox to help you get organized and save time finding e-mails.

3. **Select what the mailbox should contain and how the items in it should match the criteria you are about to define.**

4. **Define the criteria for items that the mailbox should (or should not) contain.** Click the plus sign (+) to the right to add a new criterion or the minus sign (–) to remove it.

5. **Decide whether to include messages that are in the Trash or Sent mailboxes, and then select or deselect the check boxes as appropriate.**

6. **Click OK to create the new Smart Mailbox.**

Writing Notes

Mail provides the convenience of letting you create Notes (to jot down ideas when you have them), and then save or e-mail them.

To take a note, follow these steps:

1. **Click the Note button (the tiny legal pad) in the toolbar.**

2. **Type the contents of the note in the New Note window.**

3. **Click the red button in the upper-left corner of the window to save and close the note, click Send to e-mail it, click Attach to add an item to it (just like with an e-mail), and click Fonts or Colors to format the text.**

Notes can easily be accessed in the Mailboxes pane under Reminders, as shown in Figure 10.21.

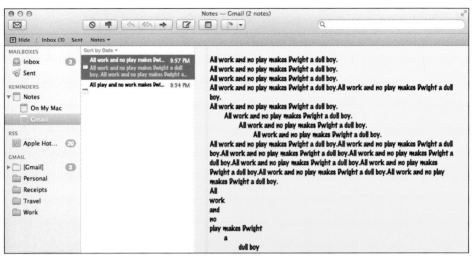

10.21 Click Notes in the Mailboxes pane to see a list of all your latest, greatest ideas and reminders.

Using RSS Feeds

RSS (Really Simple Syndication) is used by websites that update their information on a frequent basis, such as news sites. The site uses an RSS feed to broadcast when updates to the website have been posted. Mail in Lion can act as an RSS reader, meaning that you can use it to track when new articles are posted to your favorite sites. I love this feature and use it instead of third-party RSS reader applications because I can have one less application open while retaining the functionality.

To use RSS feeds in Mail, follow these steps:

1. **Find out the address of the RSS page for the site you want to track.** When using Safari as your web browser, it's very easy to detect whether a website uses an RSS feed: you see the letters RSS to the right of the address in the Safari Address field.

2. **Click the plus sign (+) in the lower-left corner of the Mail window and select Add RSS Feeds.**

3. **Select the Specify the URL for a feed radio button, as shown in Figure 10.22.**

4. **Type the address of the feed (or copy and paste it from a web browser) into the text field.**

5. **Click Add.** The feed appears under the RSS heading in the Mailboxes pane.

○ Browse feeds in Safari bookmarks
● Specify the URL for a feed

feed://www.creativeminorityreport.com/feeds/posts/default?
alt=rss

☐ Show in Inbox   Cancel   Add

10.22 Adding an RSS feed to Mail.

6. **Click the feed in the Mailboxes pane to see its latest postings.**

7. **If the article snippet intrigues you, click Read More to open the full article in Safari.**

Troubleshooting

Occasionally you may find yourself having trouble with Mail. The most common problem is the inability to send or to receive e-mails. The final two topics in this chapter attempt to help resolve these problems.

Unable to send messages

Sometimes you may find that you can't send messages. The reason may be that the Send button is grayed out, or you might receive an error message stating that you cannot connect to the SMTP server for your ISP. Here are a few things for you to try when facing this daunting situation:

● **If you have an Internet connection, open Safari and see if you can load a web page.** If not, choose Apple menu ➪ System Preferences ➪ Network and make sure you have a connection.

- **Check the SMTP settings for your account.**

  a. **Choose Mail ⇨ Preferences.**

  b. **Click the Accounts button and click the account with which you are having trouble.**

  c. **Be sure the Outgoing Mail Server (SMTP) option is set correctly.**

  d. **If your SMTP server isn't set up at all, check with your ISP for the proper settings.**

- **Make sure you have the latest software updates for Lion.** Choose Apple menu ⇨ Software Update and install any available updates.

Unable to receive messages

Starting to feel lonely? Maybe it's because you haven't received an e-mail from your friends and family lately. Well, don't feel too unloved yet; check the following to see if Mail is receiving e-mail:

- **Is your account offline?** If so, that prevents you from being notified of any new messages. You can tell that an account is offline because it has a small lightning bolt icon to the right of it in the sidebar, as shown in Figure 10.23. To put it back online, click the lightning bolt and select the Take All Accounts Online option.

10.23 An account is offline if you see the lightning bolt next to it.

- **Are you currently connected to the Internet?** If not, then be sure to connect.

- **Send a message to yourself to test your connection settings.** Check with your e-mail provider to make sure you are using the correct settings for your account.

- **Is the name of your mailbox grayed out?** If so, choose Window ⇨ Connection Doctor and follow any instructions that may be given for any accounts that are having difficulty connecting to your ISP.

How Can I Use iTunes with Multimedia?

Gotta have that music! And those movies. Don't forget about the television shows and podcasts, too! In today's world, we want our entertainment now. We want it affordable, portable, and we prefer it digital. Lion meets all of those needs with a nifty tool called iTunes. Since its introduction in 2001, iTunes has become an integral part of our entertainment arsenal. When you throw an iPod, iPad, or iPhone into the mix, iTunes becomes an absolute necessity. Thankfully, it's just as intuitive and easy to use as everything else Mac; you'll be addicted to its charms before you know it!

Getting Around in iTunes

iTunes can handle most of your digital entertainment needs, but you need to know how to use its menus, buttons, and features before you can get much use out of it. The first two sections of this chapter cover where to find everything and setting the iTunes preferences. You'll be an expert iTunes user in no time.

Understanding the iTunes window layout

Figure 11.1 shows the iTunes default interface and points out the multitude of buttons and menus.

11.1 iTunes is your personal entertainment hub.

246

Table 11.1 describes what some of the buttons and menus can help you do in iTunes. More are covered later in the chapter.

Table 11.1 iTunes Functionality

Item	Description
Library	Lists all of the items available for you to use in iTunes.
Store	Click to access the iTunes Store.
Playlists	Lists the playlists and Smart Playlists that you have created.
Album artwork/Video viewer	See the album artwork for the song you are listening to or watch videos.
Cover Flow slider	Drag to fly through the album covers when in Cover Flow view.
Genius	Click to start the Genius playlist.
Show/hide Genius sidebar	Hides or shows the Genius sidebar on the right side of the iTunes window.
Full screen	Puts iTunes into Full Screen mode.
Search	Type text to help you find items in your iTunes library, such as the name of a song or the artist who sings it.
View options	Choose to view items in a list, grouped together by their albums or using Cover Flow.
Status window	Shows the status of songs currently being played, CDs being burned, or items being copied.

Using Full Screen mode

I'm a creature of habit so I still prefer the standard view in iTunes, but I'm beginning to understand why others tend to like Full Screen mode even better. Full Screen mode lets iTunes take over your entire screen, but with a bare minimum of controls at your disposal, as shown in Figure 11.2.

iTunes can also be used in a third mode called Mini Player, which is a miniature version of the iTunes window. To enable the Mini Player, click the green zoom button in the upper-left corner of the iTunes window. Click it again to access the full iTunes interface.

11.2 iTunes in Full Screen mode.

Setting iTunes Preferences

iTunes preferences is where you tell iTunes how to interact with you, as well as with items such as iPods, iPads, iPhones, and Apple TV. Let's explore these preferences because they determine how iTunes functions to best suit your needs. Choose iTunes ⇨ Preferences to get started.

General

The General tab lets you change the name of your library, choose what items are shown in the Source pane (such as Ringtones, Ping, Podcasts, and so on), adjust the size of the text in the Sources list and for items in your library when in List view, adjust the background when in Grid view, how iTunes should react when a CD is inserted, and whether to automatically check for updates.

Playback

The Playback preferences, shown in Figure 11.3, determine how iTunes plays your music and videos.

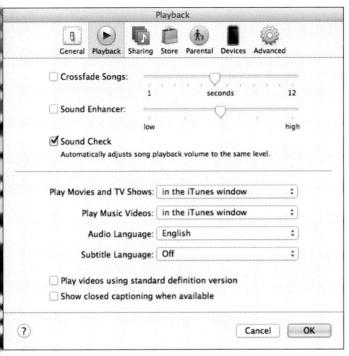

11.3 The Playback preferences allow you to listen to music, and watch movies and television shows the way you want.

Caution

Selecting the Sound Check option is a good idea. This prevents you from listening to one song that may have a lower volume level and then having your eardrums blown out by another song with a much higher volume level. Sound Check evens all the volume levels of items in your library so that there are no surprise attacks.

Sharing

The Sharing preferences, shown in Figure 11.4, determine how (if at all) you share your libraries with other users. You can share your iTunes library with up to five other computers on your network as long as they are in the same network subnet as your Mac. While you can listen to music and watch video shared by other computers on your network, you cannot add them to your iTunes library.

You can share your entire library, or only selected libraries or playlists.

Select the Require password option to allow others to see your library, but not play any of the items it contains unless they have a password that you assign.

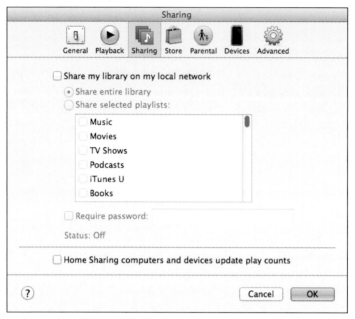

11.4 Share your library with other users on your network.

Select the Home Sharing computers and devices update play counts check box to update the play counts for items in your library when they are played by other devices (such as another Mac, iPhone, iPad, or iPod). After you make your selections, click OK to put them into effect.

Store

You can decide how iTunes handles your purchases.

- **Automatic Downloads.** If you enable this feature, you put iTunes in touch with purchases you make on your iPhone, iPad, or iPod touch. Purchases made on any of these devices are automatically downloaded to iTunes the next time you launch it.

- **Automatically download missing album artwork.** This one speaks for itself.

- **Always check for available downloads.** iTunes informs you if it finds items in the iTunes Store that you've purchased but haven't yet downloaded.

- **Automatically download pre-orders when available.** If you select this option, iTunes automatically downloads any items you've preordered as soon as they become available.

Parental

Most parents don't like to think of their kids having unfettered access to any and everything on the Internet, so why should items in iTunes be any different? The Parental Control preferences, shown in Figure 11.5, let Mom and Dad decide what limits to place on iTunes content for their children.

The available options are:

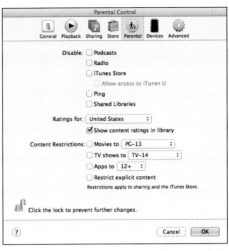

11.5 Take control of what your children can do in iTunes.

- **Disable.** Select the check boxes next to the items to which you would rather your prodigies not have access. The Shared Libraries is a big one — you never know what others may be sharing, so be cautious.

- **Ratings for.** Many countries use their own rating systems for entertainment. Select the country you need from the pop-up menu. Next, select the Show content ratings in library check box to show the ratings right next to the items in your library.

- **Content Restrictions.** Restrict users from accessing items that don't match the ratings you set up in these options. The ratings available here depend on the country you select in the Ratings for option.

After you make your selections, click OK to put them in effect.

Devices

The Devices preferences pane helps determine how iTunes interacts with devices you connect to your Mac.

- **Device backups.** This is a list of iPods, iPads, or iPhones that are backed up on your Mac. You can delete a backup file by selecting it from the list and clicking Delete Backup. Confirm the removal by clicking Delete when prompted or click Cancel.

- **Prevent iPods, iPhones, and iPads from syncing automatically.** Select this check box to keep your Mac from trying to sync automatically every time one of these devices is connected. This is a good idea if you like to have more manual control over what is synced and what isn't.

● **Allow iTunes control from remote speakers.** Selecting this option allows you to control iTunes via a third-party remote that connects to an AirPort Express.

● **Forget All Remotes.** The iPad, iPod touch, and iPhone can act as a remote control using an app called Remote. Click this button to cause iTunes to disconnect from these devices.

Note Consult your iPhone, iPod, or iPad documentation for instructions regarding how to synchronize the device with iTunes, and how to use iTunes to change the settings for the device.

Advanced

The Advanced preferences, shown in Figure 11.6, is where you can make the most useful settings in iTunes.

11.6 The Advanced tab of the iTunes preferences.

Table 11.2 breaks down some of the major features in each section.

Table 11.2 iTunes Advanced Preferences

Option	Description
iTunes Media folder location	Lets you choose to keep your imported media in a location other than the default, which is the Music folder of your user account (*your home folder*/Music/iTunes). Click Change to move the folder to another location or click Reset to move it back to the default location.
Keep iTunes Media folder organized	I highly recommend selecting this check box because it allows iTunes to organize its folder, as opposed to just throwing tracks in willy-nilly.
Copy files to iTunes Media folder when adding to library	Makes a copy of a file in your iTunes Music folder when adding the track to your library. You can deselect this option if you don't want to have multiple copies of the same file strewn throughout your system. I prefer to make the copy and delete the original.
Reset all dialog warnings	Clicking this reactivates iTunes warnings. For example, if you've told iTunes to stop asking you if you're certain that you want to make a purchase, clicking Reset causes iTunes to start asking again.
Reset iTunes Store cache	Much like a web browser, iTunes stores the iTunes Store pages you visit in a cache file. If you visit these pages again, iTunes pulls them from the cache, which is much faster than having to download them from the Internet again. If you have problems loading pages, or if the information appears to be out of date, click Reset cache to clear the cache and download the page from scratch.
Keep Mini Player on top of all other windows	Select this check box to keep the Mini Player from being hidden under other open windows.
Keep movie window on top of all other windows	Select this option to keep movies playing over other open windows.
Display visualizer full screen	Sets the default size of your Visualizer to full screen, which rocks! The Visualizer displays some amazing graphics on your screen synchronized to the music that is playing.

Organizing and Playing Media

iTunes is a pretty useless application without content. It's also a master at helping you organize that content. This section quickly teaches you how to import your own music from CDs or files, and how to use the iTunes Store to find and add new content to your collection.

Setting the viewing options

iTunes lets you decide what information about your files that you want to view. As a matter of fact, it provides a huge list of possible columns to help you sort your media. To adjust your views, follow these steps:

1. **Choose View Options from the View menu.**

2. **Select the check boxes next to the columns you want to appear in the iTunes window, such as Composer, Date Added, or Year.**

3. **Click OK and your iTunes window displays the columns you've added to your view.**

Importing music

Bringing your music into iTunes is the first order of business. Apple makes it ridiculously easy to import your CD collection, as well as music files that you have stored on other computers or discs.

Importing from CDs

When you insert a CD into your Mac, you're asked if you want to import its contents into iTunes, as shown in Figure 11.7. Click Yes to automatically import all the content on your CD into iTunes.

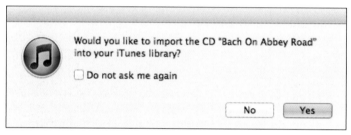

Would you like to import the CD "Bach On Abbey Road" into your iTunes library?

☐ Do not ask me again

No   Yes

11.7 A confirmation dialog appears when you insert a music CD.

Your newly imported content now appears in your library.

Importing individual files

iTunes lets you import music files that exist on other media as well, such as a folder on your hard drive or another computer on your network. To import music files, follow these steps:

1. **Press ⌘+O.**

2. **Browse your Mac or your network for the music file (or files) you want to import from within the Add to Library window.**

3. **Highlight the music files and click Choose.**

The new music is now available in your library.

Creating playlists

You can create playlists using the songs in your library. Playlists are collections of songs that you arrange in the order that you want them to play. Here's how to make a playlist:

1. **Press ⌘+N.** A playlist called Untitled appears in the Playlists section of the Source pane.

2. **Type a name for your new playlist.** I'm creating a playlist for a compilation of songs by Fleetwood Mac.

3. **Find the items you want to add to the playlist in your library, and then drag and drop them onto the name of the new playlist, as shown in Figure 11.8.** You can drag the songs around in your playlist to have them play in your preferred order.

11.8 Adding songs to my new playlist.

Setting up Genius playlists

iTunes can create a playlist of songs that go well together using the songs already in your library. This Genius playlist uses anonymous information from your library to create the playlist. iTunes also uses your Genius playlist to suggest similar songs in the iTunes Store. Follow these steps:

1. **Open the Genius feature, shown in Figure 11.9, by clicking the Store menu and selecting Turn On Genius.**

2. **Click Turn On Genius in the lower right to start the feature.** Sign in using your iTunes Store account.

3. **Select a song from your iTunes library.**

4. **Click the Genius button in the lower-right corner to create a playlist based on the song you selected.** View the playlist by clicking Genius under the Playlists heading on the left side of the iTunes window.

11.9 The Genius window explains what Genius playlists are.

Using Smart Playlists

Smart Playlists automatically add songs based on criteria that you set for them. iTunes already comes with a few Smart Playlists, such as Recently Played and Recently Added. To create a new Smart Playlist, follow these steps:

1. **Press ⌘+Option+N.**

2. **Type the criteria the Smart Playlist should use when adding songs.** In Figure 11.10, I'm creating a new Smart Playlist that adds any songs by Randy Travis (yes, you could say my taste in music is fairly eclectic).

3. **Add more criteria by clicking the plus sign (+) on the right side of the window or the minus sign (-) to remove it.** Select the Live updating check box to have the Smart Playlist check every time you add an item to your library and see if it meets your criteria.

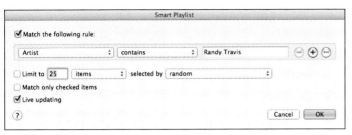

11.10 Creating a new Smart Playlist.

4. **You can limit the number of items to be found and how they are chosen for play-back by selecting the Limit to check box.**

5. **Select the Match only checked items check box to have iTunes include only songs that have a check mark next to them in the library.** Feel free to uncheck any titles you don't want added to your Smart Playlist.

6. **Click OK when you're finished.** Your Smart Playlist automatically populates itself based on the criteria you entered.

Burning CDs

I enjoy a variety of music, and I love having the ability to create my own albums and burn them to CDs. There's nothing to it:

1. **Create a playlist of the music you want to burn to a CD.**

Print Your Music

The old days of handwriting the names of your songs onto those boring blank CD labels are over! iTunes lets you create custom CD jewel case inserts, or song and album lists in a snap. Follow these steps:

1. **Highlight the playlist, artist, or album about which you want to print information.**

2. **Press ⌘+P to open a print window.**

3. **Choose whether to print a jewel case insert, a song list, or an album list.**

4. **Select from one of the available themes.**

5. **Click Print in the lower-right corner.**

6. **Choose the printer to which you want to send the job and click Print.**

2. **Right-click (or Control+click) the playlist you want to burn and select Burn Playlist to Disc, as shown in Figure 11.11.**

3. **Select a recording speed from the Preferred Speed pop-up menu.** If you have trouble burning the CD, try recording at a lower speed.

4. **Choose Audio CD as the format of choice.**

5. **If you would like a gap of silence between each track, choose its duration from the Gap Between Songs pop-up menu.**

6. **Check the Sound Check box if you want the volume of each track to be about the same.**

7. **Some CD players can show information about the tracks being played, such as their title and artist.** Check the Include CD Text box to burn this information to the CD.

8. **Click Burn, insert a blank CD into your Mac, and iTunes takes care of the rest.**

11.11 Burning a playlist to a CD.

Managing file information

iTunes allows you to manage the information contained in your tracks, which helps you organize your library, and find tracks faster and easier. The Info, Video, Sorting, Options, Lyrics, and Artwork tabs in the information window let you specify items such as the composer of the track, the album to which it belongs, the year it was composed, and more. You can also add lyrics and album artwork to the track.

To edit the information for a file:

1. **Select the audio track in your library.**

2. **Press ⌘+I to open the information window, as shown in Figure 11.12.**

11.12 You can check or modify audio track information in the information window.

3. **Click one of the tabs at the top of the window to edit the information it contains.**

4. **When finished, click OK.**

Adding album artwork

To add the album cover artwork to your music files, choose Advanced ⟿ Get Album Artwork. iTunes automatically scans your library and adds artwork to your songs. You must have an iTunes login to perform this action, but that's easy enough. If you aren't already logged in, iTunes prompts you to create one. An iTunes login performs several functions, including allowing Apple to access your billing and shipping information, and unlocking files you purchase from iTunes.

Streaming radio

The Internet is teeming with radio stations for every genre of music and talk radio you can conjure, and iTunes is more than happy to stream many of those stations for your listening pleasure.

Note You must have an Internet connection to use the Radio features in iTunes.

Follow these steps to start streaming:

1. **Select Radio in the source pane on the left side of the iTunes window.**

2. **Choose a music or talk genre from the list, as shown in Figure 11.13, and click the arrow to the left to see stations catering to your tastes.**

11.13 There is a veritable cornucopia of options to choose from in Internet radio.

3. **Double-click a station in a genre to begin streaming its content to your Mac.**

Genius

You can save links to your favorite Internet radio stations so that you can easily access them from your library rather than browsing the various categories each time. Simply drag the name of the radio station and drop it into your Music folder in the library. When you want to launch the station, just double-click the name.

Backing up your library

Most people amass a huge volume of music and video after using iTunes for a while. No one wants to risk losing all of their entertainment and have to start all over from scratch. There are a couple of ways to back up your iTunes library: Copy your iTunes folder to another computer or hard drive, or burn your files to CDs or DVDs.

To copy your iTunes folder:

1. **Open a Finder window and click the name of your account in the sidebar on the left of the window.**

2. **Select your Music folder.**

3. **Drag the iTunes folder, as shown in Figure 11.14, to another hard drive or computer to begin copying it.**

4. **Should something happen to your iTunes library, simply copy the backup iTunes folder to the Music folder in your home directory to restore it.** You may lose files you've added since your last backup, but that's better than losing everything.

11.14 The iTunes folder contains the files in your library (unless you've specified a different location).

To back up with CDs or DVDs, follow these steps:

1. **Choose File ⇨ Library ⇨ Back Up to Disc in the iTunes menu.**

2. **Decide whether to back up your entire iTunes library or only items purchased from the iTunes Store (see Figure 11.15).**

3. **If you've made a backup in the past, you could save yourself some repetition (and drive space) by selecting the Only back up items added or changed since last backup check box.**

4. **Click Next.**

5. **Insert a blank CD or DVD to begin the backup.**

6. **iTunes prompts you to insert a new disc.** The number of discs needed depends on the size of your library, and whether you are using CDs or DVDs. DVDs can hold a lot more data than CDs, so, if possible, that's the best way to go.

11.15 Determine which files in your iTunes library you want to back up.

If you want to restore your backups, choose File ➪ Library ➪ Back Up to Disc, and select Restore.

Converting audio formats

Sometimes you may want to use your audio files with another device or share them with someone else. In some cases, the device you or the person with whom you are sharing is using may not be able to use the file because of its file format. You can create copies of your audio files in other formats while retaining the originals. To do so, follow these steps:

1. **Choose iTunes ➪ Preferences.**

2. **Click the General tab and click Import Settings to open the Import Settings window, as shown in Figure 11.16.**

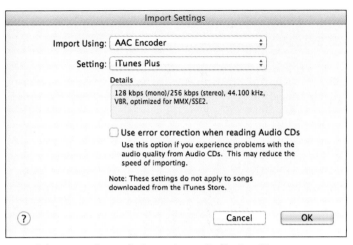

11.16 Select a new format for importing audio files into iTunes.

3. **Choose a format from the Import Using pop-up menu.**

4. **Determine the quality of the imported files using the options in the Setting pop-up menu.**

5. **Select the Use error correction when reading Audio CDs option if you have experienced problems with the audio quality of files imported from CDs.**

6. **Click OK, and then click OK again in the General preferences pane.**

7. **Select an audio file (or files) and right-click (or Control+click) it.**

8. **Choose the Create X Version, where X is the file format you selected in Step 3.**

9. **The new version of the file appears in your iTunes library along with the original.**

Creating ringtones for your iPhone

For some reason, Apple removed the built-in ability to make your own ringtones from iTunes 10, but where there's a will, there's a way.

Note Before beginning this process, find a song from which you want to create a ringtone. Next, choose a 30-second (or less) section of it with which to create your ringtone. Be sure to note the seconds at which the section starts and ends in the Status window while playing the song.

Follow these steps to create your ringtone:

1. **Find the song in iTunes that you want to be your ringtone.**

2. **Right-click (or Control+click) the file and select Get Info.**

3. **Click the Options tab, as shown in Figure 11.17.**

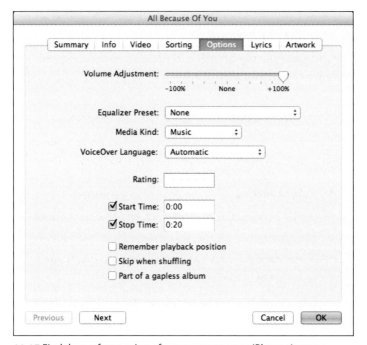

11.17 Find the perfect section of a song to use as an iPhone ringtone.

4. **Select the Start and End Time check boxes, and then type the start and end times for the section of the song from which you want to create the ringtone.** Click OK.

5. **Right-click (or Control+click) the song again and select Create AAC Version.** This creates a new version of the song using the time section you specified in the Info window. If you see a format other than AAC, go to the General preferences pane, click Import Settings, and change the Import Using option to AAC.

6. **Right-click (or Control+click) the newly created song in iTunes and select Show in Finder.**

7. **A Finder window opens and shows you the file.** Change the .m4a extension of the file to .m4r. Finder squawks at you to make sure you really want to change the extension. Click Use .m4r.

8. **Go back into iTunes, find the newly created song, and then press the Delete key on your keyboard.**

9. **iTunes asks if you want to remove the file; you do, so click Remove.**

10. **iTunes now asks if you want to move the file to the Trash and you DO NOT, so click Keep File.**

11. **Go back to the Finder, browse to the newly created ringtone file, and then double-click it to automatically import it into iTunes.**

12. **Select Ringtones in the source pane on the left side of the iTunes window and you see your newly created ringtone ready for service on your iPhone.**

Importing items from other iTunes libraries

iTunes includes a neat feature called Home Sharing that lets you import media from up to five other iTunes libraries shared by computers on your network. To use Home Sharing, follow these steps:

1. **Choose Advanced ⇨ Turn On Home Sharing.**

2. **Type your Apple ID username and password when prompted, and then click Create Home Share.** Click Done.

3. **Repeat Steps 1 and 2 on the other computers on which you want to enable Home Sharing.** Make sure you use the same Apple ID for each.

4. **To import media from another computer, select its name from the Shared list in the source pane.** Drag items from its library to yours.

Note

You must have an Apple ID in order to use Home Sharing.

Using the iTunes Store

The iTunes Store is your one-stop shop for content such as, music, movies, television shows, and podcasts of all kinds. New items are added to the iTunes Store all the time. Once you try it, you'll be as hooked as I am. To access the iTunes Store, simply click the iTunes Store icon in the source pane, as shown in Figure 11.18.

The categories of items you can get from the iTunes Store are listed at the top of the window. Simply click a category to see a drop-down menu of its subcategories. Table 11.3 lists many of the options offered by Apple.

11.18 The iTunes Store is addictive, so be careful.

Table 11.3 Items Available in the iTunes Store

Item	Description
Music	Download individual songs or entire albums. You can also download music videos and search from the extensive list of music genres.
Movies	You can rent or buy movies to watch.
TV Shows	Watch your shows on your own time instead of the networks'.
App Store	Find lots of cool applications to use with your iPhone, iPad, or iPod touch.
Books	Download and listen to audiobooks. If you prefer to read them yourself, you can download electronic books to your Mac, iPhone, iPad, or iPod touch.
Podcasts	Podcasts are radio shows or videos to which you can subscribe and download. I swear by my favorite podcasts.
iTunes U	Not only can the iTunes Store entertain, but it can also educate! Here, you can find audio and video from institutions of higher learning to listen to or view on your Mac, iPhone, iPad, or iPod touch.
Ping	Ping is a social network that concentrates on music. You can follow your favorite artists or your friends to find out what music they like, as well as what the latest trends are in the music world.

Signing in to your account

In order to use the iTunes Store you must have an account. If you do not yet have one, click the Store menu, select Create Account, and then follow the instructions.

If you have an account, follow these steps to sign in:

1. **Choose Store ⇨ Sign In.**

2. **Type your iTunes account name and password, and then click Sign In.**

3. **If you are successful, you are whisked away to the iTunes Store homepage.**

Authorizing and deauthorizing a computer

iTunes lets you authorize up to five computers to use your purchased content. To authorize a computer, follow these steps:

1. **Choose Store ⇨ Authorize This Computer.**

2. **Type your iTunes account name and password, and then click Authorize.**

3. **If you are successful, iTunes tells you so.**

To deauthorize (I think Apple made this word up) a computer, follow these steps:

1. **Choose the Store menu and select Deauthorize This Computer.**

2. **Enter your iTunes account name and password, and then click Deauthorize.**

3. **iTunes lets you know that you've successfully deauthorized this computer.**

Finding music

You can browse through the vast collection of iTunes music, or you can do what I prefer to do: perform a search. When you have an idea what you're looking for, this is the fastest way to go:

1. **At the iTunes Store homepage, click the Power Search link in the Quick Links section on the right side of the window.**

2. **Select Music in the Power Search pop-up menu.**

3. **Type any information that may help you find what you're looking for in the Artist, Composer, Song, and Album fields, as shown in Figure 11.19.** Narrow your search further by selecting a Genre.

4. **Click Search (to the right of the Genre pop-up menu) to have iTunes look for items that match your criteria.**

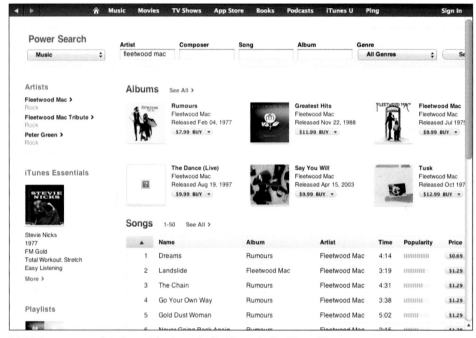

11.19 A power search is the quickest way to find items in the iTunes Store.

Renting or buying movies and TV shows

That trip to the video store just got a lot shorter because you can use iTunes to rent or buy the latest releases, as well as the classic films of yesteryear. This might not make the video store happy, but your automobile will thank you for the mileage you save. Follow these steps:

1. **Click the Movies link at the top of the iTunes Store homepage.**

2. **Browse the top ten lists to find the latest and most popular releases, choose a genre to browse through, or perform a Power Search to find your favorite movie.**

3. **Click the movie title to open its page and you see something similar to Figure 11.20.**

4. **Click View Trailer if you want to preview the movie before you rent or buy it.**

11.20 A typical movie page in the iTunes Store.

5. **Click Rent Movie or Buy Movie.** Some movies can only be rented and others can only be purchased. You can preorder some items (see Figure 11.20) before they are released.

6. **The movie then downloads and is available for you to watch in the Movies section of your iTunes library.**

Subscribing to podcasts

Podcasts are audio or video recordings you can download and play back at your leisure. There are podcasts for almost any taste, ranging from the most popular talk shows to comedy, technology, and more. To subscribe to your favorite podcast, follow these steps:

1. **Click the Podcasts link in the iTunes Store section of the iTunes Store homepage.**

2. **Find podcasts by searching in the different categories, performing a Power Search, or browsing the Top Podcasts lists.**

Genius

You can also synchronize podcasts with your iPhone, iPad, iPod, or iPod touch. This enables you to play them back on the go. Consult the documentation that came with your device for information on syncing with iTunes.

3. **When you find one that strikes your fancy, click the link to go to its page, as I've done in Figure 11.21.**

4. **Click Subscribe to have iTunes automatically download the latest episodes.**

5. **Select Podcasts from the source pane to view your subscribed podcasts and listen to or view them.**

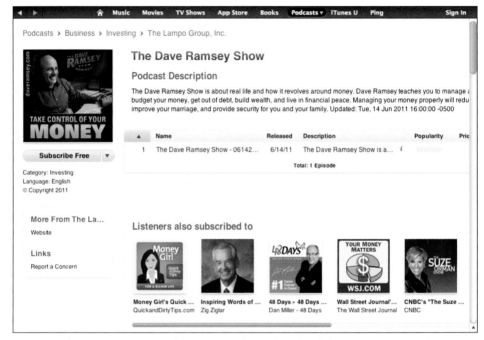

11.21 A podcast page summarizes the content and provides a list of the most recent episodes.

Enrolling at iTunes U

You don't have to be enrolled at a prestigious university to take courses there. iTunes U provides online courses from some of the premier institutions in the world, and they are yours to take for free! Follow these steps:

1. **Click iTunes U at the top of the iTunes Store homepage.**

2. **Browse the different categories, providers, and the Top Downloads section to find content, or a particular institution in which you are interested.**

3. **Click the link for the institution (or a course you want to view) and a page similar to Figure 11.22 appears.**

4. **Click Subscribe for the audio or video course you want to take.**

5. **The course downloads and can be found in the Podcast section of the source pane.** View or listen to it as you would any other podcast.

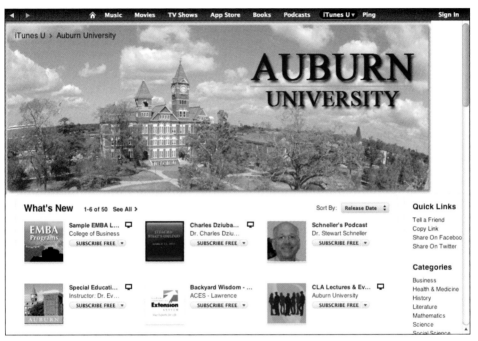

11.22 Some of the finest institutions around provide content to iTunes U.

Reading or listening to your favorite books

The iTunes Store has already taken over your neighborhood video and music haunts, and now it's time for the traditional book store to have a little competition. iTunes is also a full-scale bookstore where you can download either electronic books to read on your devices, or audiobooks to listen to in the car or on the go. To browse the store shelves, follow these steps:

1. **At the top of the iTunes Store homepage, click Books.**

2. **Browse the lists of popular books and latest selections, or perform a Power Search for a particular title or author.**

3. **Click the link for a book to see its information, as shown in Figure 11.23.**

4. **Click Buy Book to purchase one or click Get Sample to read a preview.**

5. **iTunes downloads your purchase and you can find it by clicking Books in the source pane.** Sync your iPhone, iPad, or iPod touch to read your new purchases on it.

11.23 Buy a book without a trip to the bookstore.

Downloading apps

iTunes is also home to the App Store (see Figure 11.24) for your iPhone, iPad, or iPod touch. This is where you download and sync all of those awesome apps you see in the Apple commercials.

To purchase an app, follow these steps:

1. **At the top of the iTunes Store homepage, click App Store.**

2. **Browse the categories in the Quick Links section, check out the Top Charts for the most popular apps (both free and for purchase), or do a Power Search.**

3. **When you find the app you want, select it and then click Buy or Free App to purchase it.**

4. **The next time you sync your device, the new app is ready to use.**

11.24 The App Store is crammed with the best apps for your iPhone, iPad, or iPod touch.

How Do I Work with Images and Video?

In today's digital age, you most likely use your computer to catalog and share images. Lion offers several ways to have fun with digital photography and video. In addition to taking pictures, you can use Photo Booth to record video and add special effects, including your own custom backdrops. Lion automatically works with most digital cameras and scanners. Image Capture helps you transfer images to and from your digital camera and import files using your scanner. In this chapter, I also cover viewing images in Preview, taking screenshots, watching movies with QuickTime Player, and using FaceTime for video calls.

Working with Images in Preview

Preview is an application that has been with Mac OS X from the beginning. It is commonly considered to be a jack-of-all-trades when it comes to opening and working with many file types. In this portion of the chapter, I cover how to work with images in Preview, but for more information on what Preview can do, please see Chapter 7.

Image File Types Supported by Preview

Preview can open and export many different image file types. Table 12.1 lists the image file types supported by Preview.

Table 12.1 File Types Supported by Preview

File Extension	File Type/Description
JPG	Joint Photographic Experts Group. A popular image file format used by most digital cameras. Also known as JPEG.
GIF	Graphics Interchange Format. An image file format mainly used on the Internet for small animations.
HDR	High Dynamic Range. An image file format associated with high-end digital cameras.
TIFF	Tagged Image File Format. A popular image file format used primarily by graphic artists.
PSD	Photoshop Document. The Adobe Photoshop default image file format.
PNG	Portable Network Graphics. An image file format.
BMP	Bitmap. An image file format.
RAW	A file format for an image that has not been processed in any way. This format is mostly used by digital cameras and scanners.
SGI	Silicon Graphics Image. The native raster graphics file format of Silicon Graphics workstations.

Setting the Preview preferences

Preview has its default ways of working with images, but thankfully you can customize it to fit your needs.

The Preview preferences are divided into five categories: General, Images, PDF, Bookmarks, and Signatures. I discuss the General and Images preferences in this chapter; the other three are covered in Chapter 7.

To get started, open Preview and then press ⌘+, to open the Preview Preferences window.

General

Table 12.2 breaks down the settings in the General tab of the Preview Preferences window.

Table 12.2 General Preferences

Preference	Function
When opening files	Determine how you want Preview to open multiple files: open all files in one window, open groups of files in the same window, or open each file in its own separate window.
Window background	Change the default background color of the windows you open in Preview by clicking the color box and then choosing a new color from the color palette window.

Images

There is only one item to set options for in the Images preferences pane: Define 100% scale as. The options available are self-explanatory:

- **1 image pixel equals 1 screen pixel (default setting).** This setting causes the image to appear on-screen at different dimensions depending on the screen resolution.

- **Size on screen equals size on printout.** Choose this setting to display images at the same size regardless of the screen resolution.

Viewing and editing images in Preview

Preview is more than happy to fill the role of basic image editor if you don't already have one with more frills, like iPhoto or Adobe Photoshop. While it's not able to manipulate photos and add effects like the two applications I just mentioned, Preview can handle standard resizing, rotating, and a few other nifty tricks. Open an image in Preview to get started.

Get the Inside Scoop on Images

Most people simply want to open, view, and perhaps minimally edit their pictures. However, others (and you know who you are) want the lowdown on every element of the picture, including the camera used, the compression type, the aperture, the Photometric Interpretation, and other information that only a professional photographer could appreciate.

Preview can get all that stuff for you if you simply choose Tools ⇨ Inspector, or press ⌘+I, when your image is open.

Opening and saving images

Preview can open any of the file types mentioned in Table 12.1. To open a file in Preview, do the following:

1. **From within Finder, choose Go ⇨ Applications, and then double-click the Preview icon to open it.** You can also click the Preview icon in the Dock to launch it.

2. **Choose File ⇨ Open, or press ⌘+O, to display the Open dialog.**

3. **Browse your Mac for the file you want to open, click the file icon once to highlight it, and then click Open, as shown in Figure 12.1.**

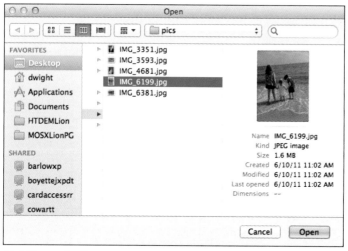

12.1 Choose the file you want to open in Preview.

Genius

If the Preview icon is in your Dock, whether it's already open or because you keep an alias for it there, you can simply drag and drop a file onto it to open it.

If you make changes to an image you've opened in Preview, those changes are automatically saved as you work. Even new images are saved automatically as you work with them, but when you're ready to name the image file press ⌘+S; you can also choose File ⇨ Save. If you've made changes to an image file, but you want to save it under a different name, press ⌘+Shift+S (or choose File ⇨ Export) to open the Export As dialog, as shown in Figure 12.2. Type a new name for the image file and choose the location to which you want to save it on your Mac. Next, select the format and quality of the image and then click Save.

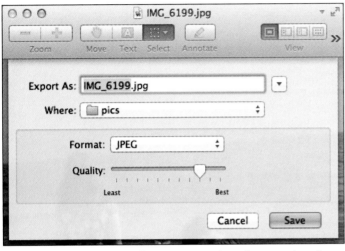

12.2 Name your file, choose where to save it, select a format and quality, and then click Save.

Note If you can't seem to find the location to which you want to save your file, click the light gray square containing the black arrow (just to the right of the Export As text field). This expands your Export As window, allowing you to browse your entire hard drive.

Importing new images

You can use Preview to import new images from a scanner or camera connected to your Mac via a USB, FireWire, or network (assuming your scanner or camera supports one or all of these connection types).

Importing images from a scanner

To import images into Preview from a scanner, follow these steps:

1. **Choose File and hold your mouse over Import from Scanner.** Select your scanner from the pop-up menu.

2. **When your scanner window opens, choose the appropriate settings for the type of file you're importing, as shown in Figure 12.3.**

3. **Click Scan to initiate the scanning sequence.**

4. **Browse your Mac for the location to which you want to save the file and then click Choose Destination.** The file you scanned opens in Preview.

Importing images from a camera

To import images into Preview from a camera, follow these steps:

1. **Choose File ⇨ Import from *camera name*.**

2. **When the camera window opens, browse to find the pictures you want to import into Preview, as shown in Figure 12.4.** To select multiple pictures, hold down the ⌘ key while clicking each picture.

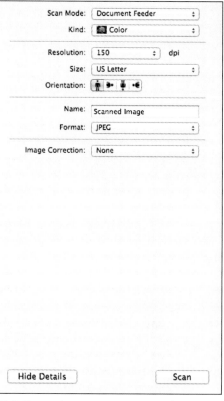

12.3 Choose the appropriate settings for the type of file you want to scan into Preview.

3. **Click Import to import pictures you've selected.** If you want to import every picture on your camera, click Import All.

4. **Browse your Mac for the location to which you want to save the file and then click Choose Destination.** The pictures you imported open in Preview.

Genius

When viewing your pictures in the Import window, you can change the way they display by clicking the List or the Icons buttons found in the lower-left corner. You can also rotate and delete images from here.

12.4 Choose the pictures you want to import into Preview.

Resizing and rotating images

If a photo or image is just too big dimensionally, Preview can easily squeeze it until it fits the spot in which you want to place it.

To adjust the size of your image, choose Tools ⇨ Adjust Size. The dialog shown in Figure 12.5 opens.

Make the necessary changes to these settings to adjust your image, and click OK when you are finished. Table 12.3 explains the options and how they affect the image.

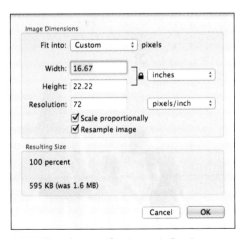

12.5 Adjust the size of an image in Preview.

Table 12.3 Size Adjustments

Option	Function
Fit into	Lets you choose automatic size settings from the pop-up menu. Use Custom to create a custom size.
Width and Height	Changes the physical size of the image.
Resolution	Changes the quality of the image. Increasing this number may have adverse effects on the image.
Scale proportionally	Keeps the dimensions of the image intact when selected. For example, if you change the width, the height changes proportionally.
Resample image	Deselect this check box if you want to reduce the dimensions of a file without losing image details.

Genius

You can also crop an image in Preview. Notice that the mouse cursor changes to a cross hair when you move it over your image; use this to select the area on your image that you want to crop. Place the cross hair underneath or over the area you want to crop, and then click and drag to draw a box around it. Once the area is selected, press ⌘+K, and then save your new image (File ➪ Export in the menu).

Preview also lets you rotate images to change their orientation. If you have a picture that was taken by holding the camera sideways (for example, to take a full-length shot of someone), you can rotate it so that the subject is standing upright instead of on her side. To rotate an image to the left, press ⌘+L; to rotate it to the right, press ⌘+R.

You can also flip an image to make the subject face a different direction, as shown in Figure 12.6. I flipped my image both vertically and horizontally to give you a better idea of what these functions do.

To flip your image horizontally, choose Tools ➪ Flip Horizontal; to go vertical, choose Tools ➪ Flip Vertical.

12.6 My kids are flipping out in this picture!

Adjusting color in images

Sometimes the colors in your pictures just don't look quite right. What is someone who isn't a color specialist to do? Preview has the answer! Preview can handle basic color adjustments very well.

To make color corrections in Preview, choose Tools ⇨ Adjust Color, or press ⌘+Option+C. The color adjustment sliders in the Adjust Color window, shown in Figure 12.7, can work wonders on your images. When you move the sliders, your image is automatically updated to reflect the adjustments.

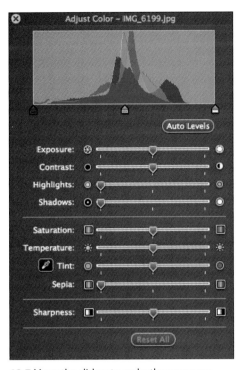

12.7 Move the sliders to make the necessary color adjustments to your image.

Taking Screenshots

At some point during your Mac adventure you may need to take a shot of your screen. There are many reasons for taking screenshots. For example, you may want to share information about your system with someone else, or you may want a quick snap of some settings you've made so that you can refer to them later. You can take screenshots manually with just a couple of key presses, or you can gain a little more control over the shots by using the Grab utility that ships as part of Lion.

Capturing screenshots manually

The quick and easy way to take screenshots is to incorporate a little manual dexterity:

- **Press ⌘+Shift+3.** This takes a shot of the entire screen.

- **Press ⌘+Shift+4.** This narrows the scope of your screenshot. Your cursor turns into a cross hair which you then drag over the section of your screen that you want to shoot. As soon as you let go of the mouse or trackpad button, a screenshot is taken of the area you highlighted.

Genius

You can also take a shot of an individual window. Press ⌘+Shift+4 again, but don't drag the cross hair. Instead, press the spacebar and the cross hair changes to a camera icon. Position the camera icon over the window you want to shoot and click your mouse or trackpad button.

Taking screenshots in Preview

There are three ways to take a screenshot within Preview. Choose File⇨Take Screen Shot and select one of the following options:

- **From Selection.** When you choose this option, your cursor turns into a cross hair. Click and drag the cross hair over the portion of the screen you want to capture and the screenshot opens in Preview.

- **From Window.** When you choose this option, the cursor turns into a camera icon. Move the camera icon over the window (or the menu) that you want to shoot and click your mouse or trackpad button to capture it. The screenshot then opens in Preview.

- **From Entire Screen.** When you select this option, Preview displays a countdown to when it will take the shot. This gives you time to position the windows where you need them on-screen or to select an item from a menu before the screenshot is taken. It then displays in Preview.

Using Grab to capture screenshots

Grab is a utility that helps you take screenshots that include various types of mouse pointers, take timed screenshots, and more. Grab can be found in the /Applications/ Utilities folder. Double-click to open Grab and use the Capture menu to choose the type of screen capture you want it to perform.

The Grab Preferences, shown in Figure 12.8, let you choose from a variety of mouse pointers.

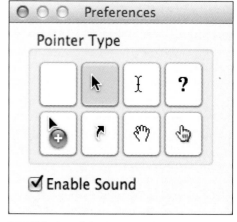

12.8 Select a pointer to appear in your screen captures.

Discovering QuickTime

QuickTime Player allows you to watch, create, and share movie files in Lion. To open QuickTime Player, go to the Applications folder and double-click its icon.

Playing back video and audio files

QuickTime Player can open and play back video and audio of various formats.

Video formats supported are:

- **QuickTime Movie (.mov extension)**
- **MPEG-4 (.mp4 or .m4v)**
- **MPEG-1**
- **3GPP**
- **3GPP2**
- **AVI**
- **DV**

Audio formats supported include:

- **iTunes Audio (.m4a, .m4p, and .m4b)**
- **MP3**
- **AIFF**
- **AU**
- **SD2**
- **Core Audio (.caf)**
- **WAV**
- **SND**
- **AMR**

Note

If the tiny playback window isn't your style, click the Full Screen button (the two diagonal arrows) in the upper-right corner of the controls window.

You can open any file using one of the afore-mentioned formats by simply double-clicking it in the Finder. QuickTime Player automatically launches and affords you the controls necessary to play back your media, as shown in Figure 12.9.

If you move your mouse pointer off the video or audio playback window, the controls disappear. Don't worry; to get them back just hover the cursor over the playback window.

Creating new video or audio recordings

QuickTime Player isn't just a player; it can take on the role of recorder as well. You can create video from the built-in Mac camera, a digital video camera connected with FireWire, or a USB webcam (if supported by the manufacturer). Audio can be recorded using the microphone built in to your Mac, an external microphone, or a musical instrument connected to your Mac.

12.9 The QuickTime Player controls are similar to those found on a DVD player.

To create a new video or audio recording, follow these steps:

1. **Choose File⇨New Movie Recording, or File⇨New Audio Recording.** A preview window opens.

2. **Make sure you have everything set up correctly and that you are ready to record before clicking the Record button.**

3. **Change the input source, adjust the quality of the recording, or select a folder in which to save the finished file by clicking the arrow in the preview window, as shown in Figure 12.10.**

4. **Click the Stop button when finished recording.**

12.10 Make adjustments to the input source and quality of the recording if necessary.

Recording your on-screen movements

If you teach classes or make presentations regularly that include demonstrations of actions you can take on a computer, you'll love QuickTime Player's ability to record your on-screen movements. To enable this feature, follow these steps:

1. **Choose File ⇨ New Screen Recording.** A preview window opens.

2. **Make sure you have everything set up correctly and that you are ready to record before clicking the Record button.**

3. **Change the input source, adjust the quality of the recording, choose to show mouse clicks in the recording, or select a folder in which to save the finished file by clicking the arrow in the preview window.**

4. **Click the Stop button to finish recording your on-screen movements.**

Sharing your recordings via the Internet

The Internet has become the number one way to share information with friends, family, and colleagues. QuickTime Player allows you to easily share your movies and recordings using several methods.

To do so, open the file you want to share, choose the Share menu, and then select one of the following:

- **iTunes.** Select iTunes and a copy of your movie is placed in the iTunes library, where it can be played on an iPhone, iPod, iPad, or Apple TV.

- **MobileMe Gallery.** You must have a MobileMe account to select this option. Once selected, you can give the movie a name, determine access options for those you want to view it, and make it compatible for playback on an iPhone or iPod touch.

- **YouTube.** Select this option to upload your file (it must be shorter than 15 minutes and smaller than 2GB) to your YouTube account. Give the file a title and description, as shown in Figure 12.11, to become the next YouTube sensation.

- **Vimeo.** If you have a Vimeo account, upload your file there to share it with others. Be sure to set the option to make the file personal if you only want to view it yourself or share it with only those you deem privileged.

- **Flickr.** If you have a Flickr account, you can share your Oscar-worthy performances. Simply log in to your Flickr account, set up the appropriate options (name, description, and so on), and upload your file.

12.11 Upload your movies to YouTube so the rest of the world can enjoy them.

- **Facebook.** It's a safe bet that most, if not all, of the folks with whom you want to share your recordings have Facebook accounts, so this might be a preferable option for some. Simply log in to Facebook and upload your file.

- **Mail.** Select this sharing method to open a new e-mail in Mail that automatically contains a copy of the file as an attachment. You can then type the e-mail addresses of your intended recipients and click Send.

Using Photo Booth

Apple has moved the old-fashioned photo booths that we used to cram ourselves into with our friends on Friday nights at the mall to our Macs. Simple as it is, there are still a few features that could use an explanation. When I purchase something new, I'm one of those people who actually like to read the instructions and learn what all the buttons and gadgets are for. Hence, my insistence on covering the Photo Booth features shown in Figure 12.12.

12.12 The main Photo Booth window in Snapshot mode.

Taking snapshots

Any kind of picture that you take with Photo Booth is considered a snapshot, whether it's a still picture or a video. You can take three kinds of snapshots: Single still picture, four quick snapshots (which are much more fun than you might think), and video. Use the snapshot-type buttons under the bottom-left corner of the viewer window to select the kind that you want to take.

Taking a single snapshot

Single snapshots (or still pictures) are so easy to take, it's ridiculous. Follow these steps:

1. **Click the single still picture button under the bottom-left corner of the Viewer window.**

2. **Position yourself in front of the Mac camera so that your image fits inside the Viewer window.**

289

3. **Click the Camera button.**

4. **Photo Booth begins its countdown from 3, flashes, and then takes the picture.**
   That's it!

Taking four quick snapshots

Taking four quick snapshots lets you create different poses in rapid succession. Follow these steps to try it out:

1. **Click the four quick snapshots button in the middle under the bottom-left corner of the Viewer window.**

2. **Position yourself in front of the Mac camera so that your image fits inside the Viewer window.**

3. **Click the Camera button to begin the countdown.** Get into your first pose before the first flash goes off.

4. **After the first flash, immediately change to your next pose and continue to do that through all four pictures.** You have only about a second between snapshots, so you have to move quickly.

5. **When all four snapshots are taken, you see a preview of your images, similar to Figure 12.13.**

Creating a video snapshot

To create some movie magic in Photo Booth, follow these steps:

1. **Click the video button on the right under the bottom-left corner of the viewer window.**

2. **Position yourself in front of the Mac camera so that your image fits inside the viewer window.**

3. **Click the Camera button to begin the countdown.**

4. **Begin your video after the flash goes off.**

5. **When finished, click the Stop button.**

Viewing your snapshots

All of your snapshots are stored in the Thumbnail bar at the bottom of the Photo Booth window. You can scroll through the list of snapshots by clicking the right and left arrows on either side of the bar.

12.13 A preview appears in the viewer window so that you can see your four-up handiwork.

To view a snapshot, click it in the Thumbnail bar and it displays in the Viewer window. To find a snapshot on your Mac, right-click (or Control+click) the snapshot in the Thumbnail bar and then select Reveal in the Finder. A Finder window opens, displaying the location of the file on the hard drive.

Genius You can access your snapshots without opening Photo Booth each time you need them. Photo Booth stores snapshots in the Photo Booth Library package, which resides in the Pictures folder of your home folder (Hard drive/Users/*your account name*/Pictures/).

Using special effects

You've only seen the tip of the Photo Booth iceberg. Photo Booth can do something the old photo booths at the mall could only dream of: add awesome special effects and backdrops!

Adding effects to Snapshots

To use visual effects like filters or distortions for your snapshots, follow these steps:

1. **Position yourself in front of the Mac camera so that your image fits inside the Viewer window.**

2. **Click Effects to see the cool filter effects shown in Figure 12.14.**

12.14 The filter effects available in Photo Booth.

3. **Click the right arrow next to Effects to see the distortion effects like those shown in Figure 12.15.**

4. **Select the effect you want to use by clicking it and then click the Camera button to take the picture.**

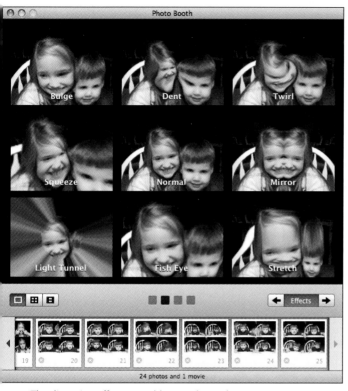

12.15 The distortion effects are a blast to play with!

Adding a Video backdrop

Video backdrops are really neat to use. They place a moving video of some exotic location behind you so that it appears as if you're really there. Impress family and friends by creating a video of yourself in front of the Eiffel Tower, swimming with the fishes, or flying through the clouds!

Here's how to do it:

1. **Position yourself in front of the Mac camera so that your image fits inside the Viewer window.**

2. **Click Effects.**

3. **Click the right arrow next to Effects twice until it brings you to the video backdrops.**

4. **Select the backdrop you want to use.**

5. **Step out of the frame when prompted until you see the backdrop you chose in the Viewer window.**

293

6. **Move into the frame of the Viewer window and click the Camera button to make your video, as shown in Figure 12.16.**

12.16 Her hair isn't even wet!

Adding custom backdrops

My favorite feature of Photo Booth is the ability to use my own photos and videos as backdrops. To create a custom backdrop, follow these steps:

1. **Click Effects and then click the right arrow next to it three times to see the Custom Backdrop window.**

2. **Drag and drop a picture or video from the Finder, iPhoto, or iMovie into one of the Drag Backdrop Here windows.**

3. **Select the new backdrop to use it for your picture or video.**

Using your pictures and videos

What to do with all these great snapshots you've been taking? You can save your snapshots in iPhoto if you like, e-mail them to family and friends, or use them to represent you in an online chat session.

Click the snapshot you want to use in the Thumbnail bar. Notice in Figure 12.17 that when you open the snapshot in preview mode, you now have several new icons underneath the Viewer window.

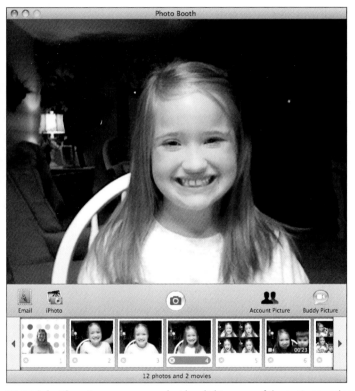

12.17 Select how to use your snapshot by clicking one of the options under the viewer window.

Note You can print from Photo Booth just as you can from any other application. To print your snapshots, choose File ➪ Print or press ⌘+P. When the Print dialog opens, click Show Details and choose one of the options in the Photo Booth pane. You can print the picture normally, or you can print proof sheets (either several different sizes of the same picture on the same page or eight pictures of the same size).

Table 12.4 explains what each icon does.

Table 12.4 Using Your Photo Booth Snapshots

Icon	Action
Email	Opens the Mail application and automatically creates a new e-mail containing the snapshot. Type the e-mail addresses of your intended recipients and send it right along.
iPhoto	Launches iPhoto if you have it (iPhoto is not part of Lion, but is part of the Apple iLife application suite) and automatically imports the picture from Photo Booth.
Account Picture	Automatically opens the Users & Groups pane of System Preferences, selects your user account, and changes your account picture to the one you selected in Photo Booth.
Buddy Picture	Opens iChat and changes the picture that the people with whom you chat see.

Working with Image Capture

Image Capture is a great tool that may surprise you with its versatility. You can use it to do any of the following:

- **Transfer images from your digital camera.**
- **Delete images from your digital camera.**
- **Scan and import images with your scanner.**
- **Find shared devices on your network.**

To open Image Capture, press ⌘+Shift+A from within the Finder. Find Image Capture in the resulting Finder window and double-click its icon. If you don't have a digital camera or scanner attached to your Mac when you start Image Capture, you are notified in the main window that no device is connected. If this is the case, read on to discover how to connect your device.

Note You may wonder why iPhoto, the amazing Apple photo-organizing and editing program, isn't covered in this book. iPhoto is actually part of the iLife application suite, which Apple sells separately from Lion. Because I concentrate on Lion in this book, Image Capture gets all the glory.

Connecting your device

If you haven't already done so, attach your device to the Mac with whatever connection its manufacturer recommends (most use a USB). If Image Capture is already open, when you attach a camera or scanner it should automatically display under Devices on the left side of the Image Capture window.

If you have multiple devices attached to your Mac, you can choose the device you want to use by selecting it in the Devices menu.

Note In addition to pictures, Image Capture is also versatile enough to import movies and MP3 files, assuming your camera has the ability to record such files.

Using a digital camera

A digital camera is your window to the world and it allows you to keep your memories for a lifetime. However, the memory cards cameras use to store your precious keepsakes have a finite amount of space. Therefore, they need to be emptied of their contents every now and again. This is where Image Capture comes in handy.

Transferring images from your camera

As stated earlier in this chapter, when you connect your camera to your Mac with Image Capture already up and running, a window opens similar to the one shown in Figure 12.18. This gives you access to — and a measure of control over — your camera.

The options are:

- **Connecting this camera opens.** This pop-up menu lets you choose an application to open automatically when the camera is connected to your Mac.

- **List or Icons buttons.** Click one of these viewing options at the bottom left of the window to change the view.

- **Rotate buttons.** Click these to rotate images before downloading them.

Importing files

Click Import All to do just that: import all of the pictures and files from your camera to your Mac. However, if you only want to import a few files, the Import button is your best option.

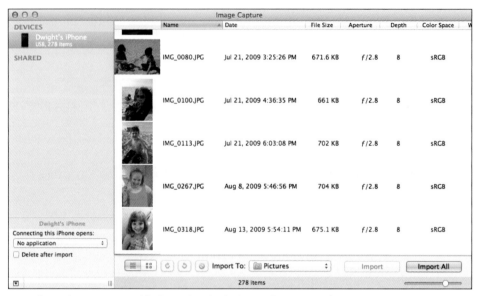

12.18 Control your camera with the options in the Image Capture window.

To import only certain files from your camera, click those you want to import from within the Image Capture window. To choose multiple files, as shown in Figure 12.19, hold down the ⌘ key while making your selections.

12.19 You can select only the pictures you want to download rather than downloading them all at once.

Next, click Import to proceed with the transfer. The files you downloaded can then be found in the Pictures folder of your home directory. You can change the location to which your pictures are imported by clicking the Import To pop-up menu at the bottom of the window.

Deleting images from your camera

Sometimes you may only want to delete some of the images on your digital camera as opposed to all, but deleting individual images can be a chore. Image Capture comes in handy in this situation. To delete individual files from your camera, follow these steps:

1. **Select the files you want to remove from your camera.** Hold down the ⌘ key while clicking to choose multiple files.

2. **Click the Delete button at the bottom of the window.**

3. **Click OK to confirm the deletion or click Cancel to stop it.**

Note Image Capture is a great application, but if you need to touch up photos, such as removing the red in your subject's eyes or cropping part of the image, you need other software. iPhoto is the perfect application for such common tasks, and it's also great for organizing and sharing images. You can purchase iPhoto from Apple as part of the iLife suite of applications.

Scanning images

Your Mac happily uses Image Capture to import images and documents from a scanner. Simply connect your scanner to get started.

Note You need to install the scanner software before connecting the scanner to your Mac. The software probably came on a CD with the scanner, but it's always a good idea to visit the manufacturer's website for any updated drivers it may have released.

Open the Applications folder on your hard drive, double-click the Image Capture icon, and then choose the scanner from the list. Place the item you want to scan onto the glass of the scanner if it is a flatbed scanner, or into the feeder if it is a document-feed scanner. This is where the fun begins!

Using the Image Capture scanning options

The default scan window that opens offers a few basic options for scanning your documents into your Mac, as shown in Figure 12.20.

To scan an item using these options, follow these steps:

1. **Highlight the scanner under Devices on the left side of the Image Capture window.**

2. **Choose the type of scanner you are using from the Mode pop-up menu.**

3. **Select the paper size of the original from the Scan Size pop-up menu.**

4. **Choose a location in which to store the scanned file or an application with which to open it using the Scan To pop-up menu.**

5. **Click Scan.** Once the scan is completed, you can find the document in the location you chose in Step 4.

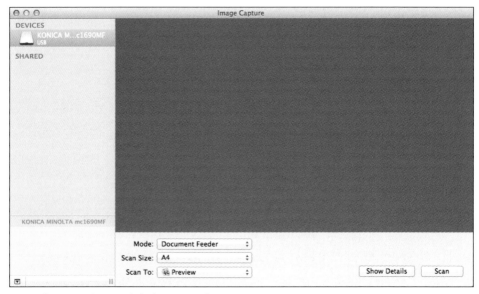

12.20 The Image Capture default scan window.

Using the scanner software options

Your scanner software may offer many options that are not available in the Image Capture standard scan window. To access those features, follow these steps:

1. **Highlight the scanner under Devices on the left side of the Image Capture window and click Show Details in the lower-right corner to see the scanner options, as shown in Figure 12.21.** Your options may be different, depending on your scanner and the driver it uses.

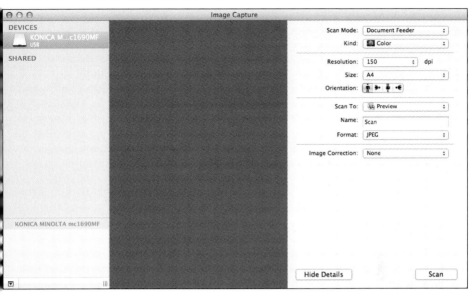

12.21 You have more control over the quality of your scans when using the software provided by the scanner manufacturer.

2. **Select the type of scanner you are using from the Scan Mode drop-down menu.**

3. **Choose what type of image you are scanning from the Kind drop-down menu.**

4. **Select the Resolution you want to use from its drop-down menu.** Resolution plays a major role in the quality of the image. Again, the higher the better, but this also increases your file size.

5. **Determine the size and orientation of your image.**

6. **Choose a location on your Mac in which to save the scanned images or an application you want to use to open them by using the Scan To drop-down menu.**

7. **Name the file and select the format in which you want to save the scanned image.**

8. **If your scanner offers other options, such as Image Correction, Unsharp Mask, and so on, make any corrections you feel are necessary using these options.**

9. **If you are using a document-feed scanner, simply click Scan to begin scanning the pages and skip the rest of the steps.** If using a flatbed or transparency scanner, continue to Step 10.

10. **Click Overview scan to see a preview of the item on the glass.**

11. **Click and drag your mouse over the portion of the preview that you want to scan, and then click Scan.**

301

Using FaceTime

FaceTime is the latest communication technology from Apple that allows you to make video calls to anyone who has an iPhone 4, iPad 2, Mac, or iPod touch. FaceTime uses the built-in cameras on these devices to send a crystal-clear video of you to the person you're calling, and you can see the other person talking back to you on your device.

FaceTime requirements

You need all of the following to use FaceTime for making video calls from your Mac:

- **An Internet connection using Ethernet or Wi-Fi.**

- **A Mac running Mac OS X 10.6.6 or later (you have Lion, which is 10.7, so you're okay).**

- **A camera, of course, or there won't be much video for your video call.** You can use the built-in Mac camera, an external camera that connects to FireWire, or an external USB camera that supports DV/HDV cameras and the UVC specification.

- **A microphone or the call will be a quiet one.** Your Mac has a built-in microphone or you can use an external microphone connected to the audio port. USB and Bluetooth microphones or headsets also work.

- **An Apple ID to sign in to FaceTime.**

- **Contacts in your Address Book.** FaceTime uses phone numbers to call iPhone 4 users and e-mail addresses to call Mac, iPad 2, and iPod touch users.

Signing in to FaceTime

When you first open FaceTime, you are asked to sign in using your Apple ID, as shown in Figure 12.22.

To sign in to FaceTime, follow these steps:

1. **If you don't have an Apple ID, click Create New Account, follow the instructions, and then continue on to Step 2.** If you do have an Apple ID, continue to Step 2.

2. **Type your Apple ID username and password in the appropriate fields, and then click Sign In.**

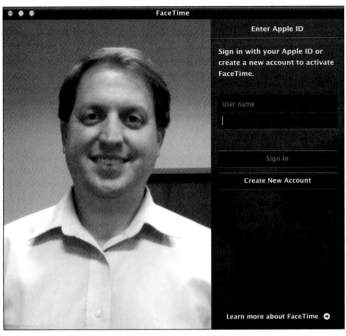

12.22 Sign in with your Apple ID to begin using FaceTime.

3. **Type the e-mail address with which you want other FaceTime users to call you and click Next.**

4. **Apple sends a verification e-mail.** Once you receive the e-mail, respond to it by clicking the Verify Now link it contains.

5. **On the web page that opens, sign in with your Apple ID username and password, and then click Verify Address.**

6. **When the e-mail address is verified, go back to FaceTime and click Next again.** FaceTime shows that your address is verified.

7. **Press ⌘+K to turn on FaceTime and your Address Book contacts appear in the FaceTime window.**

Placing a call with FaceTime

Once you're signed in, it's time to make some calls. The best thing is that no long-distance fees apply! You can feel free to call folks who are using an iPad 2, a Mac running 10.6.6 or later, or an iPod touch (4th generation) or iPhone 4 running iOS 4.1 or later.

303

To place a call, follow these steps:

1. **Find a contact to call in one of three ways:**

   - **Type the contact's name in the search field near the top of the FaceTime window.** Names that match appear as you type.

   - **Add a new contact by clicking the plus sign (+) in the upper-right corner.** Type the contact's name and information, and then click Done.

   - **At the bottom right of the FaceTime window, click Favorites, Recents, or Contacts, as shown in Figure 12.23.** Scroll through the list until you find the person you want to call.

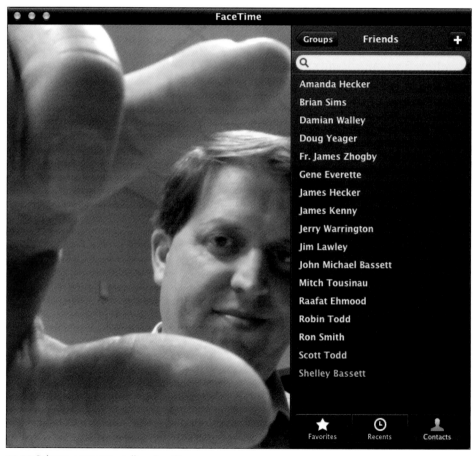

12.23 Select a contact to call on FaceTime.

2. **Click the contact you want to call and you see the contact information.**

3. **Call the person by clicking the contact information:**

   - **If the person you're calling is using an iPhone 4, click the phone number to initiate the call.**

   - **If the person you're calling is using a Mac, iPad 2, or iPod touch, click the e-mail address to place the call.**

4. **The person you are calling can then either accept or decline your call.** If the call is accepted, commence the conversation.

Managing FaceTime calls

Once on a call, you can manage it in various ways, such as:

- **Enlarge the call window by dragging the lower-right corner of the window outward.** Shrink the window by dragging the lower-right corner inward.

- **Press ⌘+Shift+F to enter Full Screen mode.**

- **Click and drag the picture-in-picture display (the picture of you) to any corner of the window.**

- **Change the orientation of the call window by choosing Video ⇨ Use Portrait or Video ⇨ Use Landscape from the menu.**

- **Mute the sound on a call by choosing Video ⇨ Mute from the menu.**

- **Pause a video call by choosing FaceTime ⇨ Hide FaceTime.**

- **Resume a paused video call by clicking the FaceTime icon in the Dock.**

- **Click End to end a video call in progress.**

You can block an incoming call by clicking Decline or receive it by clicking Accept.

Setting Up a Printer

Installing a printer in Mac OS X is a snap, provided that everything the Mac needs to communicate with the printer is installed (software and drivers) and the necessary hardware (devices and cables) is functioning as it should.

Before you purchase a printer, make absolutely certain that it is Mac-compatible (the vast majority sold today are, but it's best to be sure). Don't just trust the well-meaning employees at the electronics superstore — check it out yourself by going to the printer manufacturer's web page and checking the specifications for the printer.

You can also look for familiar Mac logos on the printer box. Logos to look for would include the large X logo with the Made for Mac OS X tagline and the happy Mac, as shown in Figure 13.1, which also appears on the left side of your Dock as the Finder icon. If you buy your printer directly from Apple, it's a safe bet the printer is Mac-compatible.

13.1 This is one of the familiar Mac logos to look for on the box of the printer you want to purchase.

There are three main steps that you must take before you can use your printer with your Mac:

1. **Install the software that came with your printer.**

2. **Connect your printer to your Mac or network.**

   - **If your printer has a USB connection, connect one end of the USB cable to the printer and the other to your Mac.**

   - **If your printer has a network or Ethernet interface, use an Ethernet (or RJ-45) cable to connect it to the network router or switch.**

3. **Use the Print & Scan System Preferences pane to create a print queue for the printer (in other words, install the printer).**

Installing printer software

Mac OS X needs special software called a driver, to be able to communicate effectively with your printer, just as it does to speak to any other device you may connect to it. Mac OS X comes pre-loaded with tons of printer drivers from several of the most popular printer manufacturers, so chances are pretty good that you won't need to install any additional software.

Caution Be sure the driver files you download are for the version of Mac OS X you are using. If you're reading this book, the automatic assumption is that you're running Lion (Mac OS X 10.7).

However, the safest way to go is to install the software the manufacturer provides in the box, typically on a CD. You can also download the latest software from the manufacturer's support website.

Note It's always a good idea to just go to a printer manufacturer's website and download the drivers right from the beginning. This ensures that you have the latest and greatest software for your printer.

Unfortunately, there's not only one way to install drivers. Printer manufacturers provide drivers and software in a number of ways using different installer applications. So, the way you install your HP printer software may be different than the way you install your Konica Minolta, Brother, Xerox, or Epson software.

Some printer manufacturers may install other software in addition to the printer driver, such as utilities that allow you to monitor the printer consumables (such as toners, ink cartridges, and drums), perform maintenance tasks, or run diagnostics for troubleshooting. These utilities are typically installed in the Hard Drive ❖ Applications folder. Consult your printer manufacturer if you're not sure what software should be installed to maximize your use of the printer (other than the driver, of course).

Generally, you should follow the installation instructions included with the printer, but here is the typical process used to install printer drivers and software:

1. **Insert the CD that came with your printer or download the software from the printer manufacturer's website.**

2. **Double-click the CD icon to open a window (if one doesn't open automatically) and see its contents and then double-click the software installer icon.** If you download the driver from the web using Safari, Safari automatically opens and mounts the disk image, and displays a window showing the contents. Double-click the installer icon in the disk image window.

3. **Type your user account login password when prompted during installation.**

4. **When the software installation is complete, you see a prompt similar to Figure 13.2.** Click Close to complete the process.

13.2 Click Close to finish the driver software installation process.

Your Mac should now have the necessary drivers and utilities to communicate with your printer. You can now move on to the second major step in your printer setup — connecting your printer.

Note

The Mac OS X installer application no longer installs several gigabytes of printer drivers by default. Instead, it installs drivers as needed when a printer is detected. For example, if you have a printer connected to your Mac or network during installation of Mac OS X Lion, the installer detects it and installs the necessary drivers. This process only works with printers made by manufacturers that have supplied drivers to Apple. Software Update finds new drivers as they become available.

Connecting your printer

How you connect your printer is just as important as having the correct driver software installed. Some printers come with only one connection type (usually USB), but others may have multiple connection options. The most common is an Ethernet interface for directly connecting the printer to your network.

USB

Connecting with USB is certainly the easiest way for your Mac to get its print on, and USB is reasonably fast for most printing needs. There's not much to it — connect one end of the USB cable to the printer, the other to the Mac, and voila! The printer is connected.

Note

Check the contents of the printer box for a USB cable, as most don't include one and you may have to pick one up before you leave the store. A USB device cable has a standard A plug on one end (the flat, rectangular connector with which most of us are familiar), and a standard B plug on the other (a smaller, almost completely square connector). The standard B plug is the end that you connect to your printer.

Network

Connect your printer to your network if you want multiple Macs to be able to print from it. Typically, connecting to a network involves hooking up your printer to a router or network switch through an Ethernet cable. There are other methods of using your printer with a network, such as sharing the printer from a Mac, using *print servers* (devices designed to connect a printer that doesn't have an Ethernet port to an Ethernet router), or using a wireless network adapter. Sharing a printer is covered later in this chapter.

Using print servers and wireless network adapters to connect your printer to a network achieves the same goal as using an Ethernet cable — they all assign a network or IP (Internet Protocol) address to the printer. Because Ethernet cable is the most common method (this may change one day, but for now it's still the norm), I stick with that as the default network connection.

Here are general instructions for connecting your printer to a network:

1. **With the printer off, insert one end of the Ethernet cable into the Ethernet port on your printer.**

2. **Insert the other end of the Ethernet cable into an available Ethernet port on your network router or switch.**

3. **Turn on the printer.** If your printer is running DHCP (Dynamic Host Configuration Protocol) right out of the box (most do), it is automatically assigned an IP address by the router or a DHCP server on the network. Consult the printer documentation to find out how to determine what IP address is assigned to your printer by your network router.

Which Network Protocol Should I Use?

Network printers can communicate with your Mac using one of two protocols: Bonjour (known as Rendezvous in an earlier incarnation) and/or IP Printing.

- **Bonjour.** This is the latest, no-configuration-needed protocol from Apple. Like AppleTalk before it, your Mac simply sees a printer running the Bonjour protocol and printer queue installation is a snap. Older printers most likely won't have Bonjour, so AppleTalk will have to suffice.

- **IP (Internet Protocol) Printing.** This is the most difficult to set up because you must know the IP address of the printer being installed. I say it's the most difficult, but the only real difficulty with IP Printing is that it is more time consuming to set up than Bonjour.

If you're on a small network, Bonjour is your best bet because of its extreme simplicity. Consult your IT administrator if you are on a larger corporate network to find out how he or she prefers you to install the printer. I would only use IP Printing if your IT department prefers it.

If you're a fan of AppleTalk, I'm sorry to disappoint you, but Mac OS X no longer supports that protocol.

Note If you plan on using only Bonjour as the connection protocol to your printer, there's no need to worry about what the IP address is.

Creating a print queue

The next step on your printer installation odyssey is to create a print queue. Creating a print queue allows you to print to the printer from your Mac, as well as manage print jobs. Later, I show you how to set up a print queue for your printer regardless of the connection type it uses.

Note If you connect your printer with a USB after installing the software, your Mac sometimes automatically creates a print queue; you don't have to lift a finger! To see whether this is the case, choose Apple menu ➪ System Preferences ➪ Print & Scan. If a print queue has been created, you see it in the Printers list on the left side of the window. Now, get to printing!

Opening the Add Printer window

Now that you have the printer connected, let's get it rolling. Follow these steps:

1. **Choose Apple menu ➪ System Preferences, or click the System Preferences icon in the Dock.**

2. **Click the Print & Scan icon in the Hardware section of the System Preferences (see Figure 13.3) to open the Print & Scan preferences pane.**

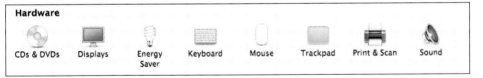

13.3 Click the Print & Scan icon to open its preferences pane.

3. **Click the plus sign (+) in the lower-left corner of the pane (see Figure 13.4) to add a printer to the list.** To delete a printer from the list, highlight it and click the minus sign (–).

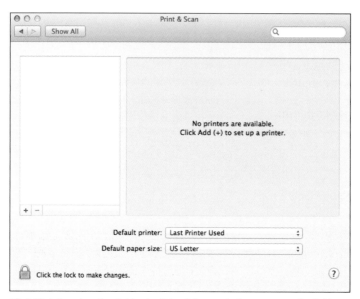

13.4 Click the plus sign (+) in the Print & Scan window to open the Add Printer window.

When the Add Printer window opens, you can use one of the following methods to create a print queue for your printer.

Installing a printer using USB or Bonjour

If you are installing the printer through USB or Bonjour, do the following:

1. **Click Default in the upper-left corner of the window's toolbar.**

2. **Click the name of the printer in the window.**

3. **The Print Using pop-up menu should automatically show the name of the printer you are setting up.** If not, click the pop-up menu, choose the Select Printer Software option, and browse the list of installed printer drivers. Select the one you need, click OK, and then click Add in the bottom-right corner.

Installing a printer using IP Printing

If you are using IP Printing as your protocol, do the following:

1. **Click IP in the toolbar.**

2. **Select the correct protocol from the Protocol pop-up menu.** Consult your printer manufacturer's documentation, website, or technical support department for more information on which protocol to choose.

3. **Type the printer's IP address in the Address field.**

4. **Type the printer's queue name into the Queue field.** Again, consult your printer manufacturer's documentation for the proper setting.

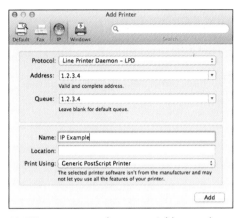

13.5 Be sure to type the correct Address and Queue information when using IP Printing.

5. **Edit the Name and Location fields to your liking.**

6. **The Print Using pop-up menu may show the name of the printer you are setting up.** If not, click the pop-up menu and choose the Select Printer Software option. Browse the list of installed printer drivers, select the one you need, click OK, and then click Add in the bottom-right corner (see Figure 13.5).

Your newly installed printer queue is now visible in the printer list of the Print & Scan window, similar to the one shown in Figure 13.6.

13.6 My newly installed printer queue is now ready to feed jobs to my printer.

315

To make certain you can now enjoy the fruits of your labor, you need to try a test print. Follow these steps to do so:

1. **Click the printer name in the printer list to highlight it.**

2. **Click Open Print Queue.**

3. **In the print queue menu (the name of the print queue is to the right of the Apple menu), choose Printer ⇨ Print Test Page, as shown in Figure 13.7.**

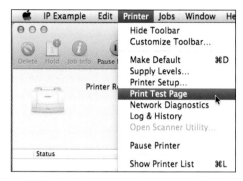

13.7 Print a test page to make sure everything is working properly with your printer.

Note

At some point, you may run across the term *CUPS*. CUPS stands for Common UNIX Printing System, which is the print system utilized by Mac OS X. It has no relation to the containers that hold our liquid refreshment, nor is it referring to protective athletic wear. CUPS controls all aspects of printing in Mac OS X, including creating print queues, creating print jobs using the information provided by the printer driver software, and managing jobs in the print queue.

Printing Documents

Now that you have a printer installed, you can get busy printing those pressing sales figures, your family vacation photos, or that map to Aunt Linda's house.

TextEdit is the application I use to show you how to print documents in Lion. From the Finder, choose Go ⇨ Applications (or press ⌘+Shift+A), and then double-click the TextEdit icon.

TextEdit automatically opens a new blank document when it first starts. Type something interesting in the document and print it.

To print from just about any application in Mac OS X, do one of the following processes:

1. **Choose File ⇨ Page Setup.**

2. **Select the printer in the Format for pop-up menu (see Figure 13.8).**

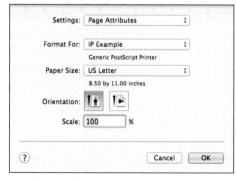

13.8 The standard Page Setup dialog used in most Mac OS X applications.

3. **Choose the paper size on which you want to print in the Paper Size pop-up menu (also shown in Figure 13.8).**

4. **Make adjustments to the Orientation and Scale as you see fit.**

5. **Click OK.**

If the first process doesn't work, try this one:

1. **Choose File ➪ Print, or press ⌘+P.**

2. **The standard Print dialog box opens, as shown in Figure 13.9.**

3. **Click Show Details to expand the Print dialog, as shown in Figure 13.10.**

4. **Change any print options, if necessary.** See the next section for a description of the print options that are available.

5. **Click Print to send your print job to the printer queue, where it is passed on to the printer.**

13.9 This is the standard Mac OS X Print dialog used by most applications.

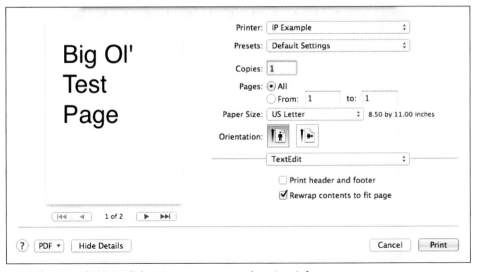

13.10 The expanded Print dialog gives you access to the printer's features.

Genius

Some printers — typically PostScript-capable laser printers — can print certain files (such as PDFs, JPEGs, or TIFFs) directly. To do so, you simply drag and drop the file into the print queue; you don't even have to open the file in an application. Check with your printer manufacturer to see whether yours can handle such a cool task.

Discover the Lion printing options

Lion has many built-in print options that allow you to configure your print jobs in so many ways it can make your head spin. I cover the most popular options in this section.

Note

Some applications, such as QuarkXPress and Adobe InDesign, use their own print dialog. This can really throw you for a loop if you're used to the standard Mac OS X way of doing things. Peruse the application documentation to learn how to navigate the myriad options they provide.

The main sheet of the standard Print dialog offers some bare-bones basics as well as application-specific print settings. Figure 13.10 shows the main sheet of the standard Print dialog when using TextEdit.

Table 13.1 breaks down the basic print options.

Table 13.1 Basic Print Options

Option	Function
Printer	Select a printer from the pop-up menu.
Presets	Choose a preconfigured set of options.
Copies	Enter the number of copies you want to print.
Two-Sided	Select this check box to duplex your print job automatically. This option is only available if you have a duplexer installed on your printer (contact the manufacturer of your printer if you need more information).
Pages	Specify whether you want to print all pages of a document or a specific page range.
Paper Size	Select the size of the paper on which you are printing.
Orientation	You can select Portrait or Landscape.
Options menu	This pop-up menu allows you to select from several option sheets (see Figure 13.11). This menu is typically set to the application-specific settings in the main sheet of the Print dialog. For example, Figure 13.10 shows TextEdit.

To access the other printing options that Mac OS X Lion provides, click the options pop-up menu, as shown in Figure 13.11. Note that some of the options that appear here are specific to the printer you're using.

Tables 13.2 through 13.6 list the other printing options and their functions.

13.11 Choose from several option sheets to customize your Lion printing experience to the max.

Table 13.2 Layout Options

Option	Function
Pages per Sheet	Use this option to print multiple pages of your document on a single side of your paper.
Layout Direction	Choose how the pages are laid out on the page when printing multiple pages per sheet.
Border	Place a border around the individual pages when printing multiple pages per sheet.
Two-Sided	This option is only available if your printer supports a duplexer option, which allows the printer to print on both sides of the sheet.
Reverse Page Orientation	This option causes the job to print out upside down. This is useful if you have paper, such as letterhead, that needs to be printed in a certain direction but you can't place it on the printer in that direction.
Flip horizontally	Anything on the page flips and prints as if being viewed in a mirror.

Table 13.3 Color Matching Options

Option	Function
ColorSync/In Printer	Choosing ColorSync allows Lion to handle color matching, while choosing In Printer lets the printer do all the grunt work.
Profile	This option allows you to associate a color profile with this print job. This option is only available when using the ColorSync option.

Table 13.4 Paper Handling Options

Option	Function
Collate pages	Select this check box to print all pages of the document sequentially before printing the next copy.
Pages to Print	Print all pages, or just odd- or even-numbered pages.
Page Order	Choose from Automatic, Normal, or Reverse page order.

continued

Table 13.4 continued

Option	Function
Scale to fit paper size	Select this check box to scale the page contents to fit the size selected in the Destination Paper Size pop-up menu.
Destination Paper Size	Allows the document to be printed on a different paper size than specified in the Page Setup dialog. This option is only available if the Scale to fit paper size check box is selected.
Scale down only	Select this check box to prevent the items on the page from being scaled larger than they presently are.

Table 13.5 Paper Feed Options

Option	Function
All pages from	Select a paper tray from which to print the job. This option is only useful if your printer supports multiple paper trays.
First page from	Print the first page of a document using a particular paper tray. For example, use this option if you want to print the first page of a job on your company's letterhead, which is in one tray on your printer.
Remaining from	Print the remainder of the print job from the paper tray you select. This option is only available when selecting the First page from option. Continuing the example from the First page from option, select the paper tray on your printer that contains plain paper to finish the rest of your job, as opposed to wasting letterhead.

Table 13.6 Cover Page Options

Option	Function
Print Cover Page	Select either Before document or After document if you want to print a cover page that differentiates your jobs from those of other people using the printer.
Cover Page Type	Select the type of cover page to print. This option is only available if Before document or After document is selected in the Print Cover Page options.
Billing Info	This information is used to identify you if you are being billed for each job you print.

Why and how to create PostScript files

When you first click Print in the Print dialog, Lion immediately creates PDF information for the print job. Sometimes you may need to generate a PostScript file for a certain job, especially if you work in the publishing industry and outsource your printing, or to troubleshoot a printer or printing issue. Because PDF uses a subset of the PostScript language, it's relatively easy for Mac OS X to convert the PDF data generated when you first click Print into a PostScript file. To create a Postscript file, follow these steps:

1. **Choose File ➪ Print in your application's menu.**
2. **Click PDF in the lower-left corner of the Print dialog.**
3. **Select Save as PostScript from the pop-up menu.**
4. **Give the document a name, select a location to save it to, and click Save to generate a PostScript file.**

Assigning ICC profiles to a printer

Having spent many a year in the printing industry, I know that a frequently asked question is how to use ICC profiles with a printer. An ICC profile is a data file that characterizes how a device handles color. ICC profiles may be either generic or specific to a particular device, such as a monitor or printer. Consult the manufacturer of your device to inquire about its support of ICC profiles. These profiles can be assigned to single print jobs using the application that designed the document or to printers on an individual basis. Consult the application documentation to find out how to use ICC profiles with it. Below, I've taken the liberty of showing you how to use the ColorSync Utility to assign profiles to individual printers. Follow these steps:

1. **From the Finder, press ⌘+Shift+U to open the Utilities folder.**
2. **Double-click the ColorSync Utility icon.**
3. **Select Devices from the toolbar at the top of the window.**
4. **Click the arrow next to Printers to expand the list.**
5. **Highlight the printer to which you want to assign the profile, as shown in Figure 13.12.**
6. **Click the arrow to the right of Current Profile and select Other.**
7. **Browse your Mac for the ICC profile you want to use with the device, select it, and then click Open to assign the profile.**
8. **When you print using the printer to which you assigned the profile, turn off any color matching options provided by the manufacturer in the Print dialog to force the printer to use the profile you just created.**

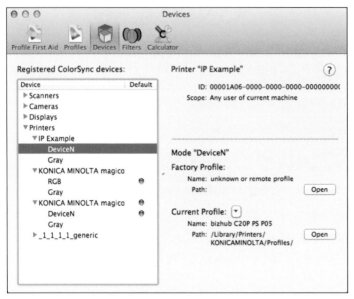

13.12 Assign color profiles to devices using ColorSync Utility.

Using the Sharing System Preferences

Sharing System Preferences is where all the action begins. That's where you go to enable and con-figure sharing of all types. Choose Apple menu ⇨ System Preferences and then click the Sharing icon to open the Sharing preferences window, as shown in Figure 13.13.

First things first — if the Computer Name field is blank at the top of the Sharing pane, type a name for your computer. Other users can see your computer on the network using this name.

Your Mac can share many different items, but some don't demand the same amount of coverage as others. For that reason, Table 13.7 gives a brief overview of each sharing option and the rest of this chapter is devoted to the areas of sharing that need a bit more attention.

Note

Lion uses a network protocol called Bonjour that allows almost effortless networking between devices that are running Bonjour. Bonjour requires no configuration of any kind; devices that are using Bonjour simply see one another on the network. While Bonjour is built in to Lion, you might be pleased to know that Apple has developed Bonjour for Windows as well. See how simple networking can be between Mac OS X and Windows by downloading and installing Bonjour for Windows from http://support.apple.com/kb/DL999.

13.13 This is where you tell Lion how to share with friends.

Table 13.7 Sharing Preferences

Sharing Type	Description
DVD or CD Sharing	Select this option to allow other computers to remotely connect to and use the Mac optical drive. This option is helpful if your computer doesn't have a built-in optical drive (like the MacBook Air, for instance). With this option, you can share the optical drive from another Mac.
Screen Sharing	This feature allows other users to remotely access your Mac and see your screen on their screens. They can also move and open items, such as folders and applications, on your computer.
File Sharing	Select this option to give other users access to folders that you are sharing from your Mac. There's much more about this later on in this chapter.
Printer Sharing	To share printers for which you have created a queue in your Print & Scan preferences, select the Printer Sharing check box. See more on this feature later in this chapter.
Scanner Sharing	Select the check box next to a scanner connected to your Mac to share it with others on your network.
Web Sharing	You can create and store web pages on your Mac. Select the Web Sharing check box to allow others on your network to access those web pages from a web browser on any computer. Your computer's website addresses are displayed once you enable Web Sharing.

continued

323

Table 13.7 continued

Sharing Type	Description
Remote Login	Select this option to let users on other computers remotely access your Mac through a Secure Shell (SSH) in Terminal. Even though you can restrict which users have access, I would not recommend using this option due to security concerns unless you are otherwise directed by someone in your company's IT department.
Remote Management	If you or your network administrators use Apple Remote Desktop to access your computer remotely, you must enable Remote Management. I discuss this option further later in this chapter.
Remote Apple Events	Select this option to allow applications and users on other computers to send Apple Events to your Mac. Apple Events are commands that cause your Mac to perform an action, such as printing or deleting files. I don't recommend using this option unless you know what you're doing and trust other users on your network.
Xgrid Sharing	Select this option if you want to allow an Xgrid server on your network to remotely use your Mac's processing power. Large computing labs use this kind of setup to process gigantic tasks; using the processing power of other computers on the network can greatly help speed up those tasks. Basically, if you don't know what an Xgrid server is, you don't need to enable this option unless told to do so by your IT department.
Internet Sharing	You can share your Mac's Internet connection with other computers through Ethernet, AirPort, or FireWire. This comes in handy if only one Mac has access to the physical Internet connection in your home or office. If you enable this option, you must check which of the afore-mentioned connection types you want to share.
Bluetooth Sharing	Use the Mac Bluetooth connection to communicate with other devices, and then select this check box to share files. I cover more about Bluetooth later in this chapter.

Sharing Files

File sharing is what most people think of when you mention sharing on a computer. Lion lets you decide which folders and volumes to share from your Mac, and who can access those shared items. Select the File Sharing check box to enable it on your Mac (see Figure 13.13).

Adding shared folders and users

The Shared Folders window lists the folders on your hard drive that are set up to share files. To add folders to this list, follow these steps:

1. **Click the plus sign (+) beneath the Shared Folders window.**

2. **Browse your Mac and select the folder you want to share.**

3. **Click Add to begin sharing items in this folder.**

Next, you need to specify which users can access the folders you are sharing. Follow these steps:

1. **Click the plus sign (+) under the Users window.**

2. **Select a group of users from the list in the left pane and then choose the user with whom you want to share the specified folder from the right pane, as shown in Figure 13.14.**

3. **Click Select to add the user to the list of authorized users.**

4. **Choose the user's name in the list and assign permissions to him by clicking in the pop-up menu, as shown in Figure 13.15.**

   - **Read & Write.** This allows the user to modify and delete the files in the shared folder, as well as copy new files into it.

   - **Read Only.** This means the user can only see and open the files being shared in the folder.

   - **Write Only (Drop Box).** This allows users only to copy files into the folder; they can't see or open its contents.

You can remove folders or users by highlighting them and clicking the minus sign (−) under the appropriate window.

13.14 Click the user with whom you want to share your folder.

13.15 Assigning file-sharing permissions for a user.

Enabling file-sharing protocols

Lion is very advanced in its sharing capabilities and can share using multiple protocols. Click Options on the right side of the File Sharing pane to see which protocols are available, as shown in Figure 13.16. Selecting the check box next to the protocols you want to use enables them, allowing you to share items over your network with other users running the same protocols.

Table 13.8 briefly explains the protocols.

☐ Share files and folders using AFP
File Sharing: Off

☑ Share files and folders using SMB (Windows)
When you enable SMB sharing for a user account, you must enter the password for that account. Sharing files with some Windows computers requires storing the Windows user's account password on this computer in a less secure manner.

On	Account
☑	Dwight

⑦   Done

13.16 Select the check boxes next to the protocols you want to use for sharing your files.

Table 13.8 File-sharing Protocols

Protocol	Description
AFP	Apple Filing Protocol. This is an older network protocol that Lion uses for talking to ancient AppleTalk networks.
SMB	Server Message Block (Microsoft Windows Network to former Windows users). This allows Lion to work seamlessly with a Windows-centric network. Select the check boxes next to the accounts you want to enable for SMB sharing. You must type the password for each account you enable.

Sharing Printers and Scanners

When you share a printer from your Mac, you aren't physically sharing it. You're actually sharing the print queue that you created for the printer in the Print & Scan preferences. This means that when you share a printer, the clients who send jobs are sending them to your Mac, not directly to the printer. It's your Mac's responsibility to funnel the job to the printer after it has received it. Select the Printer Sharing check box to enable this feature for Lion, as shown in Figure 13.17.

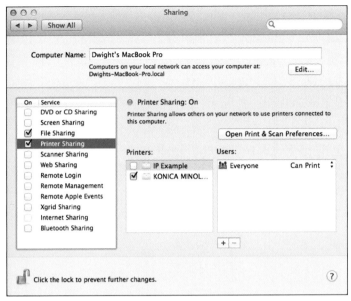

13.17 Share printers you have installed on your Mac using Printer Sharing.

Sharing a printer with Mac OS X users

It's pretty easy to share printers with other Mac OS X users. Simply select the check box next to the printer you want to share in the Printer Sharing pane and the shared printer is then visible to users when they go to add a printer.

Sharing a printer with Windows users

To share any printer on your Mac with other computers running Windows, follow these steps:

1. **Select the check box next to the printer you want to share in the Printer Sharing pane (see Figure 13.17).**

2. **Enable File Sharing by selecting the File Sharing check box in the Service list.**

3. **Click Options in the File Sharing pane.**

4. **Select the Share files and folders using SMB (Windows) check box.**

5. **Choose which accounts can access the printer and type their passwords.**

327

To add the printer to a Windows PC, follow these steps:

1. **Open the Printers control panel in Windows 7 or Windows Vista.** In Windows XP, open the Printers and Faxes control panel.

2. **Click Add Printer and install a network printer.** See the Windows documentation for instructions on installing a network printer if you're unfamiliar with the procedure.

3. **Select the generic PostScript printer driver during the installation, even if the printer isn't a PostScript printer.** Anyone who understands printer drivers is probably slapping his forehead at this point, but here's the cool part: When the PC sends a print job, Lion automatically translates the PostScript code generated by the PC into a code the printer understands. This further proves how awesome Lion is.

Note

A Windows user must be logged in as an Administrator account on the PC in order to install a shared printer.

Sharing scanners

Lion allows you to share scanners that are physically attached to your Mac with other Macs on the network. The Scanner Sharing preferences pane makes this a snap. To do so, select the check box next to Scanner Sharing. Next, find the scanner you want to share in the list and select the check box next to it.

Remote Management

When you first select the Remote Management check box, you are prompted to configure what level of access other users can have to your Mac, as shown in Figure 13.18. The options are self-explanatory.

All local users can access this computer to:

- ☐ Observe
  - ☐ Control
  - ☐ Show when being observed
- ☐ Generate reports
- ☐ Open and quit applications
- ☐ Change settings
- ☐ Delete and replace items
- ☐ Start text chat or send messages
- ☐ Restart and shut down
- ☐ Copy items

[Cancel] [OK]

13.18 Decide what users can do after they access your Mac.

After you enable Remote Management, you can add local users to the access list. Follow these steps:

1. **Click the plus sign (+) under the access list.**

2. **Browse the list of available users, click the user you want, and then click Select.**

3. **Configure the access options for this user as you did when you first enabled Remote Management.** You can change these options at any time by clicking Options.

Sharing Via Bluetooth

The Bluetooth Sharing feature, shown in Figure 13.19, lets you configure how your Mac interacts and shares files with other devices running the Bluetooth protocol.

13.19 Bluetooth Sharing options.

Once again, first things first — you must enable Bluetooth on your Mac in order to share files with other devices running the protocol. If Bluetooth is not already on, follow these steps:

1. **Click Bluetooth Preferences in the Bluetooth Sharing window to open the Bluetooth preferences pane.**

2. **Select the check boxes next to On and Discoverable.**

3. **Click the Back button in the upper-left corner of the Bluetooth pane to go back to the Sharing pane.**

Table 13.9 briefly explains the options in the Bluetooth Sharing pane.

Table 13.9 Bluetooth Sharing Options

Option	Function
When receiving items	Decide how your Mac reacts when another Bluetooth device sends an item to it.
Folder for accepted items	Set the default folder for files received from other devices.
When other devices browse	Determine how your Mac reacts when another Bluetooth device wants to browse your shared folders.
Folder others can browse	Set the default folder on your Mac that users of other Bluetooth devices can browse.

Note

You must pair a device with your Mac in order to exchange files with it.

Using Bluetooth File Exchange

Bluetooth File Exchange is the utility you use to browse and exchange files with other Bluetooth devices. Open Bluetooth File Exchange by pressing ⌘+Option+U in the Finder, and then double-click the Bluetooth File Exchange icon.

Send a file from your Mac

To send a file from your Mac to another Bluetooth device, follow these steps:

1. **Choose File ⇨ Send File, or press ⌘+O.**

2. **Browse your Mac for the file you want to send, highlight it, and then click Send.**

3. **Select the device to which you want to send the file from the list in the Send File window (see Figure 13.20) and click Send.**

4. **The receiving device may prompt you to allow the incoming traffic from your Mac.** The transfer is complete once the receiving device has received all the data from your Mac.

13.20 Select the device to which you want to send a file.

Browse another Bluetooth device

You can browse another Bluetooth device to find files you want to copy, or to send files from your Mac to a specific location on that device. Follow these steps:

1. **Choose File ⇨ Browse Device, or press ⌘+Shift+O.**

2. **Select the device you want to browse from the Browse Files list and click Browse.**

3. **Browse the folders on the device from within the Browsing window, as shown in Figure 13.21.**

4. **If you are sending a file, open the folder on the device in which you want to place the file, and then click Send.** Browse your Mac for the file you want to send, select it, and click Send.

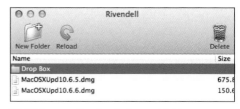

13.21 Browse the directories and folders on another Bluetooth device from your Mac.

5. **If you want to get a file from the device, find and select it, and then click Get.** Name the file, choose where to save it, and then click Save.

6. **You may also delete a file from the remote Bluetooth device by highlighting it and clicking Delete in the upper-right corner of the Browsing window.**

How Can I Automate My Mac?

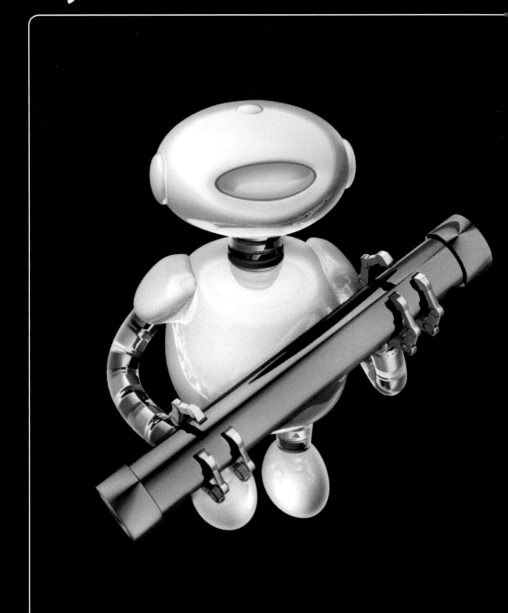

What if your Mac could perform routine (and possibly mundane) tasks for you automatically? Sounds pretty tempting, no? Lion is fully equipped to make your Mac life more enjoyable with a handy application called Automator. Automator uses actions (or steps) to create workflows that you can run any time to complete repetitive tasks quickly and easily. Services and AppleScripts can automate repetitive steps even further. Another way Lion can help with your Mac housework is with Time Machine, the Mac OS X backup utility. Time Machine literally takes you back in time to retrieve lost data.

Getting Around in Automator

It's most helpful to know your way around Automator before trying to create workflows and actions. Open Automator by pressing ⌘+Shift+A in the Finder and then double-clicking the Automator icon. After Automator opens, make a selection in the Choose a type for your document window, as shown in Figure 14.1.

Choose a type for your document:

Workflow   Application   Service   Print Plugin

Folder Action   iCal Alarm   Image Capture Plugin

Workflow

Workflows can be run from within Automator.

Open an Existing Document...   Close   Choose

14.1 Select an item from the list to move into the main Automator window.

For this example, select Workflow and click Choose. You are now in the main Automator window. Figure 14.2 points out the most important features in Automator.

Table 14.1 gives a brief description of each Automator feature.

Library column

Media Browser   Action column

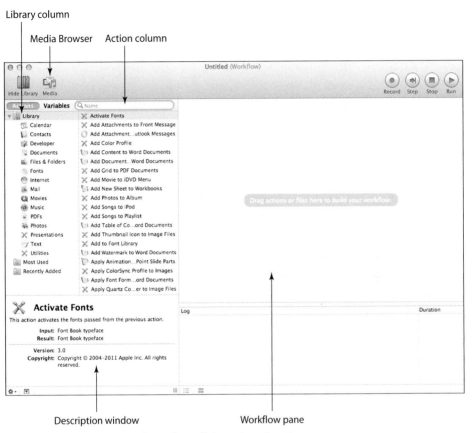

Description window   Workflow pane

14.2 The main Automator window, where all the action takes place.

Table 14.1 The Main Automator Window

Item	Description
Library column	Lists the available applications and other items from which you can choose actions.
Action column	Lists the available actions for each application or item in the Library column.
Workflow pane	Allows you to arrange actions in the order they are to be performed.
Description window	Displays a brief explanation of the selected action.
Media Browser	Lets you browse your Mac for audio, photos, or videos that you may want to include in your workflows.

Using Workflows

Workflows are groups of actions that are combined to help you accomplish a task. When you run a workflow, the actions in it are carried out in sequential order until the last action has been performed. The results, or output, of the first action become the input for the next action, and so on, until the workflow is completed.

Designing a workflow

Building a workflow from scratch is much simpler than you may think. To help you get started with Automator, I've created a new workflow and walk you through its creation step by step. First, here's what I want to do with my new workflow:

- **I want to rename images that I've saved from my camera to a folder on my desktop called New Pics using Image Capture.** My camera automatically adds IMG to the beginning of every file and then numbers them sequentially. I want to name the files a little more descriptively and Automator is the perfect tool to accomplish this task.

- **Once renamed, I want to open my files in Preview so that I can check them out.**

- **I want my images to automatically print so that I can have a hard copy of each.**

- **I want to e-mail my new pictures to friends and family.**

As I mentioned, my camera automatically saves files with an IMG prefix, so that's the convention I use in this short tutorial. You may want to adjust the variable in Step 3 of the following list to match the default naming conventions of your camera.

Follow these steps to begin building the workflow:

1. **Tell Automator which files you want.** Select Files & Folders from the Library column, and then drag and drop Find Finder Items into the Workflow pane, as shown in Figure 14.3.

2. **Choose Other from the Search drop-down menu and select Desktop on the left side of the resulting window.** Click New Folder, name the folder New Pics, click Create, and then click Choose.

3. **In the criteria section, leave the All pop-up menu alone, change the Any content pop-up menu to Name, leave the contains pop-up menu alone, and finally type IMG in the text field.** This tells Automator that you are looking for files with names that start with IMG.

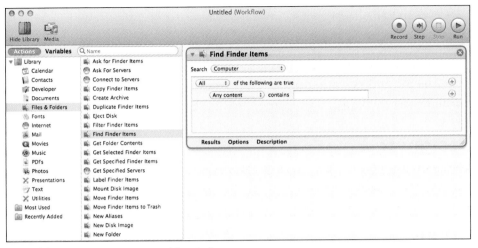

14.3 Adding actions to my new workflow in Automator.

4. **Tell Automator that you want to rename the items in the New Pics folder.** Select Files & Folders from the Library column, and then drag and drop Rename Finder Items into the Workflow pane beneath the Find Finder Items action. A caution window appears; click Don't Add to proceed.

5. **Choose Make Sequential from the first drop-down menu, select the new name radio button in the Add number to option, and type the name with which you want to begin each of your files in the text field.** I use dwightpix at the beginning of my picture files, as shown in Figure 14.4. This action causes Automator to replace the prefix IMG on all files with dwightpix, followed by a sequential number. However, I'm not quite finished renaming.

6. **Add the date the files were imported to my Mac to the end of the filenames.** Select Files & Folders from the Library column, and then drag and drop Rename Finder Items into the Workflow pane beneath the previous Rename Finder Items action. Click Don't Add to proceed as before. The default criteria, as shown in Figure 14.4, are appropriate for the needs of this example, so nothing needs to be changed.

7. **I want my renamed images to open in Preview so that I can see how they look.** Select Photos from the Library column, and then drag and drop Open Images in Preview to the Workflow pane beneath the second Rename Finder Items action. This causes Automator to start Preview (if it's not already running) and automatically display the new images.

339

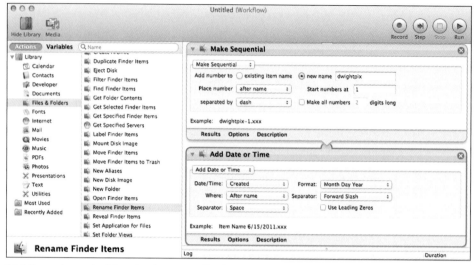

14.4 Renaming and adding the date to my files in Automator.

Note You may notice as you drag new actions into the Workflow pane that those already there move down a bit until the one you are dragging is beneath them. You can easily reposition actions in a workflow by simply dragging and dropping them into the order you need.

8. **Have Automator print hard copies of the photos automatically.** Select Photos from the Library column, and then drag and drop Print Images to the Workflow pane beneath the Open Images in Preview action. Make any additional adjustments that you deem necessary; for example, I chose to center and scale my images to fit the page, as shown in Figure 14.5.

9. **Have Automator open Mail and create a new message, automatically attaching the new images so that all you have to do is type the recipients' addresses and click Send.** Select Mail from the Library column, and then drag and drop New Mail Message to the Workflow pane beneath the Print Images action. Type any items that you want automatically added to your new e-mail, such as the e-mail address or a subject, as shown in Figure 14.5.

10. **Click Run (see Figure 14.4) in the upper-right corner to run the workflow.** Automator performs the actions and warns you if there are any problems.

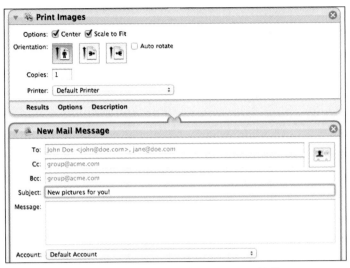

14.5 Automator automatically prints and creates a new Mail message containing the new images.

Saving a workflow

You will certainly want to save your workflows so that you don't have to create them every time you need them — that kind of defeats the purpose of Automator. You can save your workflows as workflows, applications, or plug-ins. Table 14.2 gives a brief explanation of each.

Table 14.2 Different Ways to Save Your Workflows

Save As	Description
Workflow	Saves the actions you brought together as a workflow. You can then open it in Automator to run or edit it.
Application	Saving a workflow as an application makes it a stand-alone file. Double-click to launch it as you would any other application.
Services menu, Script menu, Print Workflow, Folder Action, iCal Alarm, Image Capture	Your workflow is saved as an application-specific plug-in that the application (such as Finder, iCal, or Image Capture) can use to automatically perform tasks.

To save your workflow as a new workflow, an application, or a plug-in type, follow these steps:

1. **Press ⌘+S.**

2. **Give the workflow a descriptive name and choose where to save it.**

341

3. **Select a format from the File Format pop-up menu.**

4. **Click Save.**

To save an existing workflow that you are modifying, press ⌘+S.

Recording Your Actions

The coolest feature in Automator for Lion is the ability to create custom actions based on your keyboard and mouse events. Automator can record your keyboard and mouse events and execute them as part of a workflow.

Genius Scripters who write their own AppleScripts or developers who create their own applications will be delighted to know that they can develop their own actions specific to their needs. Xcode, which is an API (application programming interface) distributed by Apple with Lion, provides all the tools necessary for programmers to make unique actions.

To record your actions, you must enable access for assistive devices in the Universal Access preferences. To do so, choose Apple menu ⇨ System Preferences, select Universal Access, and then select the Enable access for assistive devices option at the bottom of the window.

Note Before you start recording, make sure that your Mac is set up exactly the way it needs to be to perform the necessary actions. For example, if you are using an application as part of your action, you want to have it open before beginning to record.

To get started on your custom action, follow these steps:

1. **Open a workflow and click Record in the upper-right corner.**

2. **Perform the steps necessary to complete your action.**

3. **Click the Stop button, shown in Figure 14.6, when you are finished.**

4. **Click Run to test your new actions.**

5. **Edit actions in the list by deleting unnecessary actions, changing the timeout setting for each action, or modifying the Playback Speed.**

6. **Save your action as a workflow, application, or plug-in.**

14.6 Automator records your actions until you click the Stop button.

Using Services to Perform Tasks

Services are yet another way that Mac OS X can automate tasks and make your computing life easier. Essentially, services are Automator workflows available for you to use, depending on the type of file or item you have selected in the Finder or in an application. For example, if you right-click (or Control+click) a JPEG image in the Finder, you see services related to JPEGs at the bottom of the contextual pop-up menu, such as Set Desktop Picture or New Email with Attachment. Another example would be highlighting text in Safari; right-click (or Control+click) the highlighted text and you can select the Add to iTunes as a Spoken Track service.

To see all of the preconfigured services at your disposal in Lion, open the System Preferences by choosing Apple menu ⇨ System Preferences. Select Keyboard from the Hardware section of the System Preferences window and then click Services under the Keyboard Shortcuts tab, as shown in Figure 14.7.

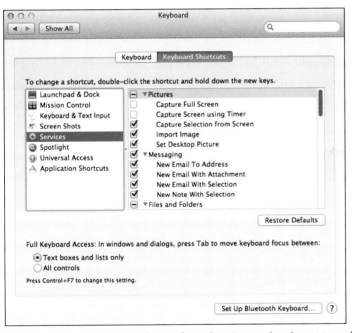

14.7 Lion has an extensive list of preconfigured services ready to be put to work.

Scrolling through the list of services you are sure to notice that they are divided into types, such as services dedicated to pictures or text. You can enable or disable a service (that is, make it available or unavailable for a particular type of file or item) by selecting the check box next to it in the list.

Table 14.3 lists the preconfigured services built in to Lion. You may see other services if the application you are using provides them.

Table 14.3 Lion Preconfigured Services

Service Type	Function
Pictures	Capture Full Screen.
	Capture Screen using Timer.
	Capture Selection from Screen.
	Import Image.
	Set Desktop Picture.
Internet	Open URL.
Files and Folders	Open Selected File in TextEdit.
	New Terminal at Folder.
	New Terminal Tab at Folder.
	Encode Selected Video Files.
	Folder Actions Setup.
	Open.
	Reveal.
	Show Info.
	Send File to Bluetooth Device. Keyboard shortcut: ⌘+Shift+B.
Messaging	New Email to Address.
	New Email With Attachment.
	New Email With Selection.
	New Note With Selection.
Searching	Look Up in Dictionary.
	Search With %WebSearchProvider@ (uses the Safari default search engine). Keyboard shortcut: ⌘+Shift+L.
	Spotlight. Keyboard shortcut: ⌘+Shift+F.
Text	Add to iTunes as a Spoken Track.
	Convert Selected Simplified Chinese Text.
	Convert Selected Traditional Chinese Text.
	Convert Collection From Text.
	Create Font Library From Text.
	Make New Sticky Note. Keyboard shortcut: ⌘+Shift+K.
	New TextEdit Window Containing Selection.
	Open main Page in Terminal. Keyboard shortcut: ⌘+Shift+M.
	Search main Pages in Terminal. Keyboard shortcut: ⌘+Shift+A.
	Show Address in Google Maps.
	Summarize.

Service Type	Function
Development	Compare Files.
	Compare To Master.
	Create Service.
	Create Workflow.
	Get Result of AppleScript. Keyboard shortcut: ⌘+*.
	Make New AppleScript.
	Run as AppleScript.

Genius

You can create and edit shortcuts for services. Select Services in the Keyboard Shortcuts tab of the Keyboard preferences pane. Click to highlight the service for which you want to create or edit a shortcut, and then click to the right of the highlighted area to see a text field. Type the new shortcut (or edit the existing one) and it appears in the text field. Click out of the text field and close System Preferences.

Discovering Time Machine

One of the Lion features that Apple is most proud of — and rightly so — is Time Machine. Oh, there have been backup utilities out there made by third-party companies (even a few good ones), but Apple has delivered something above and beyond in terms of simplicity and information retrieval.

Time Machine backs up your system behind the scenes — you can work while it handles its business undetected in the background. The initial backup takes quite a while, as Time Machine backs up everything on the Mac hard drive (again, it all happens in the background, so you can continue to use your Mac). After the initial backup, Time Machine continues to automatically back up your files every hour, but only those items that have changed. Because it is only backing up changed items, these backups are performed much faster.

Why it's important to back up your files

I want to take a small section of this chapter to preach the doctrine of backing up your computer. You have too many precious memories and too many important documents on your Mac to count on it lasting forever (yes, even Macs do eventually have issues, as I cover in Chapter 16). Take a few minutes out of your iLife and, perhaps, spend a few dollars on an external hard drive, to get Time Machine up and going. Backing up your data is something you never regret.

The Apple Time Capsule

The Apple Time Capsule acts as both a wireless network router (like AirPort), and a central backup point for all Macs running Lion and Time Machine. The Time Capsule automatically backs up every file from every Mac wirelessly and in the background, eliminating the need to connect an external drive to your Mac. This is one serious backup tool, and I highly recommend getting your hands on one. Check it out by visiting www.apple.com/timecapsule/.

Hardware requirements for Time Machine

Time Machine can back up your data to any of these four configurations:

- **A network volume, such as a file or backup server.** This is a good idea for large networks.

- **An external hard drive.** This is my recommendation. Be certain that the data capacity of the external drive is large enough to save all the data on the hard drive.

- **A USB flash drive.** Be sure the data capacity of the flash drive is large enough to save all of your backup data.

- **A partition on the Mac hard drive (if the drive is, indeed, partitioned).** Partitioning a drive is the act of using a disk utility to divide a single hard drive into several sections, fooling the computer into believing that one drive is actually multiple drives. I do not recommend using this sort of configuration because if your hard drive has a problem, you lose all of your data in spite of having backed it up.

Setting Up a Backup Drive

There are a couple of steps necessary to get started with Time Machine: You need to format your backup drive, and then you need to tell Time Machine that it can use this drive for its backups.

Formatting a hard drive

You must format any drive you connect to your Mac before you can use it with Time Machine. To format a drive (see the Caution before continuing this procedure), follow these steps:

1. **From within the Finder, open Disk Utility by pressing ⌘+Shift+U, and then double-clicking its icon.**

2. **Connect the drive to your Mac.**

3. **Select the drive in the list on the left of the Disk Utility window.**

4. **Click the Erase tab near the top of the window, as shown in Figure 14.8.**

Caution

If this is a drive you've used before, be sure that you copy all the data from it before performing a drive format. Once the formatting process has started, all data on the drive is lost forever.

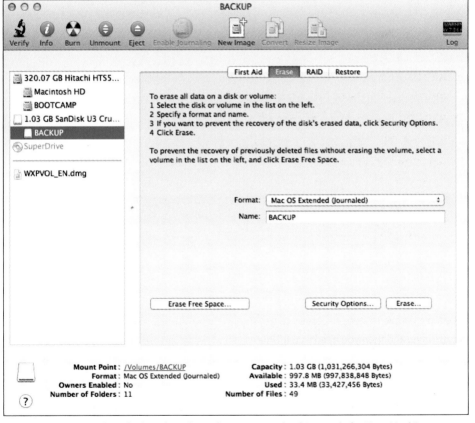

14.8 Click the Erase tab and select the volume format to get the drive ready for Time Machine.

347

5. **Set the Format option to Mac OS Extended (Journaled).**

6. **Click Erase, and then click it again in the verification window.**

7. **Once the formatting is finished, click Eject in the Disk Utility toolbar at the top, and disconnect the hard drive from the Mac.**

Configuring a backup drive for Time Machine

When you first connect an external drive (you may have to format it first) to your Mac, Time Machine detects its presence and asks if you want to use it for backups. If you say yes, Time Machine sets everything up automatically, and away you go. In most cases, this is fine; you are never bothered about it again and Time Machine does its duty.

You may be asking why you would say no to the question, if that were the case. Well, if this is a drive you've used in the past or one that you want to partition, you may not want Time Machine hijacking it for its sole use. To manually set up a drive, follow these steps:

1. **Open the Time Machine preferences (shown in Figure 14.9) by choosing Apple menu ⇨ System Preferences, and then clicking the Time Machine icon.**

2. **Click Select Disk.**

3. **Choose a drive and click Use Backup Disk.**

14.9 The Time Machine preferences allow you to manually configure how it works.

4. **Time Machine begins a countdown, similar to the one shown in Figure 14.10, for when it will perform the first backup.**

5. **If you want Time Machine to automatically begin backing up everything on the system, just sit back and relax.** However, if you want to back up only a portion of the hard drive, click the On/Off switch on the left side of the Time Machine preferences pane to toggle the switch to Off. Next, follow the directions in the next section.

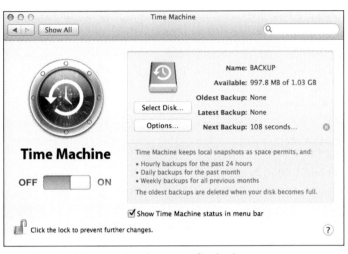

14.10 Time Machine counting down to its first backup.

Excluding files from a backup

There may be several good reasons why you don't want Time Machine to back up every file on your Mac. For example, perhaps there isn't enough storage space on the backup drive or you simply don't want to back up all the information for each user on the computer. Whatever the reason, you need not fear because I'm about to show you how to exclude information from your backup sessions. Follow these steps:

1. **Be sure Time Machine is Off so that it doesn't begin a backup process while you choose the files you don't want to back up.** Simply click the On/Off switch to toggle it.

2. **Click Options in the middle of the preferences pane.**

3. **Click the plus sign (+) in the lower-left corner of the Exclude these items from back-ups window.**

4. **Browse your Mac to select the folders and files you do not want included in the backup, and then click Exclude to add them to the list, as shown in Figure 14.11.**
Refer to the Estimated size of full backup (mine is being calculated in Figure 14.11) to see if your backup drive can store that much data. Click Save when finished.

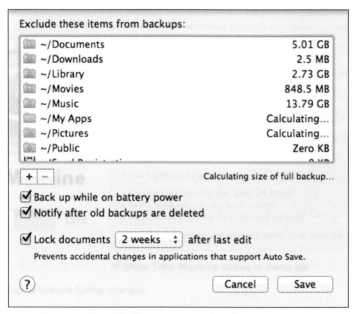

14.11 You can exclude files from a Time Machine backup.

Running a Backup

As mentioned, the entire backup process is handled behind the scenes, but that doesn't mean you can't check out what's going on, or even stop and restart a backup that's already in the works. Open the Time Machine preferences pane to see the progress of a backup procedure.

Performing a manual backup

You don't have to wait for Time Machine to get around to backing up your system. In fact, you can start the process right now if you want. Follow these steps:

1. **Choose Apple menu ➪ System Preferences and click the Time Machine icon.**

2. **Select the Show Time Machine status in menu bar check box.**

Caution When you manually select files to back up, the preference files and other items necessary for Time Machine to completely restore your Mac should it fail may not be included in the process.

3. **Be sure Time Machine is On.** Toggle the On/Off switch, if necessary.

4. **Click the Time Machine icon in the menu bar.**

5. **Select Back Up Now, as shown in Figure 14.12.**

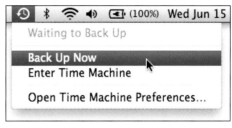

14.12 Select Back Up Now to back up your information immediately.

Pausing or resuming a backup

You can stop and start a backup if you need to. To pause a backup, click the Time Machine icon in the menu bar (see Figure 14.12), and then select Stop Backing Up. To resume a backup process, click the Time Machine icon in the menu bar, and then select Back Up Now. Your backup should begin where it left off. Nothing to it!

Retrieving Information from Time Machine

Now that you know how to back up your system, it's time to learn how to retrieve that information should you ever need to do so. Let's see how to restore individual items and even an entire drive.

Restoring individual files

Time Machine lets you restore individual files and folders that you may have lost or of which you want to get previous versions. To do so, follow these steps:

1. **Open Time Machine by clicking its icon in the Dock or press ⌘+Shift+A, and then double-click its icon in the Applications folder.**

2. **Time Machine opens and you see a Finder window, similar to the one shown in Figure 14.13.**

3. **Use the timeline on the right side of the screen (or the arrows next to it) to navigate through time to the date the item you need was backed up.**

14.13 Traveling through time!

4. **Browse the files in the Finder window to find the item you want to retrieve.**

5. **Select the item in the Finder window and then click Restore in the bottom-right corner of the Time Machine window.** The file is zipped forward in time to today and Time Machine closes. You have to admit, that's one of the coolest things you've ever seen on a computer!

Restoring an entire drive

Time Machine lets you restore an entire drive which, on its own, is worth the price of upgrading to Lion. This saves you countless hours because you don't have to reinstall the OS or all of the applications you had on your system. To restore a drive, follow these steps:

1. **Connect your backup drive to the Mac.**

2. **Choose Apple menu ⇨ Restart, and then press and hold ⌘+R while your Mac restarts.**

3. **Select your language from the Language Chooser and click Continue (the arrow).**

4. **Perform one of the following depending on the type of backup drive from which you are restoring your system:**

    - **If backing up from an external drive (hard drive, USB flash, and so on), select it and click Continue.**

    - **If backing up from a network drive, select it and click Connect to Remote Disk.**

    - **If backing up from a Time Capsule, select your AirPort network using the AirPort menu on the menu bar, select your Time Capsule, and then click Connect to Remote Disk.**

5. **Type your name and password to connect to your backup drive if required, and then click Connect.**

6. **Choose the date and time for the backup you want to restore and follow the instructions from that point to finish the restoration process.** This can take a while, but not nearly as long as starting from scratch.

Delete Files from Time Machine Backups

What if you want to delete a file from your backed-up folders, instead of restore it? Simple! Just follow these steps:

1. **Open Time Machine.** Use the Finder window and timeline to find the item you want to delete from the backup.

2. **Select the file or folder you want to delete.**

3. **Click the Action menu (which looks like a gear) in the Finder toolbar and select Delete Backup.** To get rid of all references to the item in Time Machine, select Delete All Backups.

How Do I Install Windows 7 on My Mac?

Now that newer Macs come equipped with Intel processors, you can install Windows on your Mac just as you would on any other Intel-based PC. If you're switching from a Windows computer to the wonderful world of Mac, having Windows installed can make the transition a little smoother. However, if you are anything like the Windows converts I know, you will find yourself booting up into Windows less and less as you become more familiar with Lion.

Understanding the Boot Camp Assistant

Boot Camp is a tool provided with Lion that helps walk you through the process of installing Microsoft Windows on your Mac. It is a very simple utility but one that performs some very big jobs, such as:

- **Partitioning your hard drive.**
- **Booting from the Windows installation disc.**
- **Installing drivers in Windows that you need in order to use hardware that comes with Macs, such as the built-in camera (if you have one).**

Benefits of installing Microsoft Windows

If you're a longtime Mac fan, you may be dubious about the title of this section, but former Windows users probably understand the upside of having Windows at their fingertips. Here are a few of the most obvious benefits:

- **Some companies use software that only runs in Windows.** If you work for one of those companies but are one of the smart folks who insist on having a Mac, you can have the best of both worlds.

- **Windows converts probably have a lot of Windows-only software — including games — that they don't want to trash because they now have a Mac.** Boot Camp enables them to keep their software.

- **On increasingly rare occasions, you may run across a website that only works with a Windows operating system.** Those sites are no longer off limits to Mac users.

- **Some new Mac users may have printers that work only with Windows (this is also becoming increasingly rare).** Installing Windows ensures that they won't have to chuck the printer, which can be pretty painful if you have a stockpile of consumables (such as toner and ink) tied up in the device.

What you need to install Windows

Here are the requirements that must be met before installing Windows on your Mac:

- **At least 16GB of available space on the hard drive for 32-bit versions of Windows 7, and at least 20GB for the 64-bit version.**

Note

You must install the 32-bit version of Windows 7 unless you have a Mac Pro or MacBook Pro introduced in early 2008 or later, in which case you can install the 64-bit version.

- **Your Mac must have an Intel processor at least as fast as 1GHz, which is a foregone conclusion because you're running Lion.**

- **You must install all available firmware updates for your Mac.** Run Software Update (choose Apple menu ⇨ Software Update) or go to the Apple support website for your particular model to find any updates for your computer.

- **A Mac OS X Lion installation disc, a blank CD or DVD, or an external hard drive.** You must **use one of these** to install Windows support software.

- **At least 1GB of memory, which is also a foregone conclusion because you're running Lion.**

- **A Windows installation disc.** You can install Windows 7 Home Premium, Professional, or Ultimate.

Genius

To install Windows XP, the installation disc must contain Service Pack 2. If the disc doesn't include Service Pack 2, search Google for "slipstream Windows XP Service Pack 2 disc" to find several sites with instructions for creating a bootable installation CD that does include Service Pack 2.

Using the Boot Camp Assistant to Install Windows

Open the Boot Camp Assistant to get started:

1. **From within the Finder, press ⌘+Shift+U to open the Utilities folder.**

2. **Double-click the icon for Boot Camp Assistant to see a window like the one shown in Figure 15.1.**

3. **Click Print Installation & Setup Guide to do just that (assuming you have a printer).** This guide is necessary, so you need to either print it or gain access to it on another computer.

4. **Click Continue.**

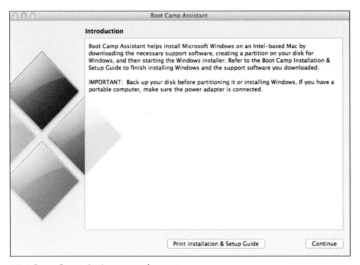

15.1 Boot Camp Assistant ready to go.

Caution Printing the Boot Camp Installation & Setup Guide is necessary in order to continue with this chapter. It is 12 pages long and chock-full of information that you must have before continuing. If you can't print it, run or view it from the Apple support website on another computer (www.apple.com/support/bootcamp/).

Downloading the Windows support software

Your Windows installation requires special drivers provided by Apple in order for Windows to use Mac hardware, such as the trackpad, mouse, and display. Your Mac OS X Lion installation disc contains these drivers. If you don't have the disc handy, Boot Camp allows you to download the drivers, as shown in Figure 15.2. You can then either save them to an external hard drive or burn them to a CD or DVD by following these steps:

1. **Select the Download the Windows support software for this Mac radio button and click Continue.**

2. **Boot Camp contacts Apple via the Internet and downloads the software.** This may take quite some time, depending on the speed of your Internet connection.

3. **Once the support software is downloaded, decide whether to burn it to a disc or save it to an external hard drive.** Click Continue to move to the next step.

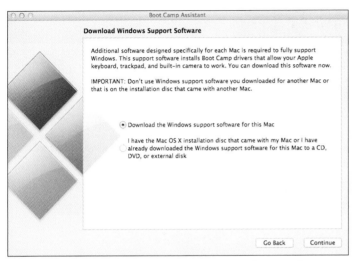

15.2 You must download special drivers for your Windows installation to successfully utilize Mac hardware.

Partitioning the hard drive

Boot Camp Assistant now wants to help you partition the Mac hard drive. Partitioning the hard drive essentially marks off a section of it and fools Lion into thinking your Mac has two hard drives instead of one. This partition is used exclusively for Windows, so keep this in mind when deciding how much space to allocate to it because you cannot recover that space for Mac usage.

Note If you previously partitioned the Mac hard drive, you may see a window asking if you want to create or remove a Windows partition, or start the Windows installer. To install Windows, choose to start the Windows installer and click Continue.

At this point, you need to decide how much of the Mac hard drive to allocate to Windows. There is no set number that I can recommend to you for the size; it depends entirely on your needs. Keep in mind that you also need additional space to install applications and store files. To divide the drive, click and drag the little dot between the Mac OS X and Windows boxes to the left or right to increase or decrease the size for each partition.

If you have a lot of Windows applications that you plan to install, it might be best to click Divide Equally. This gives half of the hard drive to Windows.

Follow these steps:

1. **Set the size of your Windows partition and click Partition.** Boot Camp Assistant checks the hard drive for any potential problems and then continues the process.

2. **Insert the Windows 7 installation disc when prompted by Boot Camp Assistant.**

3. **Click Start Installation, as shown in Figure 15.3.**

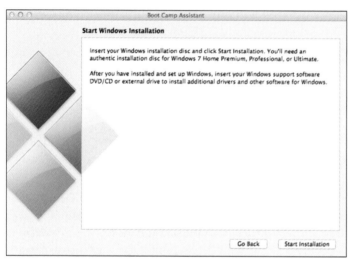

15.3 Click Start Installation to begin installing Windows.

Caution

If you mistakenly select the wrong partition on which to install Windows, you could potentially wipe out your Mac OS X Lion installation during the steps in the next section. Be careful, particularly in Step 2, or you may run into more problems than you bargained for.

Installing Windows

By now, your Mac should have booted into the Windows 7 installer disc, which is where I pick up:

1. **Follow the instructions on your computer for installing Windows.** Be sure to follow along with the Boot Camp Installation & Setup Guide you printed earlier.

2. **At a certain point, you are asked on which partition to install Windows.** Be certain to choose the one labeled BOOTCAMP! This is the key to your success or failure.

Note If you are using a MacBook Air, you need to install Windows and the Boot Camp drivers using a compatible external drive connected directly to your computer.

3. **Click the Drive options (advanced) on the lower-right side of the window to reformat the Boot Camp partition.**

4. **Click Format and then click OK. Click Next and the Boot Camp partition is correctly formatted.**

5. **Continue through the on-screen prompts.** Once Windows is installed, your Mac reboots into Windows 7.

Note If you are prompted by a message saying the software hasn't passed Windows Logo testing, click Continue Anyway.

6. **Eject the Windows installation disc by choosing the Start menu in the bottom-left corner and selecting Computer.** Click to highlight the drive containing the Windows installation disc, and then click the Eject option in the menu near the top of the window.

7. **Insert either your Mac OS X Lion installer disc or the disc (or external hard drive) on which you saved your Windows support software.** The Boot Camp installer program runs. Follow the instructions on your screen and never cancel any part of the installation! Remember to read the guide. Your Mac restarts when the installation is completed and you have finished your Windows installation process.

Note When you first boot your Mac into Windows following the Boot Camp installation, you see the Boot Camp Help window. Use this resource! It has invaluable information on how to use your Mac and its hardware, such as the keyboard, with Windows software. There are some differences when using a Mac compared to using PC hardware, but nothing that you can't easily overcome by reading through a Help window.

Choosing a Start-up Disk

Now that you have a Mac with two operating systems, you need to decide which one will be its default: Lion or Windows? You can easily select either of the two disks to be your default start-up disk, and you can just as easily switch between the two.

From Windows

To select a start-up disk from within Windows, follow these steps:

1. **Click the Start menu and select Control Panel.**

2. **Change the View by option to Large icons to see all the control panels that are installed.**

3. **Double-click the Boot Camp icon.**

4. **Under the Startup Disk tab shown in Figure 15.4, select the operating system to which you want to boot by default, and then click OK.** Click Restart if you want to reboot right now.

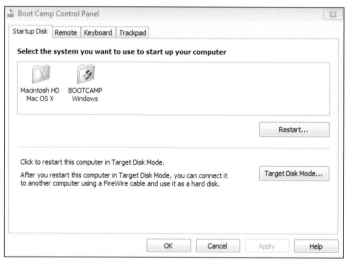

15.4 The Boot Camp Control Panel in Windows.

From Lion

To select a start-up disk from within Lion, follow these steps:

1. **Choose Apple menu ⇨ System Preferences.**

2. **Click the Startup Disk icon.**

3. **Select the operating system that you want to be your default from the list, as shown in Figure 15.5.** Close the System Preferences unless you want to reboot the Mac now, in which case click Restart.

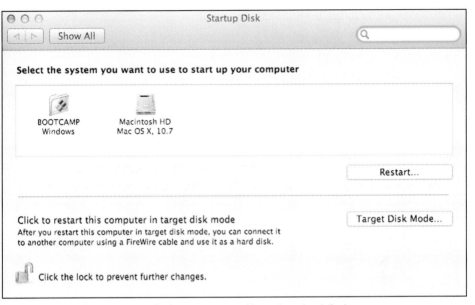

15.5 Select the disk partition to which you want your Mac to boot by default.

Removing Windows from Your Mac

If you get tired of Microsoft's operating system taking up a large chunk of your hard drive, you may want to safely remove it. Easy enough:

1. **Open the Boot Camp Assistant by pressing ⌘+Shift+U from within the Finder and double-clicking its icon.**

2. **Click Continue.**

3. **Select the I have the Mac OS X installation disc radio button, and then click Continue.**

4. **Select the Create or remove a Windows partition option, and then click Continue.**

Caution   When you wipe out your Windows partition, all of your Windows content is permanently lost. If you have important files or documents on the Windows side, back these up before restoring the Mac hard drive.

5. **Click Restore, as shown in Figure 15.6, to completely wipe out your Windows partition and restore the Mac hard drive to a single partition.**

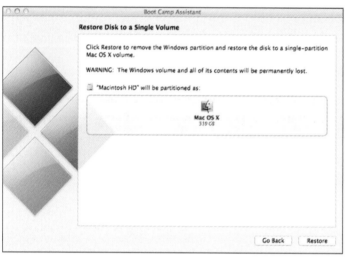

15.6 Easily restore your hard drive to a single partition.

Alternative Methods for Running Windows on Your Mac

You may be happy to know there is another way to install and run Windows (and other operating systems) on your Mac that doesn't require partitioning a section of the hard drive. My biggest beef with the Boot Camp method is that the partition you create for Windows has a fixed size — it doesn't increase or decrease, which can waste a lot of space if you don't use all of the partition. On the other hand, it may not be large enough to contain all of your data. My second beef is that I'm limited to installing Windows and not alternative operating systems like Linux. Thankfully for folks like me, there is another way: virtualization.

Virtualization is a method that allows you to install multiple Intel-capable operating systems on your Mac at the same time (as many as your hard or external drive can hold) and run them simultaneously within Mac OS X. There are several software packages out there that can help you achieve this dream, some of which I mention here. These applications help you create virtual machines on which you can install operating systems. These virtual machines access the computer hardware and run at almost native speeds. Another great upside to virtual machines is that they can be made to expand or contract based on the amount of data they contain, which prevents you from wasting hard drive space.

Note

I do not endorse any one of the upcoming software titles over another. All three have their pros and cons, and one may suit me better than it suits you. The two titles that you have to buy offer free trials you can download. The third option is free, so there's no reason not to give each one a go and determine which you like best.

Parallels Desktop for Mac

Parallels Desktop for Mac from Parallels was the first viable virtualization option for Macs with Intel processors. The latest release (as of this writing), version 6, introduced many new and powerful features, such as improved battery life for laptops, faster start-up and shutdown for Windows, better compatibility for Linux systems, and up to 80 percent better 3-D performance. All of this allows you to simultaneously run multiple virtual machines even more efficiently than before, as shown in Figure 15.7.

15.7 Parallels Desktop for Mac in action.

For more information or to download a trial copy of Parallels Desktop for Mac, visit www.parallels.com/products/desktop.

VMWare Fusion

VMWare Fusion, shown in Figure 15.8, is the brainchild of VMWare, one of the most trusted virtualization applications in the PC and Linux markets for years. In 2007, VMWare decided it was time to apply its knowledge of virtualization to the Mac platform and a wonderful competition (from the consumer's standpoint) began with Parallels. This resulted in both companies trying to outdo each other by making great leaps in software capabilities. This competition caused VMWare to gain a significant chunk of ground technology-wise between versions 1 and 2, and to go even further with version 3 (the latest version as of this writing).

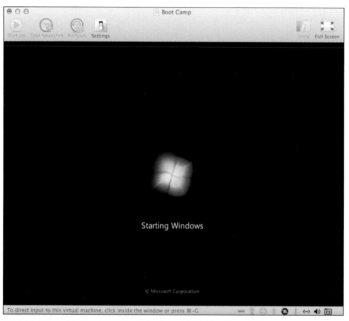

15.8 VMWare Fusion booting Windows 7 within Mac OS X.

Features such as Unity View (the ability to run Windows programs as if they were native Mac applications) and Data Sharing (you can drag and drop files between operating system windows) make VMWare a viable option for anyone who needs to run multiple operating systems on her Mac. To learn more about VMWare Fusion or to download a trial copy, visit http://vmware.com/products/fusion.

VirtualBox

If you want to use Parallels Desktop for Mac or VMWare Fusion, you have to shell out some cash. Don't have any to spare? Don't worry; you're not completely without options. As a matter of fact, Oracle has provided you with a very nice option that not only supports multiple operating systems, but is also free: VirtualBox, shown in Figure 15.9. VirtualBox doesn't have all the bells and whistles that accompany the previously mentioned apps, but if you simply need the ability to run Windows, Linux, or another Intel-based operating system within Mac OS X, VirtualBox can get the job done. Check it out at www.virtualbox.org.

15.9 VirtualBox running Windows 7 within Mac OS X.

Do You Have Any Troubleshooting Tips?

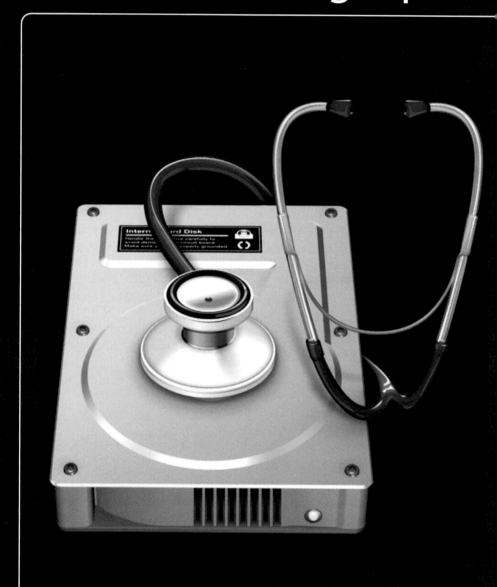

Macs have a well-earned reputation for being as rock-solid reliable as it gets in the tech realm, but nothing, not even Cupertino engineering, lasts forever. Things happen, and the information in this chapter can point you to the help you need, if not lend a hand in resolving the issue altogether.

Start Problem Solving

I realize that if you're reading this book, you are most likely a savvy computer user and that you may already be beyond the basics. However, by nature, any troubleshooting chapter must begin with the basics, so let's dive right in.

Restarting your Mac

Most issues with a Mac are fairly simple to resolve. As a matter of fact, the resolution to most problems is to simply restart your Mac.

Restarting is something that most computer users have to do at some point, and it's always the first recourse when you notice quirky things beginning to happen. To restart your Mac, choose Apple menu ⇨ Restart. Lion asks if you're sure you want to restart (see Figure 16.1). Click Restart to reboot the computer.

Hopefully your woes are gone once your Mac boots back up; if not, the rest of this chapter should help you get to the heart of the matter.

16.1 Click Restart to perform the oldest troubleshooting trick in the book.

Backing up your Mac

Before continuing any further, I cannot stress enough the importance of backing up your information. Maintaining a backup of your files prevents you from losing them should something catastrophic happen to your Mac, not to mention the peace of mind it fosters. I learned the hard way that files should always be backed up. I hope in the following section to prevent you from experiencing the same nightmare I did.

Chapter 14 covers the use of Time Machine for keeping an external hard drive continuously updated with backed-up files. While Time Machine is an easy way to keep your backups current, it's not the only way you can back up your Mac. You can also do one of the following to keep things current:

- **Purchase backup software.** Why lay down your hard-earned cash for a backup application when you have Time Machine as part of Lion? Time Machine is a great utility, but it may not be enough (or offer enough control) for some users. That's where third-party applications come in. Here are a few I've personally used:

  - **Carbon Copy Cloner by Bombich Software.** This one has been a tried-and-true app for a very long time on the Mac platform. Carbon Copy Cloner can even create a bootable backup of your system, which is quite a keen feature. CCC is donationware, so you can try it out as long as necessary before paying for it. Learn more about CCC at www.bombich.com/software/ccc.html.

  - **Retrospect.** This is another backup stalwart that I remember using as far back as Mac OS 8. Download a trial, and even find a comparison to Time Machine, at www.retrospect.com/products/software/retroformac/.

  - **MacKeeper.** MacKeeper is a system utility that also provides a great backup utility as part of its total package. This app is the newest of the three I mention here, but it's already garnering wide attention and support for its capabilities. You may download MacKeeper for a 15-day free trial. Give it a look at http://mackeeper.zeobit.com.

- **Back up manually (the old-fashioned way).** Simply attach an external hard drive, install an internal drive (if you have a Mac Pro this is a cinch), use a flash drive, or connect to another computer, and then drag and drop your files to that device.

Make Sure You Are Up to Date

There could be a bug in your operating system or application software that is causing your problems. Check to be sure you are using the latest versions of Mac firmware and Lion by running Software Update. To do so, choose Apple menu ⌕ Software Update. If Software Update finds new versions of your firmware or software, install them and see if this resolves your issues.

If the problems you are experiencing are related to a particular application, visit the website of the application developer to see if there are any updates to the software or if there are any known issues with it. Table 16.1 lists the web addresses of some of the most popular Apple software vendors and a list of their more popular products.

Table 16.1 Third-Party Apple Software Vendors

Company	Popular Applications	Website
Adobe	Photoshop, InDesign, Illustrator, Acrobat	www.adobe.com/go/gn_supp
Quark	QuarkXPress	http://support.quark.com
Microsoft	Word, Excel, PowerPoint, Outlook	www.microsoft.com/mac/
Mozilla	Firefox, Thunderbird	http://support.mozilla.com/
Intego	VirusBarrier, FileGuard	http://support.intego.com/
Intuit	TurboTax, Quicken, QuickBooks	www.intuit.com/support/
FileMaker	FileMaker Pro, Bento	http://filemaker.com/support/index.html
Roxio	Toast, Popcorn	www.roxio.com/enu/support/default.html

Start-up Issues

When your Mac won't start, it's pretty scary. I won't insult your intelligence by telling you there's nothing to worry about, but most of the time this can be solved with a few quick-and-easy steps. If you told me you had start-up issues, the first question I would ask is if the Mac literally won't power up, or if it is getting hung up in the boot process. Let's take it from there.

Your Mac won't power up

Here are a few questions and tips to try if your Mac simply won't power up:

- **Is the power cable connected?**

- **Does the power outlet you are connected to work with other devices?**

- **If you are using a laptop, is the power adapter connected or are you running off the battery?** If so, is the battery charged? Does the Mac work with the power adapter connected?

- **Is the Mac powering up, but the display won't come on?** If so, you could have a bad display. Try connecting another display to your Mac to determine if that is the issue. If a new display doesn't work or if your display works with another computer, there could be a problem with your Mac's video card.

- **Have you added any devices (such as an external hard drive) or parts (such as memory) to your Mac, either internally or externally?** If so, remove or reconnect the device or part, and try to reboot. You may have a defective device, cable, or part.

- **If all else fails, try to reset the System Management Controller (SMC).** There are three ways to reset the SMC, depending on the model of your Mac:

  - **Mac Pro, iMac, or Mac mini.** Shut down the computer and remove all cables (mouse, keyboard, power cord, and so on). After waiting at least 15 seconds, reconnect only the power cable, mouse, and keyboard (in that order), and then push the power button.

  - **MacBook or MacBook Pro.** Remove the battery and unplug the power adapter if it is connected. Hold the power button down for at least 5 seconds and release. Install the battery and connect the power adapter, and then press the power button.

  - **MacBook Air.** Connect the power adapter to the computer. While holding down the Shift, Option, and Control keys on the left side of the keyboard, press the power button once. Wait at least 5 seconds before pushing the power button again to turn on the computer.

Your Mac hangs at start-up

It can be even more maddening if you're able to start up your Mac but unable to boot into Mac OS X. All sorts of things may occur: You might see a folder with a blinking question mark; the screen may be stuck at the gray Apple logo with the spinning gear; a blue screen may appear but nothing happens past that point, and so on. These issues can hopefully be resolved by one of the following steps:

- **Force your Mac to restart.** Hold the power button down for several seconds until the Mac turns off. Restart and see if it boots normally.

- **Reset the parameter RAM (PRAM).** This is also known as zapping the PRAM. Lion stores information about your Mac in the PRAM, such as speaker volume levels, time zone and display settings, and so on. Restart your Mac and immediately press ⌘+Option+ P+R simultaneously. Continue to hold down all four keys until you hear the Mac start-up sound at least twice (wait for three, just for good measure). Release the keys after the second or third start-up sound, and hopefully you are then able to start up normally. You may need to adjust the settings back to what they were before resetting the PRAM.

- **Boot your Mac in Safe Mode.** Hold down the Shift key immediately after the start-up sound. Don't let go until you see the gray Apple logo. Booting in Safe Mode causes your Mac to delete several cache files that may be corrupt and causing problems with your Mac. Reboot normally to see if this resolves your issues.

● **Boot your Mac with the Lion installation disc.** Select Disk Utility from the Utilities menu, click your hard drive icon in the left column of the list, and click Repair Disk in the lower-right corner of the window. Once the repair is completed, reboot your Mac to see if it starts normally.

If you still can't start up your Mac at this point, it's time to take some drastic measures. Contact Apple technical support, as your Mac may need a bit more hands-on expertise.

Handy start-up keyboard shortcuts

Apple has developed a toolbox of keyboard shortcuts that allow you not only to boot up your Mac, but also to perform specific tasks, such as choosing a different start-up drive. Table 16.2 lists the shortcut key combinations and the tasks they facilitate.

Table 16.2 Start-up Keyboard Shortcuts

Task	Shortcut
Start up from a disc	Insert the disc into the Mac optical drive and press C until the disc begins to boot.
Choose a start-up drive	Press and hold Option as soon as you hear the start-up sound. Release the button after you see available start-up drives. Select the drive from which you want to boot.
Start in Safe Mode	Press the Shift key as soon as you hear the start-up sound. Don't release it until you see the spinning gear under the gray Apple logo.
Start up in Target Disk mode	Press and hold T immediately after the start-up sound. Release it when you see the FireWire logo on your screen.
Zap the PRAM	Press and hold ⌘+Option+P+R immediately at start-up before you hear the start-up sound. Release the keys after you hear the third start-up sound.
Start in Single User mode	Press ⌘+S immediately after the start-up sound. You may release the keys once you see the command-line screen.
Start in verbose mode	Press and hold ⌘+V immediately after the start-up sound to see detailed messages during the boot process.
Eject a disc at start-up	Hold down the mouse button or the eject button on your keyboard at start-up. This is particularly useful if you have an optical disc that just won't eject via conventional means.

Isolating Software Trouble

Let's say you're typing away in your favorite word processor and you suddenly see the wait cursor, known fondly as The Spinning Wheel of Death. The application crashes, and you lose about an hour's worth of work because you forgot to save your document. Or, perhaps you are making a bank transaction in your favorite web browser when it freezes and you find out that your transaction was lost in the process. What do you do if you have an application that just won't behave? Following are some questions and tips for troubleshooting a software issue:

- **Have you installed the latest updates for your software?** If not, visit the website of the application developer and see if there are any updates.

- **Did the issue occur only after you installed an update (either for an application or Mac OS X)?** Check with the application developer for any known issues with the update or to explain the issue you're experiencing.

- **Do you experience problems with only one document?** There may be an element in that particular document, such as a font or graphic, that is corrupted and causing the issue. Try creating a new document, copy and paste elements from the old document into the new one, and see if the issue is resolved.

- **Do you get a specific error message?** If so, consult the application documentation or the manufacturer's website for help interpreting the message.

- **Is the issue related to a software/hardware combination (such as a certain scanner or camera) with a particular application?** For example, if you have a problem with Image Capture crashing when you try to import images from your camera, check to see if you can import images with a different application. If other applications also have this issue, see if another camera works. If other applications do not exhibit the problem, it's quite likely that the single misbehaving application is the culprit.

- **Discard the application's preferences files.** Consult the application documentation or contact the manufacturer to find out where the application stores its preferences in Lion. When you restart the application, new preference files are created. You may need to check your preferences to make sure they are set the way you want them to be.

- **Is the application frozen?** If so, force it to quit by pressing ⌘+Option+Esc. Select the offending application from the list in the Force Quit Applications window and click Force Quit.

Unfortunately, if the issue isn't cleared up by now, you may need to reinstall the application. Again, be sure to contact the manufacturer or read the documentation included with the application to see if there are any special instructions that you need to follow to properly reinstall it.

Utilizing the root account

Sometimes the problem is that something has become corrupted in your user account. To find out, log in to a different account and see if the issue persists. I prefer to use the root account, which gives you complete control over the Mac. Follow these steps:

1. **Open Directory Utility, which is found in the System/Library/CoreServices folder.**

2. **Click the lock icon in the lower-left corner (see Figure 16.2).** Type your username and password when prompted.

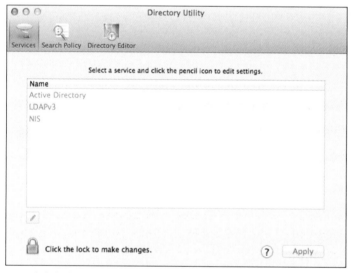

16.2 Click the lock to make changes to the Directory Utility.

3. **Choose Edit ⇨ Enable Root User to enable the root account.**

4. **Type the root account password twice to confirm it.** Do not forget this password!

5. **Quit Directory Utility.**

6. **Log out of the account you are currently using.**

7. **In the login window, click Other.** Type root for the username and then type the password you assigned to the root account in Step 4.

8. **To log in to the root account, click Log In (in the lower-right corner).**

9. **Test your issue while logged in as root.** If the symptom persists, it is a system-wide problem. If the issue does not present itself while logged in as root, you've isolated the problem to the account you were previously using.

Deleting preference files

Most applications installed on a Mac create preference files somewhere on the system. These files tell the application how it should behave, what customizations have been made, what passwords may be necessary for someone to use it, and lots of other information it may need to function properly. If these preference files (there may be more than one, depending on the application) have been corrupted, your application may engage in some very odd behavior. In fact, it may not start up at all. If this is the case:

1. **Contact the developer of the application to find out what preference files are used by the app and where you can find them on your Mac.**

2. **Find the preference files and delete them.**

3. **Reopen the offending application and the preference file(s) is correctly rebuilt.**

Killing a process

If your Mac is super-sluggish, there may be an errant application hogging up all of the memory. When this happens, you could restart your Mac to effectively kill all processes and start over. If you have other tasks running that you need to leave alone, Apple has made Activity Monitor for just such occasions.

To find and stop a memory-hogging process via Activity Monitor, follow these steps:

1. **From the Finder, press ⌘+Shift+U to open the Utilities folder.**

2. **Double-click the icon for Activity Monitor.**

3. **Browse through the processes list (see Figure 16.3) and see if there are any processes using a large percentage of the computer's cycles.** To see the percentage being used by each process, look under the % CPU heading. You can click the % CPU heading to arrange the processes in order by highest percentages.

4. **Highlight the offending process and click Quit Process in the upper-left of the window to stop it in its tracks.**

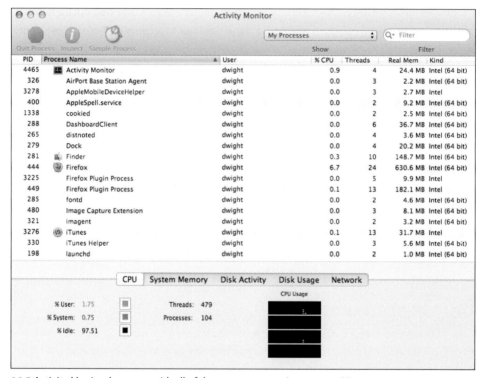

16.3 Activity Monitor keeps up with all of the processes running on your Mac.

Correcting permissions issues

Every file in Mac OS X has a set of permissions assigned to it. These tell Lion exactly who can access the file and how he can use it. Sometimes these permissions can get a little out of sorts and need to be repaired in order for your Mac to function in its normally spectacular way. Here are some symptoms to look for:

● **You are unable to empty a file from the Trash.**

● **An application can only be launched by one user account even though it is installed for use on all accounts.**

- You cannot open a document that you know you should be able to open.
- The Finder restarts when you are trying to change permissions for a file.
- You are unable to open folders on your Mac (or the network) to which you are supposed to have access.
- An application crashes when you try to print from it.

There are several other issues that may be related to permissions problems as well, but these are the most common. Repairing permissions is, thankfully, an easy task to accomplish. Follow these steps:

1. In the Finder, open Disk Utility by pressing ⌘+Shift+U and double-clicking its icon.

2. Select the drive that contains the files with the permissions issues.

3. Click Repair Disk Permissions in the lower-left corner of the First Aid tab and the process of repairing the permissions begins, as shown in Figure 16.4.

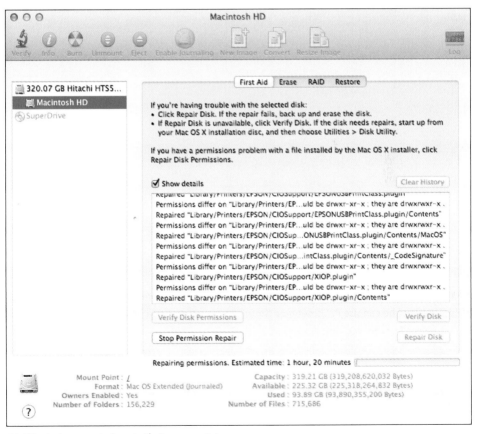

16.4 Restoring permissions to their proper states.

Note
You can also run Disk Utility from the Lion installation disc, which is especially help-ful if you can't boot up with the drive in question. To boot a Mac with the installation disc, choose Utilities⇨Disk Utility and run the repair as described in the previous steps.

When All Else Fails — Reinstall

If you've tried everything suggested above (and you may have dug further into the issues than this book does) and your Mac still doesn't work properly, it's time to completely back up and reinstall Lion. See Chapter 14 for help on backing up your system and Chapter 1 for instructions on install-ing Lion over an existing copy of Mac OS X.

Note
If you aren't comfortable reinstalling Lion without taking a few more stabs at resolv-ing the issue (and you live in the United States), give Apple Technical Support a call at 1-800-APL-CARE (1-800-275-2273). If you live outside the United States, visit the Apple Technical Support contacts website to find support numbers for your country: www.apple.com/support/contact/.

Appendix A

Mac Online Resources

The Internet is an awesome tool for finding more information regarding Mac OS X and all other things Mac. The plethora of sites dedicated to Mac are capable of keeping you up to date with all the latest Mac news, software updates, issues experienced by other users, help with troubleshooting, and the most recent rumors, as well as the latest, greatest tips and tricks for squeezing all the juicy goodness you can get out of Mac OS X.

Official Apple Sites

The Apple site should be the first stop for any self-respecting Mac user on his or her quest for more information. Here are some helpful links to the most important sections of the site:

www.apple.com/mac/

This is the portal to all things Mac-related on the Apple site. From here you can check out the latest hardware and software Apple has to offer.

www.apple.com/macosx/

This is the Apple Mac OS X site, solely dedicated to the best operating system on earth.

www.apple.com/downloads/

Visit this site to find all the latest software downloads from Apple and the Mac community.

www.apple.com/support/

The Mother of Mac Support Sites; this is where you should go first when troubleshooting an issue with your Mac.

www.apple.com/itunes/

Need to get your groove on? This site will take you to iTunes and iPod nirvana.

https://discussions.apple.com

This site is where you can connect with other Mac users about issues, tips, and all the neatest tricks regarding your Apple hardware or software.

www.apple.com/usergroups/

Would you like to join up with other local Mac users to discuss all things Mac? If so, then a Mac User Group is right up your alley. Go here to find the Mac User Group in your area and get involved.

http://store.apple.com/

Your one-stop Apple shop, where you can buy all things Apple and many others that are Apple related.

www.apple.com/why-mac/compare

Are you having a difficult time deciding which new Mac you want to use with Lion? If so, this site gives a very nice head-to-head comparison of Apple's latest personal computer offerings.

http://support.apple.com/specs/

This is hands down the best site for finding specifications for almost any Apple product.

www.apple.com/findouthow/mac/

Mac OS X Lion Portable Genius is the first place you ought to go for help and information regarding Mac OS X. However, should you find yourself without this preferred resource, you can go to this site for help with Mac basics.

www.apple.com/wifi

Because you are running Lion on your Mac, it no doubt has an AirPort card installed, allowing you to connect to a network wirelessly. Should you find yourself needing to buy a wireless router, you might consider one from Apple. This site gives you the information you need to decide which product may be best for your needs.

http://training.apple.com/#certification

If you find you want to delve even more deeply into the whole Mac experience, certification by Apple may just fit the bill. This site lists the kinds of certification available, what courses you can take to achieve your goals, and where to find classes.

More Mac Sites

The web is packed with third-party sites catering to the needs of Mac users. Here are a few of my favorites, in no particular order:

www.macworld.com

You can find all sorts of Mac stuff here, from how-to articles to reviews of the newest products. It is the premier Mac news and reviews site.

www.appleinsider.com

Rumors are a part of life for many Mac fans, and this site relays all the online gossip regarding Apple's latest and greatest offerings.

www.macintouch.com

One of my favorites since the 1990s (I'm dating myself a bit), this is a great source for Mac news and reader reviews.

www.macnn.com

News, podcasts, reviews, blogs, and forums can be found on this Mac news site.

www.macosxhints.com

This site is great for Mac OS X tips and tricks, from the simplest to the most difficult to implement.

www.microsoft.com/mac

Find all the latest updates for your Microsoft Office applications and learn how to better use those with which you currently work.

http://mactimeline.com/

A great history of Apple updates and when they were offered to users, this site benefits the nerdiest of Mac users (obviously, including myself), but I've included it for all Mac nerds-to-be, as well.

http://macscripter.net/

Everything you want to know about scripting for your Mac, and more! AppleScript and Automator are favored topics on this forum.

www.macfixit.com

A great site for learning about Mac hardware, how to solve hardware issues, and where to find tutorials about how things work.

http://macosrumors.com

Another of the great rumor sites, this one has been in my bookmarks since the days of Mac OS 8.

www.versiontracker.com

Find the latest versions of your favorite third-party software, as well as offerings from the best Mac developers around.

http://db.tidbits.com

This is another tried-and-true (and old) site that faithfully caters to the news and tips needs of Mac users.

Appendix B

Mac Shortcut Keys

Through all the years that computers have been around, the remaining constant has always been the keyboard. While it has gone through some subtle changes, the basic layout of the keys has remained the same since man first walked upright (which is ironic because we have to lean over to use them). The keyboard can be quite an efficient tool for quickly executing tasks on your Mac, and this section lists some of the more common keyboard shortcuts.

Finder Shortcuts

Use the shortcuts in Table B.1 to switch Finder window views, open a new Finder window, eject a disc, duplicate files and folders, maneuver through the Finder sidebar, and manage your Trash.

Table B.1 Finder Shortcuts

Shortcut	Description
⌘+A	Select all items in the current window.
⌘+D	Duplicate the selected item.
⌘+E	Eject the current disc.
⌘+F	Display the Find dialog.
⌘+I	Open the Get Info window for the selected item.
⌘+J	Show the View options.
⌘+L	Create an alias for the selected item.
⌘+N	Open a new Finder window.
⌘+O	Open the selected item.

Shortcut	Description
⌘+R	Show the original item for the current alias.
⌘+T	Add the currently selected item to the sidebar.
⌘+W	Close the current Finder window.
⌘+Delete	Move the selected item to the Trash.
⌘+1	Switch the active window to Icons view.
⌘+2	Switch the active window to List Flow view.
⌘+3	Switch the active window to Columns view.
⌘+4	Switch the active window to Cover Flow view.
Shift+⌘+A	Go to the Applications folder.
Shift+⌘+C	Go to the Computer folder.
Shift+⌘+D	Go to the Desktop folder.
Shift+⌘+G	Display the Go to Folder dialog.
Shift+⌘+H	Go to the Home folder.
Shift+⌘+I	Go to the iDisk folder.
Shift+⌘+K	Go to the Network folder.
Shift+⌘+N	Create a new folder in the current Finder window.
Shift+⌘+U	Go to the Utilities folder.
Shift+⌘+Delete	Empty the Trash (with the confirmation dialog).
Option+Shift+⌘+Delete	Empty the Trash (without the confirmation dialog).
Option+⌘+N	Create a new Smart Folder in the current Finder window.
Option+⌘+W	Close all open Finder windows.

Application Shortcuts

Table B.2 shows you how to cycle through the current application's icons, how to open an application's preferences, and how to maneuver through windows without resorting to your mouse.

Table B.2 Application Shortcuts

Shortcut	Description
⌘+Tab	Cycle forward through active application icons with each press of the Tab key; release ⌘ to switch to the selected application.
⌘+,	Open the current application's preferences.
⌘+H	Hide the current application.

continued

Table B.2 continued

Shortcut	Description
⌘+`	Cycle forward through the current application's open windows.
Shift+⌘+`	Cycle backward through the current application's open windows.
Shift+⌘+Tab	Cycle backward through active application icons with each press of the Tab key; release Shift and ⌘ to switch to the selected application.
⌘+M	Minimize the current window to the Dock.
⌘+Q	Quit the current application.
Option+⌘+H	Hide all applications except the current one.
Option+⌘+M	Minimize all windows in active application to the Dock.
Option+⌘+Esc	Display the Force Quit Applications window.

Start-up Shortcuts

Table B.3 details shortcuts you can use for alternate booting techniques.

Table B.3 Start-up Shortcuts

Shortcut	Description
C	Press and hold to boot from the inserted CD or DVD.
T	Press and hold to invoke FireWire Target Disk mode.
N	Press and hold to start up from the default NetBoot disk image.
Option	Press and hold to display the Startup Manager where you can select a start-up drive.
⌘+.	Opens the optical drive when you are in the Startup Manager.
Mouse button	Press and hold to eject any removable discs.
⌘+Option+P+R	Press and hold to reset your Mac's parameter RAM.
⌘+S	Press and hold to start up in single user mode.
⌘+V	Press and hold to see detailed status messages during the boot process.
Left Shift key	Hold down as soon as you see the progress indicator (which looks like a spinning gear) to prevent automatic login.
Shift	Press and hold as soon as you hear the start-up sound and release as soon as you see the progress indicator to boot into Safe Mode.
Shift	Press and hold immediately after clicking the Log In button to keep Finder windows and login items from opening when you log in.

Restart and Shutdown Shortcuts

Table B.4 gives you some different options for the various dialogs you see when you restart or shut down your Mac.

Table B.4 Restart and Shutdown Shortcuts

Shortcut	Description
Control+Eject	Display the Restart/Sleep/Shut Down confirmation dialog.
Power	Display the Restart/Sleep/Shut Down confirmation dialog.
Shift+⌘+Q	Log out (with confirmation dialog).
Option+Shift+⌘+Q	Log out (without confirmation dialog).
Option+⌘+Eject	Put your Mac into Sleep mode (without confirmation dialog).
Control+⌘+Eject	Restart your Mac (without confirmation dialog) with the option to save changes in open documents.
Control+Option+⌘+Eject	Shut down your Mac (without confirmation dialog) with the option to save changes in open documents).
Control+⌘+Power	Force your Mac to restart (without confirmation dialog) without the option to save changes in open documents.
Power	Press and hold to force your Mac to shut down (without confirmation dialog) without the option to save changes in open documents.

Safari Shortcuts

Table B.5 details the shortcuts you can use to maneuver through Safari windows, manage your bookmarks, send e-mails, and perform Google searches.

Table B.5 Safari Shortcuts

Shortcut	Description
⌘+I	E-mail the contents of the current page.
⌘+L	Select the Address bar text.
⌘+N	Open a new window.
⌘+O	Display the Open dialog for opening a file.
⌘+R	Reload the current page.
⌘+T	Open a new tab.

continued

Table B.5 continued

Shortcut	Description
⌘+W	Close the current tab.
⌘+D	Open the Bookmark dialog.
⌘+n	Open the nth item (where n is a number between 1 and 9) on the Bookmarks bar.
⌘+}	Select the next tab.
⌘+{	Select the previous tab.
⌘+.	Stop loading the current page.
⌘++	Make the text bigger on the current page.
⌘+0	Make the text normal size on the current page.
⌘+-	Make the text smaller on the current page.
⌘+[	Navigate backward.
⌘+]	Navigate forward.
Shift+⌘+H	Navigate to the home page.
Shift+⌘+T	Toggle the Tab bar on and off (works only if you have one tab open).
Shift+⌘+W	Close the current window.
Shift+⌘+I	E-mail a link to the current page.
Shift+⌘+K	Toggle pop-up blocking on and off.
Shift+⌘+L	Run a Google search on the selected text.
⌘+Return	Open the Address bar URL in a background tab (you must select the URL in the Address bar for this command to work).
Shift+⌘+Return	Open the Address bar URL in a foreground tab (you must select the URL in the Address bar for this command to work).
Shift+⌘	Click a link to open it in a foreground tab.
⌘	Click a link to open it in a background tab.
Option+⌘	Click a link to open it in a background window.
Shift+Option+⌘	Click a link to open it in a foreground window.
Option+⌘+D	Add the current page to Bookmarks (without the Bookmark dialog).
Option+⌘+B	Display the Bookmarks window.
Option+⌘+L	Display the Downloads window.
Option+⌘+A	Open the Activity window.
Option+⌘+Return	Open the Address bar URL in a background window.
Shift+Option+⌘+Return	Open the Address bar URL in a foreground window.

Miscellaneous Shortcuts

Use the shortcuts in Table B.6 to cut, copy, paste, undo recent actions, manage the dock, and capture screenshots.

Table B.6 Miscellaneous Shortcuts

Shortcut	Description
⌘+X	Cut the selected objects or data.
⌘+C	Copy the selected objects or data.
⌘+V	Paste the most recently cut or copied objects or data.
⌘+Z	Undo the most recent action.
F12 or Eject	Press and hold to eject an inserted disc (which button to use depends on your keyboard).
Fn+Control+F2	Give keyboard control to the menu bar.
Fn+Control+F3	Give keyboard control to the Dock.
Option+⌘+D	Toggle Dock hiding on and off.
Option+Volume up/down/mute	Display the Sound preferences.
Option+Brightness up/down	Display the Display preferences.
Shift+⌘+3	Capture an image of the screen.
Shift+⌘+4	Drag the mouse to capture an image of the selected area of the screen.
Shift+⌘+4	Press spacebar and then click an object to capture an image of it.

Glossary

access point A network device that allows two or more Macs to connect over a wireless network.

Address Book Application for maintaining lists of personal contacts and their pertinent information, such as phone numbers, e-mail and street addresses, and relevant web pages.

administrator A powerful user account that has the ability to make permanent changes to the Mac operating system, including (but not limited to) creating and deleting other users or administrators, installing software for system-wide use, installing device drivers, and so on.

AFP Apple Filing Protocol. A network protocol used to share files and network services among Mac computers.

AirDrop A feature that allows incredibly simple drag-and-drop file sharing with other Macs running AirDrop. Click the AirDrop icon in a Finder window sidebar, find the computer with which you want to share your files, and then drag and drop your file onto the computer name or icon. The file is automatically copied to the recipient's Downloads folder.

AirPort Apple's range of wireless networking products. AirPort uses the industry standard 802.11 protocol.

Apple menu Home to a few key commands, such as Software Update and System Preferences. Also includes Sleep, Restart, Shut Down, and Log Out commands. See also *application menu, menu bar, menu extras.*

AppleTalk An easy-to-use networking protocol developed by Apple for communication among computers, servers, printers, and any other devices running the protocol.

application Software designed with a specific purpose in mind (such as word processors, web browsers, e-mail clients, page layout, and so on) that you can install on your Mac.

application menu The part of the *menu bar* between the *Apple menu* icon and the *menu extras*. It displays the menus associated with the current application. See also *Apple menu, menu bar, menu extras.*

application preferences The options and settings that you can configure for a particular application via the Preferences command. See also *system preferences.*

back up The process of creating copies of your data.

Bluetooth A wireless networking technology that allows two devices to communicate when they are within range of each other.

Bonjour A service discovery protocol implemented in Mac OS X. Formerly known as Rendezvous, it allows for the automatic discovery of other devices running the protocol, which can then share services. For example, a Mac running Bonjour can discover and print to a printer that's also running Bonjour, without having to know the printer's IP address.

bookmark An Internet site saved in a web browser so that it can be quickly accessed in future browsing sessions.

BSD Berkeley Software Distribution. UNIX-based operating system developed by the University of California, Berkeley. Mac OS X runs on a derivative of BSD called Darwin. See also *Darwin*.

ColorSync The Apple color management technology. Uses other industry-standard technologies, such as ICC profiles, to keep color consistent among applications, your Mac, and input (scanners and cameras) and output (displays and printers) devices.

command key (⌘) Located next to the spacebar on the keyboard. Can be used in conjunction with other keys to perform certain tasks. For example, pressing ⌘+P causes an application to open its Print dialog box.

command-line interface (CLI) A text-only interface used to display information for the user and to send commands to the computer.

compression The process of making a file, or a folder containing many files, smaller in data size.

Cover Flow A Finder view that shows a split screen with a List view of the contents on the bottom and a preview of the current item on the top.

CUPS The printing system used by most UNIX-based operating systems, including Mac OS X.

Darwin The name of the flavor of BSD UNIX on which Mac OS X is based. Darwin is developed by Apple and is the core of the Mac operating system services, such as networking and file systems. See also *BSD*.

Dashboard An application that runs other mini-applications called widgets. Dashboard can be accessed by pressing the F12 key on your keyboard or clicking its icon in the Dock. See also *widget*.

device driver Software developed by a hardware device's manufacturer that allows the operating system to interact with that hardware.

DHCP Dynamic Host Configuration Protocol. A protocol used to automatically assign IP addresses to client computers in a network environment.

Disk image A file created by Disk Utility that acts exactly like a physical drive in that files can be saved to it the same as they can in any other directory. Many application installers that you download from the Internet use disk images to transport their data.

discoverable Describes a device that has its Bluetooth feature enabled so that other Bluetooth devices can connect to it.

Dock Located at the bottom of the screen by default, the Dock stores links to the items or applications used most frequently.

drop box A directory in the home folder that others on your network can use to share files with you.

Eject key Press this key (on some Macs, hold it down for a second or two) to eject a previously inserted CD or DVD.

Ethernet The most common network standard in use today. Links computers together via a system of cables and hubs, or routers. Data transmission speed can range from 10 to as fast as 10,000 megabits (10 Gigabits) per second, depending on the cabling and hardware used.

event An appointment or meeting scheduled in iCal.

fast user switching A Mac feature that allows more than one user to be logged in at once. Leaves programs running when a user logs out and reinstates them just as they were when the same user logs back in.

file system A technology used by the operating system to keep track of the files stored on a drive, such as a hard drive.

Finder The one application that is always running on a Mac. Used to navigate the Mac hard drive for files, folders, applications, other volumes, and so on. See also *Spotlight*.

Firewall Software that protects a computer or network from outside intrusion.

FireWire A high-speed serial bus standard developed by Apple for the speedy transmission of large amounts of data. Also known as IEEE 1394, it is cross-platform and can transmit between 400 and 800 megabits per second, depending on which version is supported by the Mac hardware.

font A complete set of characters for a particular typeface that defines how the typeface appears on the Mac display and printed documents.

FTP File Transfer Protocol. An IP protocol used for transferring, creating, and deleting files and folders located on an FTP server.

group A collection of Address Book contacts. See also *Smart Group*.

guest operating system An operating system that runs inside a virtual machine using virtualization software.

HFS+ Hierarchical File System. The default file system for Mac OS X, which uses a hierarchical system for storing and organizing files and folders.

home directory (or folder) The directory that contains all of a user's personal documents and files. Every user account created on a Mac is assigned a home directory located in the User's folder at the root of the hard drive.

HTML HyperText Markup Language. The programming language used to render the graphics and text of a web page.

HTTP HyperText Transfer Protocol. A protocol responsible for linking and exchanging files on the Internet.

iCal The Mac default scheduling application.

iChat A Mac application used to converse with other people in real time by sending each other online text messages.

iDisk Online file storage that comes with a MobileMe account.

iLife A suite of applications that can be installed on a Mac. Includes programs such as iDVD, iPhoto, and iWeb.

Image Capture The Mac application that you use to connect to a device (such as a digital camera, scanner, or digital camcorder), and download photos or videos from that device to your Mac.

iTunes The Mac default media player application.

iWork A productivity suite that consists of three programs: Pages, a word processor; Numbers, a spreadsheet program; and Keynote, a presentation program.

Java Cross-platform software development environment used on most computer operating systems and many handheld devices. Also frequently used to display dynamic information on web pages.

JPEG Joint Photographic Experts Group. Perhaps the most common format for pictures on computers and the Internet. Can compress the data size of the image while still retaining reasonable image quality.

LAN Local Area Network. A network that is confined to one particular area, such as a small office or home business.

Launchpad Provides instant access to applications through an iOS-like interface.

LPD Line Printer Daemon. An industry-standard protocol for printing via TCP/IP over a network.

login items The applications, files, folders, network shares, and other items that start automatically when a user logs in to her account.

Mail The Mac OS X default e-mail application. Can handle multiple e-mail accounts of varying protocols, such as IMAP, POP, and Exchange.

menu bar The strip that runs across the top of the Mac screen. See also *Apple menu, application menu, menu extras*.

menu extras These icons appear on the right side of the *menu bar* and show the status of certain Mac features, such as the wireless network connection. Also allow the configuration of other features, such as the volume and Bluetooth functionality. See also *Apple menu, application menu, menu bar*.

Mission Control Provides an organized overview of every open item in Mac OS X, such as all the windows associated with an application, Dashboard, and full-screen applications.

modifier key Pressed in conjunction with one or more other keys to launch some action. Most Mac keyboard shortcuts involve the Command key (⌘).

open source The software development method that allows for free access to source code, as well as the modification and redistribution of the code.

OpenGL A cross-platform application programming interface (API) developed by Silicon Graphics to produce two- and three-dimensional graphics.

pair To connect one Bluetooth device with another by typing a passkey.

partition A portion of hard drive space that has been separated from the rest of the drive. A Mac views each partition as a separate hard drive that can be used for anything, including installing Windows or storing particular types of files.

permissions Access rights given to the owner and other users of a Mac. Without the right permissions, a user cannot view or access files or folders owned by another user. See also *user account*.

Photo Booth A standard Mac OS X application for taking pictures with the built-in Mac camera and adding special effects.

preference files A document that stores options and other data entered using an application's Preferences command.

Preview An application that ships with Mac OS X for viewing PDF files and images. Capable of opening more than 25 file formats, including almost all of the popular image formats.

printer queue Stores print jobs and data for the printer. If there is a problem, the print data is stored here until printing can resume.

protocol A set of standards or rules that govern the communication of information between two computers.

Quartz A graphics service in Mac OS X responsible for rendering two-dimensional graphics.

QuickTime The Apple default multimedia framework designed for the creation and handling of various video, sound, and animation digital media formats.

QuickTime Player The Mac default digital video player.

Safari The Mac default web browser.

Safe Boot To start a Mac in Safe Mode. See also *Safe Mode*.

Safe Mode A start-up mode in which a Mac doesn't load most of its behind-the-scenes components. See also *Safe Boot*.

sidebar The pane on the left side of any Finder window that offers a number of shortcuts to objects such as devices, network shares, and local folders.

sleep mode A low-power state in which a Mac uses only marginally more electricity than if it were powered off altogether, while still preserving all running applications, windows, and documents.

Smart Folder A kind of virtual folder where the contents depend on the criteria specified by the user. Mac adjusts the contents automatically as the files change.

Smart Group A collection of Address Book contacts in which each member has one or more things in common. Address Book automatically updates a Smart Group as contacts are added, edited, or deleted. See also *group*.

Smart Mailbox A Mail folder that consolidates all messages that meet one or more conditions.

SMB Server Message Block. Protocol used primarily by Windows computers for accessing shared files, printers, and other network services. Mac OS X has the built-in ability to communicate with Windows-based PCs through SMB.

SMTP Simple Mail Transfer Protocol. Protocol used mainly for sending e-mail, but rarely for receiving e-mail.

Spaces An application that allows a user to work with multiple desktops on which he can run applications and view documents.

Spotlight A Mac feature used to search for files, folders, applications, Mail messages, images, and other data. See also *Finder*.

synchronization A process that ensures that data (such as contacts, e-mail accounts, and events) on a Mac is the same as the data on other devices, such as cell phones, other computers, and PDAs.

System Folder Located at the root of the hard drive, it contains the core components needed to boot a Mac system and run it efficiently. A Mac does not boot correctly if this folder is tampered with (such as by changing its name), so it's best to steer totally clear of it.

system preferences The options, settings, and other data a user configures for her Mac via the System Preferences application. See also *application preferences*.

TCP/IP Transfer Control Protocol/Internet Protocol. Set of industry-standard protocols used for communications via the Internet. TCP's job is to keep up with the packets of data being sent, while IP is the actual vehicle for delivering the packets.

Terminal A program used for accessing the command-line interface of Mac OS X.

TextEdit The Mac default word processor.

Time Machine A Mac application used to create and access file backups.

user account Required for every person who uses a Mac to access personal files and folders. See also *permissions*.

utility Specialty software application dedicated to managing and tuning Mac software and, to some degree, hardware.

virtual machine Software files that virtualization applications recognize and utilize as if they were separate computers. Runs within Mac OS X, allowing a user to work with Mac OS X and the OS on the virtual machine at the same time. See also *virtualization*.

virtualization Running a guest operating system (such as Windows on a Mac) in a virtual machine. See also *virtual machine*.

widget Mini-applications launched with Dashboard. Typically concentrate on one particular task, such as local weather, movie showtimes, sports scores, and so on. See also *Dashboard*.

Index